The Female Narrator in the British Novel

The Female Narrator in the British Novel:

Hidden Agendas

Lisa Sternlieb

First published 2002 by
PALGRAVE
Houndmills, Basingstoke, Hampshire RG21 6XS and
175 Fifth Avenue, New York, N.Y. 10010
Companies and representatives throughout the world

PALGRAVE is the new global academic imprint of
St. Martin's Press LLC Scholarly and Reference Division and
Palgrave Publishers Ltd (formerly Macmillan Press Ltd).

ISBN 0–333–97372–0

This book is printed on paper suitable for recycling and
made from fully managed and sustained forest sources.

A catalogue record for this book is available
from the British Library.

Library of Congress Cataloging-in-Publication Data
Sternlieb, Lisa Ruth, 1962-
  The female narrator in the British novel: hidden agendas / Lisa Sternlieb.
      p. cm
Includes bibliographical references (p.) and index.
ISBN 0–333–97372–0
  1. English fiction–History and criticism. 2. Women in literature.
3. Man-woman relationships in literature. 4. Point of view (Literature)
5. Deception in literature .6. Marriage in literature. 7. First person
narrative. 8. Sex role in literature. 9. Narration (Rhetoric) I. Title
PR830.W6 S74 2002
823.009'352042–dc21

                                                          2001058809

10 9 8 7 6 5 4 3 2 1
11 10 09 08 07 06 05 04 03 02
Printed and bound in Great Britain by
Antony Rowe Ltd, Chippenham, Wiltshire

Acknowledgements

Reproductions from James Joyce's writings – numerous extracts from *Ulysses,*
one letter, and *The Centenary of Charles Dickens* – included with the permission
of the estate of James Joyce. © Estate of James Joyce

Material from *Possession* by A.S. Byatt, copyright © 1991 by A.S. Byatt, used by
permission of Random House Inc.

Material from *Possession* by A.S. Byatt published by Chatto & Windus, used by
permission of the Random House Group Ltd.

For

Rose Sternlieb
who taught me how to tell a story

and for

Janine Sternlieb
"there is no friend like a sister"

Contents

Acknowledgments

This book began as a dissertation at Princeton under the direction of Maria DiBattista and Deborah Nord. Maria and Deborah have been more than inspiring teachers, mentors, and advisors; they have been great and loyal friends. This book could not have been written without their wisdom, patience, and generosity. I thank Deborah for her unfailing devotion to my career and my happiness, for giving me a beautiful send-off from Princeton and for making it possible for me to come back and visit again. I thank my favorite "fast-talking dame" for her brilliant conversation, her capacious heart, and a certain visit to the Sistine Chapel.

So many others at Princeton have continued to support me. I especially want to thank Oliver Arnold, Michael Wood, Esther Schor, and Beth Harrison. The gift of *A Literature of their Own* at age twenty-two from my college mentor, Susan Brisman, started me on this journey. I thank Elaine Showalter for what she and her work have meant to me all these years. I had the good fortune to meet A.S. Byatt at Princeton and am grateful to her for a memorable conversation.

I could not imagine a more supportive group of colleagues than I have found at Wake Forest. I especially thank Nancy Cotton, Jim Hans, Barry Maine, Bill Moss, Gillian Overing, Gale Sigal, and Olga Valbuena for the intelligence, thoughtfulness, and enthusiasm with which they have evaluated my writing and teaching, and Eric Wilson for the mind-bending conversations. I thank Dillon Johnston for introducing me to the terrific Eleanor Birne, and Connie Green for just being her wonderful self. I am most grateful to my colleagues for their audacious decision to hire three Victorianists at the same time. Life as an assistant professor and a North Carolinian/Londoner would be unimaginable without my two fellow Victorianists on a bench. I am indebted to Jan Caldwell and Caroline Levine for spirited intellectual conversation, Victorian outings, a Keatsian nickname, and an indispensable dinner party. I thank Jan for unconditional love, indulgence of my hypochondria, and meatloaf. I thank Caroline for her generous soul, her indefatigable attempts to find Mr. Mister, and chicken and salad. Thanks are also due to my students at Wake and Princeton (especially Julia Lee) who have taught me more than they've learned from me. For their help with my manuscript in its final stages I am deeply indebted to Linda Hughes, Janey Fisher, Becky Mashayekh, and Beverly Tarquini.

"You haven't heard my ... story?" Maggie Debelius and my other fabulous friends – Lisa Basile, Ralph Black, Martha Born, Helen Catt, Suzanne Churchill, Jay Dickson, Ann Gaylin, Roxanna Gutierrez, Simone Hanson, Gaby Hartel, David Kasunic, Richard Kaye, Bob Knight, Katie LeBlanc, Werner Linster, Elizabeth Phillips, Eva Rodtwitt, Nancy Selleck, Mark Turner, Jane Weber, and Matt Wolf – have indulged my penchant for hyperbolic storytelling. Suzanne has it all and lets me be a part of so much of it. She made the *Wuthering Heights* chapter possible. Nancy continues to do more for my intellectual self-esteem than anyone else by deeming every wild idea which did or did not make it into this book "absolutely fabulous." She and her work have inspired me to move from monologue to dialogue. Because of Eva and Elizabeth, I no longer fear the future. And my much-loved Jane has, by her courage, helped me put all of life into perspective.

My wonderful and rapidly expanding family has put me up or put up with me, supported me emotionally or financially, and given me a great deal of joy. I thank the Bergners, Blums, Heaths, Mezers, Shermans, and Sternliebs. Amy Bergner and her family; and Joe and Janine Sternlieb and their families, have made these years of writing and revising a delight. I am grateful to Amy for our recent travels and for indulging my love of English literature. Rose Sternlieb remains my favorite female narrator.

By writing I am simply following in the footsteps of my parents – Selma, the political columnist; Herschey, the fabulist. I am lucky to have grown up in the presence of such original and independent minds. I hope they can still find evidence of their passionate politics in my prose.

I am grateful to Natalia Schiffrin and Philippe Sands for introducing me to my best reader, editor, poet, and friend.

I thank Jonathan Marks for looking twice, changing tactics, and hazarding confidences. His love has made me design a new narrative.

Introduction: Designing a Narrative

The subject of this book is the female narrator in the nineteenth- and twentieth-century British novel. My central contention is that narratives which have been noted for their artlessness, naturalness, and directness *work* because of their artfulness, artifice, and self-protectiveness. My readings will celebrate the capacity of a woman narrator to design, construct, and baffle while appearing to ingratiate with artless candor. I limit my discussion exclusively to canonical texts – *Jane Eyre, Wuthering Heights, The Woman in White, Bleak House*, and *Ulysses* (with some afterthoughts on *Possession*) – and to characters who have been the subject of much feminist criticism. For while we believe ourselves overly familiar with Jane, Nelly Dean, Marian Halcombe, Esther Summerson, and Molly Bloom, I will argue that we cannot hope to "know" these women. Rather than contributing to a vast body of work which positions the post-Freudian reader as more capable of understanding than the naive Victorian writer, I will show how the Victorians positioned us into their novels as a naive, malleable audience.

Feminist criticism of Victorian literature has tended to analyze the construction of privacy, sexual sanctions, and the plotlessness of women's lives in almost exclusively socio-historical terms, without considering how these might operate as narrative strategies. In this book I analyze not the story of plot but the plot of narration – the circumstances under which the story comes to be told at all. And I consider chastity, virtuousness, self-effacement, and submission not merely as the intractable expectations of Victorian femininity but as plot devices. In other words, I will be concerned with thinking of the plot as context, and the context as the materials of the plot.

At the same time I am interested in making narratology more accessible, less technical and abstract. Like Susan Lanser, who has done more

1

than anyone else to formulate a feminist theory of narrative, I am not trying to introduce a "new narrative poetics ... [but] a poetics attentive to issues that conventional narratology has devalued or ignored."[1]

Lanser writes that:

> When narrative theorists talk about voice, we are usually concerned with formal structures and not with the causes, ideologies, or social implications of particular narrative practices. With a few exceptions, feminist criticism does not ordinarily consider the technical aspects of narration, and narrative poetics does not ordinarily consider the social properties and political implications of narrative voice .... When these two approaches to 'voice' converge ... it becomes possible to see narrative technique not simply as a product of ideology but as ideology itself ....[2]

Lanser's important work makes a necessary effort to bridge the gap between different methodologies, but it finally uses the analysis of narrative technique to reaffirm rather than to upset previous ideological readings. That is, her narratological readings arrive at the same ideological conclusions as non-narratological feminist critics have written. For example, it is now *de rigueur* to attack *Jane Eyre*, the most beloved text of 1970s feminism, for its racism and capitulation to patriarchal values. Lanser simply finds a new way of dealing the same blow: "If the powerful voice achieved by Jane Eyre helped to foster a tradition of outspoken white female narrators in novels since the mid-nineteenth century, the very hegemony of that tradition, brought into being by the dramatized silencing of Bertha Mason, must also have helped to foreclose narrative possibilities for women novelists of color writing in the West."[3] Lanser limits her discussion to works by women. What I will do instead is to show how narratological readings of texts by both men and women can help feminist critics again appreciate texts we have been enjoined to view with suspicion.

Before positioning novels ideologically, I see it as crucial to understand them narratologically. That is, we need to consider the circumstances under which a narrative is meant to be read. Are we ostensibly reading the narrator's actual words or those transcribed by an editor? Are we privileged to watch the process of writing or can we only guess at the conditions under which the narrative was created? Is the narrative being written with a particular reader in mind? Has the narrator constructed her ideal reader? Histories of the novel seldom take such questions into account.

Thus, my study grapples with some of the deficiencies in narrative theory, feminist criticism, and histories of the novel. In the following brief survey I will show how my book challenges established notions of unreliable narration and reductive readings of what is female, how it advocates investigation of narratorial motivation and anti-realist tendencies within realist fiction, and how it promotes the study of narration to address both the unexplored literariness and unexpected politics of well-known texts. But first a word of caution. I propose to write a kind of criticism that distinguishes, in Richard Rorty's words, "between knowing what [I] want to get out of a ... text in advance and hoping that the ... text will help [me] want something different. ..."[4] An introduction demands that generalizations be made, and I will oblige. But the most important claim I can make for these extraordinary novels is that they defy categories and generalities. Each of these novels has taught me how to read fiction in a new way and has confirmed for me that no single theory or methodology can adequately account for a great work of literature.

*

Why does narratological criticism need a feminist perspective? Narrative desire in the female plot, Peter Brooks has argued, is different than in male plots. It is characterized by "a resistance and what we might call an endurance: a waiting (and suffering) until the woman's desire can be a permitted response to the expression of male desire."[5] Even if we agree that this configuration applies to Jane Eyre as a character, it cannot hold for Jane as narrator. As I will argue in greater detail in my next chapter, Jane's desire for an intimate relationship with Rochester is countered by the subterfuge of her narrative. Her pleasure in serving as his confidante is complicated by her narrative, which delights in revealing his secrets. Brooks can only conceive of female desire as either coinciding with male desire or actively reacting against it. But the desire of the female narrator to narrate, to win over or deceive a reader, to protect or betray a lover must be read as acting independently of both male desire and the stated or implied desire of the heroine. The motivations of her narrative may diverge from those of the larger narrative in which she exists; her personal agenda may have little to do with her author's larger political agenda. Her desire also exists apart from our own desires as readers. If anyone must "wait and suffer and endure" in *Jane Eyre*, it is the reader who is frustrated by Jane's underactive imagination, her unwillingness to investigate the noises in the attic. The reader of *Bleak House*, who is forever anticipating Esther's delayed confessions, must also patiently wait for her to tell her story in her own time. Far from controlling a woman's desire, Lockwood, the original auditor of Nelly Dean's narrative, ends up desiring (but not acting on) what Nelly has manipulated him into wanting all along.

The discourses of both narratology and feminist criticism have conflated the female author and the female narrator, the female narrator and the female character. Brooks uses "female plot" to describe a Grimm fairy tale, *Clarissa*, *Jane Eyre*, and *To the Lighthouse*. This term needs to be unpacked and reformulated more precisely in terms of who is writing, who is narrating, and who is the subject of the plot. For example, the position of the female narrator runs counter to that of the female author, for while the Brontës and Eliot among others hid behind pseudonyms (Eliot in particular often addressing and allying herself with a male reader), the female narrator is able to make herself known to her reader as a woman. Jane's achievement lies in appearing to engender a readerly intimacy which her narrative in fact obviates. Jane the narrator has more freedom than Brontë or the character she portrays, and yet paradoxically she chooses not to take advantage of it. She chooses modesty where her creator and her subject have it thrust upon them.

While I will challenge Brooks's description of female desire, I do not want to jettison entirely his understanding of women's stories. The phenomenon he describes reaches back to Homer, and *The Odyssey* establishes a dichotomy that obtains throughout the history of western literature. Penelope is the warp to Odysseus's weft. Her circumscribed, static existence is pitted against his larger than life experience. Each of the novels in this study might be read as following this paradigm. Jane Eyre sits quietly and listens to Rochester speak of his travels and his opera mistresses. Marian Halcombe tries to hold life together back home while Walter Hartright gets lost in South America. Esther Summerson keeps the keys so that the men in her life can ignore the domestic. Nelly Dean stays behind while Heathcliff and Lockwood disappear and return. And, of course, Molly Bloom spends her day warming the bed for her missing husband. But these female characters are not simply waiting, suffering and enduring. They are constructing their stories. They achieve power, not through what they do, but through how they tell. It is for the very reason that their lives are so restricted, so comparatively dull that women make fascinating narrators. For their experience of telling must necessarily be made more interesting than their experience of living. Each of the writers I discuss latches onto this fruitful tension; each uses a woman's telling of the story as a counter-narrative. The Brontës used counter-narratives in much the same way that they did pseudonyms, to live in two worlds simultaneously. Currer and Ellis Bell allowed Charlotte, Emily, Jane, and Nelly to live virtuously while telling subversively. Jane Eyre's narration undermines her autobiography's plot; Nelly Dean's storytelling tries for a different effect than her story. In Dickens Esther's narrative vies with the omniscient narrator's, in Collins Marian's opposes Walter's, and in Joyce Molly's undoes the previous seventeen chapters. By making them narrators these authors give these female characters more power and talent than their actual stories would suggest. What is at stake for Dickens in using a female narrator obviously differs in part from what matters to Charlotte Brontë, and the difference will become apparent from the following chapters. But the focus of this book is not on any author's feelings about or relationship to real women, but on the narrative challenge posed by having a woman tell her life.

It is a challenge that I believe differs significantly from having a male character do the same. Female narrators exploit the dissimilarities between plot and narration, past and present, deception and self-deception in markedly different ways. Yet these distinctions are never made in one of the most influential studies of first-person narration – Wayne Booth's discussion in *The Rhetoric of Fiction*. Booth defines the unreliable narrator as someone who "is mistaken, or [who] believes himself to have qualities which the author denies him, or [who] as in *Huckleberry Finn*, claims to be naturally wicked while the author silently praises his virtues behind his back."[6] In short Booth defines as reliable the narrator when he "speaks for or acts in accordance with the norms of the work (which ... [are] the implied author's norms), [and as] *unreliable* when he does not." This distance between the implied author's and the narrator's intentions Booth defines as irony.[7]

Following on from Booth, Shlomith Rimmon-Kenan defines the distinction between the reliable and the unreliable narrator thus:

> A reliable narrator is one whose rendering of the story and commentary on it the reader is supposed to take as an authoritative account of the fictional truth. An unreliable narrator, on the other hand, is one whose rendering of the story and/or commentary on it the reader has reasons to suspect .... The main sources of unreliability are the narrator's limited knowledge, his personal involvement, and his problematic value-scheme.[8]

These distinctions do not go far enough in describing the narrators in my study – liars whom we are made to believe. The narrators I will discuss are deceivers, not self-deceivers. As characters they have rarely given critics cause to suspect them, but as narrators they are game players of the highest order. As I will discuss in my *Wuthering Heights* chapter, I believe there should be a distinction made between the *deliberately* unreliable and what previous critics of narrative are describing, the *inadvertently* unreliable narrator, the narrator who believes he is telling the truth or who is telling the truth as he knows it. In the first-person narratives Booth discusses we often "take delight in communion,... even in deep collusion with the author behind [the narrator's] back."[9] I will be describing a different kind of collusion, between author and narrator. And the irony I will be examining will not be the result of distance between the author and his/her narrator, but between the intentions of the plot and its narration. The narrators on whom Booth focuses produce evidence for or against themselves. The narratives I will discuss may appear more transparent, more accessible, yet some of them destroy evidence instead. Retrospection in each of these texts (with the exception of *Wuthering Heights*) is designed to enable privacy, not self-exposure. We read Jane Eyre, Esther Summerson, and Marian Halcombe as trustworthy because of the elaborate defenses created and allowed by retrospection. The self-deceivers on whom Booth concentrates generally fail to exploit these benefits of retrospection, but the women whom I will discuss use whatever limited time they have to construct privacy, a public persona, and a plot, to commit sins of omission and commission. They are neither naive, nor unaware of the plots in which they are involved, but deeply invested in *portraying* themselves as lacking agency, as amanuenses, as artless scribblers. This performed artlessness has its most exemplary manifestation, however, in Joyce's *Ulysses*. Like her literary forebears', Molly Bloom's virtue must be understood in relation to her actual artfulness.

Unreliability in the Victorian novel has often been approached from a psychoanalytic perspective. John Kucich finds in much Victorian fiction a

> multidimensional subjectivity that by definition cannot be presented directly, truthfully, [for] the psychoanalytic model ... embedded as it is in Victorian views of the psyche, presupposes a 'lying function' as the site of intersection between the unconscious and the conscious mind .... Psychoanalytic sleuthing presumes that the conscious mind has been deceived about its unconscious contents by such duplicitous forces as Freud's dream-censor.[10]

Like Kucich, I am concerned with "the power of lies," but rather than viewing them as unconscious evasions and displacements, I will read them as the consciously designed structures upon which these narratives are built. It will be my concern throughout this book to counter a tendency in post-Freudian criticism that privileges unconscious motivations over the agency of authors, characters, and narrators. The tension I will explore will not be between conscious and unconscious, but between lived and narrated experience. Of course, as in actual lived experience fictional characters may be unaware or uninformed. But when these characters come to tell of their experience, they have insight and understanding. If relatively little has been written about any of these characters as narrators, virtually nothing has been written about them as *retrospective* narrators. Am I granting these fictional narrators too much agency, too much conscious motivation? I believe that I am countering an enormous body of criticism that chooses instead to read them as victims or incompetents. How can we hear Jane and Marian as silenced by men when we are reading their words? Why should we feel Esther, Nelly, and Jane are unaware of the plots in which they are involved when they have already lived through them? At the same time I am, of course, not suggesting that fictional constructs have lived and written these texts. By focusing on agency and motivation I am suggesting that authorial intention is at work in these novels. I am arguing that the Brontës, Dickens, Collins, and Joyce are using their narrators to show off their *own* powers of control and imagination.

More importantly, as a feminist, I am questioning feminist criticism's continued reliance on Freud. No one could express my frustration with such an unholy alliance more eloquently than Nina Baym did nearly twenty years ago:

> To accept woman as castrated is to evince a 'hegemonic' mindset that recapitulates and hence capitulates to fear, dislike, and contempt of women .... [T]his attachment to Freud – assuming that it is not simply opportunistic – manifests precisely that masochism that Freud and his followers identified with the female. We are most 'daddy's girl' when we seek ... to seduce him. Our attempt to seduce him, or our compliance with his attempt to seduce us, guarantees his authority. If Freud is right, there is no feminism .... Lacan too – or perhaps, Lacan even more.[11]

The Freudian/Lacanian grip on the feminist imagination is not nearly as tenacious as it was when Baym wrote these words, and yet much feminist criticism, under the influence of Laura Mulvey's psychoanalytic approach, is still more comfortable writing about women as objects of the "male gaze" than as subjects who look themselves.[12] Even if women's language is less and less associated with "madness, anti-reason, primitive darkness and mystery"[13] (as it was under the powerful influence of Lacanian French feminism), men's language is still regularly described as phallocentrically rational and logical.[14] My readings will make more of the mind of a woman as a site of power than her body as evidence of "lack." They will advocate the exploration of intellectual (rather than simply sexual) pleasure as a fruitful line of inquiry for feminist critics. I hope that my approach will help to further distance feminist criticism from Freudian/Lacanian misogyny.

Both Kucich and Mary Poovey have shown how honesty in Victorian England was equated with men, dishonesty with women, how Victorian medical researchers went so far as to try to discover the "physiological roots of a supposedly ingrained female mendacity."[15] While *history* may support these fascinating claims, I find little evidence of this dichotomy in either nineteenth-century fiction or contemporary literary criticism. Do any women in *Pride and Prejudice*, *Dombey and Son*, or *The Way We Live Now* have Wickham's, Carker's, or Felix Carbury's capacity for lying? Literary critics have accused Jane Eyre, Nelly Dean, and Esther Summerson of naïveté and insufficient understanding, but rarely of deliberate dishonesty. If the Victorians can be blamed for considering women too devious, we as literary critics may be criticized for finding women too transparent. But I am not attempting to refute Victorian medical research or late twentieth-century new historicism; I am not trying to prove that actual women are dishonest or that the Brontës, Dickens, Collins, Joyce, and Byatt have found them so. Instead, I am describing a *structure* that allowed fictional women to be as dishonest, artful, and deceitful as their authors wanted them to be, a purely artificial structure which allowed for artifice whether or not that artifice came naturally to real women.

Thus, I am working with realist fiction to put forth an anti-realist argument. That is, I am concerned with the ways in which these novels' modes of narration interfere with any accurate representation of their stories. For example, as Ian Watt has illustrated, the realist novel since Defoe has been concerned with showing how a narrative is occurring at a particular place and time.[16] The novels I discuss are no exception. In fact I will be stressing the implications of knowing exactly when Jane's, Nelly's, Marian's, and Molly's narratives take place. But I will do this to show how female narrators undo that reality which is so manifestly presented to us. *Jane Eyre's* structure allows the heroine to punish the husband she is ostensibly embracing. *Bleak House's* allows Dickens to work out imaginatively what can't be resolved in the harsh reality of Victorian England with its horrible social disparities and tragic children. The structure of *The Woman in White* allows Collins to posit a challenge to the novel writers, to negate the value of marriage, and to champion the cause of the poor, ugly woman. These challenges to realism necessarily culminate in *Ulysses*. The minute attention to hour and location of the novel's first seventeen chapters is pitted against the pure artifice of Molly's soliloquy that effectively erases both time and place.[17]

Watt, Gérard Genette and others have shown how the achievements of formal realism closely parallel those of the cinema.[18] Yet while the novel can simultaneously show and not show, film cannot. Each of the texts I discuss has been filmed and/or staged; each of my readings will show how these novels' narrative structures defy visual realization. How do we make visually exciting the main plot of *The Woman in White*, reading and being read to? How can we film Esther Summerson's negotiations with an unknown, unnamed narrator? How can we film a plot that takes place in the present and past concurrently? How can Molly Bloom perform a text that is being written and unwritten simultaneously? How can we give *Jane Eyre's* visually realizable plot equal time with the narration that cancels it out? To film these narratives is to turn them into tangible *products*; I will read them as ongoing *processes*.

In order to fully marvel at these novels once again, we must recognize that actors cannot do what fictional constructs can, we must see how the novelist can make his cast do what the director cannot. In the last two decades there have been scores of film and TV adaptations made of nineteenth-century novels. Perhaps their unfailing devotion to lingering over the details of pretty costumes, bucolic landscapes, and handsome leads has made it increasingly difficult for us to see how radical the nineteenth-century novel can be. And as if the novel were nothing more than the sum of ingredients necessary for Merchant/Ivory or Masterpiece Theater to turn out its latest adaptation, some of the most influential literary critics of the last two decades have insisted on reading it primarily and insistently as a propagator of dominant class values.

For example, in her "political history of the novel," *Desire and Domestic Fiction*, Nancy Armstrong traces a continuum from *Pamela* to *Jane Eyre* by following each heroine's progression from the working class into aristocratic marriage:

Critics tend to read Pamela's sexual encounters as psychological rather than political events. Thus they can pass off the ideological conflict shaping the text as the difference between a man and a woman rather than between a person of station and a person of low rank. Writing apparently gained a certain authority as it transformed political differences into those rooted in gender. To the authority that came with concealing the politics of writing in this way we can attribute the development of a distinctively female form of writing.[19]

By the time Charlotte Brontë wrote *Jane Eyre*, Armstrong argues, she could do so with the understanding that her "readership acknowledged the authority of language that had little else behind it but the force of female emotions."[20]

> She begins *Jane Eyre* in the voice of a woman who seems to be empowered by her speech alone. With neither money, nor status, nor good looks, nor charm to recommend her, Jane Eyre begins her rise to a secure position within the dominant class in a remarkably forthright manner: '*Speak* I must; I had been trodden on severely, and *must* turn: but how? What strength had I to dart retaliation at my antagonist? I gathered my energies and launched them in this blunt sentence: 'I am not deceitful: if I were, I should say I loved you; but I declare I do not love you: I declare I dislike you the worst of anyone in the world.'[21]

Of course, Jane Eyre does not propel herself into "a secure position within the dominant class" with her powerful speech, but straight into banishment to Lowood Institution. And Pamela may have had a more difficult time than Armstrong in overlooking Mr B.'s gender as he is trying to rape her! But I am less interested here in taking on Armstrong's individual readings than in questioning her method of linking these two novels: "Competing class interests are therefore represented as a struggle between the sexes that can be completely resolved in terms of the sexual contract."[22] By focusing on the politics of class, Armstrong finds complete resolution of conflict between the sexes in *Pamela* and *Jane Eyre*. By focusing on the politics of narrative authority, I find an ongoing, unresolved struggle for power between the sexes. Moreover, I see these struggles being waged in completely different terms so that, as I will argue in Chapter 1, Pamela, rather than laying the groundwork for Jane's verbal authority, is the figure against whom Jane must react in order to establish the upper hand in her own narrative. Thus, while Armstrong, by concentrating on emotional language, is able to trace a continuum of "distinctively female writing" from 1740 to 1847 and beyond, I, by focusing on retrospection, privacy, autonomy, and design, will show how *Jane Eyre* and the novels which follow it depart radically from Pamela's epistolarity.

The history of the English novel begins with men manipulating the writings of women. The editor of *Moll Flanders* admits that "the pen employ'd in finishing her Story, and making it what you now see it to be, has had no little difficulty to put it into a Dress fit to be seen, and to make it speak Language fit to be read."[23] And Mr B., after stealing Pamela's desperate scribblings, uses the poetry she has written to console herself in her solitary suffering to entertain his guests. The narrative strategies of Jane, Esther, Marian, and Molly require that men never get their hands on their texts; nor, I will argue finally, does the reader. Working with canonical texts, I hope to defamiliarize women who have engendered a profound, but false, sense of intimacy with their readers. For instance, Marian Halcombe's diary entries have always been read like Pamela's letters. Critics position themselves behind Marian's writing desk as she scribbles, and write of her as if they knew every word of her diary. But by the time we read Marian's story, it has already been written and already fallen into the hands of Count Fosco. Marian has learned a cruel lesson; in order to regain control of her story and her self-presentation she reads aloud those portions of her diary that she wants Walter Hartright to hear. What we read is what he has heard and transcribed, not what she has written for her eyes only, not what Fosco has read against her will.

Through giving them self-protective narrative strategies, the authors of Jane, Esther, Marian, and Molly have them not only defend themselves against the outrages of overzealous editors, self-interested husbands, or dangerous admirers, but forearm them against the kinds of liberties taken by today's feminist critics as well. While recent feminist criticism has chastised Jane Eyre for embracing a discourse of domesticity and Marian Halcombe for enabling the conventional union of her sister and brother-in-law, I hope to show, by studying plots of narration, that both narrators actively undermine the marriage plot. I will also challenge readings of Molly Bloom which see her dismantling patriarchy through her use of écriture feminine, her indifference to sexual morality or her performance of gender. For Molly's narrative strategy shows her desperately trying to preserve her marriage. It is now commonplace for critics to refer to Brontë's and Dickens's sexual conservatism, to Collins's and Joyce's misogyny and/or radical feminism. I hope to show through my narratological readings of these authors' texts the inadequacy of these labels.

Although I am obviously not the first to discuss the relationship between these authors and their narrators, I am challenging conventional assumptions about which narrators are or are not the authors' surrogates. Most critics of *The Woman in White* see Walter as Collins's stand-in. Some critics go so far as to conflate the two. But in my reading the joke is at Walter's expense, for Collins's sympathies lie with Marian and it is Fosco who ventriloquizes his author. The third-person narrator of *Bleak House* is often mistaken for Dickens himself. But in my reading Dickens's sympathies lie with Esther and with her efforts to distance herself from the selfish, neglectful presence that is her companion narrator. Nelly Dean has been read by many critics as more of a device than a character; I read her as *Wuthering Heights*'s main character. Joyce gives Molly Bloom, who has often been read as a misogynist afterthought to *Ulysses*, more control over his narrative than any other character.

While it would be rare to find readings that confuse/conflate Emily Brontë and Nelly, Dickens and Esther, Collins and Marian, or Joyce and Molly, Charlotte Brontë and Jane Eyre are often referred to interchangeably as in this famous analysis by Virginia Woolf:

> [M]y eye was caught by the phrase 'Anybody may blame me who likes.' What were they blaming Charlotte Brontë for? I wondered. And I read how Jane Eyre used to go up on to the roof when Mrs. Fairfax was making jellies and looked over the fields at the distant view. And then she longed – and it was for this that they blamed her – that 'then I longed for a power of vision which might overpass that limit ....'[24]

Although it is necessary (as my next chapter will show) to distinguish between Jane and her creator, Woolf has chosen for her analysis a rare moment in the novel in which Jane *does* serve as Brontë's mouthpiece, where the author "will write of herself where she should write of her characters:"[25]

> [W]omen feel just as men feel; they need exercise for their faculties and a field for their efforts as much as their brothers do; they suffer from too rigid a restraint, too absolute a stagnation, precisely as men would suffer; and it is narrow-minded in their privileged

fellow-creatures to say that they ought to confine themselves to making puddings and knitting stockings, to playing on the piano and embroidering bags. It is thoughtless to condemn them, or laugh at them, if they seek to do more or learn more than custom has pronounced necessary for their sex.[26]

This is more Charlotte Brontë's agenda than Jane Eyre's. Charles Dickens could never have written such words. His Esther could not even imagine such radical sentiments. And yet, finally, Jane, like Esther, does not use her narrative in the cause of all women (as so many critics have bitterly lamented) but to attend to her own personal relationships, to better her own life. *Jane Eyre* and *The Woman in White* are indeed radical texts; through their narratives Jane and Marian pose serious threats to the conventional marriage plot. But they do this first and foremost by furthering their own personal interests.

As I will argue in Chapter 5, Molly Bloom does not have the *time* to be a social critic. Nor do such urgent narrators as Marian and Nelly. As feminist critics *we* may have the leisure to chastise these women for their political apathy or incorrectness; but their authors (whether male or female, radical or conservative) see to it that these narrators have more pressing concerns. For they have each of these women operate under a deadline and narrate according to a man's schedule. Nelly and Marian narrate when Lockwood and Walter are ready to listen; Jane and Esther narrate when they can get time away from their husbands. None of these women are habitual storytellers. All of these narratives read as distinctive and unique opportunities to have their say. But the experience of Nelly or Marian, who "speak" their narratives, differs from that of Jane or Esther who write theirs. Jane and Esther have the opportunity to construct their ideal readers. But Nelly and Marian have a limited amount of time to tell their story to one man. Consequently, their narrative strategies are both more and less successful than those of women who have time to write. Jane and Esther have the luxury to establish what kind of relationship they want with potential readers, yet can finally only guess their readers' responses; Nelly and Marian have the advantage of personal contact and interaction with their auditors, yet have no ability to construct an audience and are therefore more dependent on the unpredictable responses and misinterpretations of Lockwood and Walter. (In the purely artificial construct of Joyce's "Penelope"

Molly Bloom is neither writing nor speaking, but she must quickly weave and unweave before her husband awakes.)

Nelly is the only narrator in this study who is invited by a man to tell him a story. He hopes that she will be a great spinner of yarns; though untested, she proves to be the very best. Nelly's is probably the quintessential example in British fiction of the retrospective moment. After decades of keeping her story to herself, she has one chance with a captive, bedridden audience to tell it whole, to get it right. Nelly's narrative epitomizes what we will see again and again in these novels. The products of retrospection are structured and designed, but the process of retrospection is an urgent and singular experience. Unlike the other narrators in this study, however, Nelly does not use retrospection to protect, but rather to expose herself. She is the one example I will discuss of the narrator who uses her story as an opportunity to confess.

Wuthering Heights is also paradigmatic of my book's central concern, to show the inherent doubleness of retrospection. As I have mentioned above, criticism too frequently conflates character and narrator. In each of my chapters I will undertake to distinguish between the past life of a character and the present experience of the narrator. This intrinsic "doubleness" also accounts in part for the duplicity which characterizes all of these texts.

For these narrators have secrets, secrets their authors are not anxious for any reader to uncover. Whether sneaky or honest, virtuous or corrupt, when flesh-and-blood Victorian women write of their lives, they invariably fasten onto the desire for privacy. Harriet Martineau, the essayist and political economist, writes of her eighteen-year-old self exploring the difficulties of finding time to study:

> When I was young, it was not thought proper for young ladies to study very conspicuously; and especially with pen in hand. Young ladies (at least in provincial towns) were expected to sit down in the parlour to sew, – during which reading aloud was permitted, – or to practice their music; but so as to be fit to receive callers .... if ever I shut myself into my own room for an hour of solitude, I knew it was at the risk of being sent for to join the sewing-circle, or to read aloud ....[27]

In her bitter essay, "Cassandra," Florence Nightingale describes this practice of women reading aloud to each other as "like lying on one's back, with one's hands tied and having liquid poured down one's throat."

Women never have half an hour in all their lives (excepting before or after anybody is up in the house) that they can call their own, without fear of offending or of hurting some one. Why do people sit up so late, or rarely, get up so early? Not because the day is not long enough, but because they have 'no time in the day to themselves' .... A married woman was heard to wish that she could break a limb that she might have a little time to herself.[28]

In her autobiography, the novelist Margaret Oliphant laments the constraints on her time and space:

How I have been handicapped in life! Should I have done better if I had been kept, like [George Eliot], in a mental greenhouse and taken care of? This is one of the things it is perfectly impossible to tell. In all likelihood our minds and our circumstances are so arranged that, after all, the possible way is the way that is best; yet it is a little hard sometimes not to feel with Browning's Andrea, that the men who have no wives, who have given themselves up to their art, have had an almost unfair advantage over us who have been given perhaps more than one Lucrezia to take care of.[29]

It is no wonder then that the heroines of Victorian fiction spend so much time trying to hide. Jane may fancy herself inconspicuous, but when she seeks shelter in window-seats at Gateshead and at Rochester's party, she is quickly discovered. When she tries to blend in at Lowood, she is placed on a chair in front of her classmates; when she tries to live anonymously, St. John uncovers her name. Esther spends half her story trying to conceal her identity only to have a cast of characters dig it up for their own purposes. Her time is taken up exclusively with helping others, caring for others, visiting others. Marian's letters and diary are opened and read, her hiding place and pseudonym easily uncovered. Yet these fictional characters, through their own narratives, create a level of privacy for themselves which actual nineteenth-century women could only have dreamt of.

I end this study by arguing that the continued dominance of invisible agency and disguised narrative authority in contemporary women's fiction suggests that there is something that we can define as female narration. In A.S. Byatt's *Possession* contemporary literary critics (as characters) discover the narratives of Victorian women. But Byatt has self-consciously constructed these narratives to protect Victorian women from the machinations of the contemporary feminist critic. The closer these critics come to thinking they understand these texts, the more slippery and evasive we, the reader, learn them to be. Byatt's novel is a brilliant example of an interplay of many different female voices. We marvel at Byatt's ventriloquy in creating Ellen Ash (the devoted wife), Christabel LaMotte (the reclusive poet), Sabine de Kercoz (the frustrated writer), Blanche Glover (the jilted lover), Sybilla Silt (the fake medium), and Gode (the servant). But of all these female voices, Byatt's herself speaks most distinctively. Like her heroines and her heroines' literary forebears, her narrative strategy shows a predilection for sometimes cruel subterfuge and blatant lying. By employing the same strategies she so eloquently condemns her creations for using, Byatt sets up a tension in her work which I define as the experience of female narration. This experience, which titillates in order to frustrate the reader, cripples in order to empower the narrator.

1
Jane Eyre: Hazarding Confidences

More than six months after publishing *Jane Eyre*, Charlotte Brontë wrote to her closest friend and constant correspondent, Ellen Nussey:

> I have given *no one* a right either to affirm, or hint, in the most distant manner, that I am 'publishing' – (humbug!) Whoever has said it – if any one has, which I doubt – is no friend of mine...you can just say, with the distinct firmness of which you are perfect mistress, when you choose, that you are authorised by Miss Brontë to say, that she repels and disowns every accusation of the kind. You may add, if you please, that if any one has her confidence, you believe you have, and she has made no drivelling confessions to you on the subject.[1]

The relationship between the secretive Brontë and the trusting Nussey finds an echo in the relationship maintained between Jane Eyre and her reader, who is repeatedly drawn in by protestations of intimacy and repeatedly encouraged to defend suspicious behavior. Today readers come to the novel armed with the tools of post-structuralist, psychoanalytic, and post-colonial theory, and yet they are as seduced by the position of confidante as was the unsophisticated Ellen Nussey.[2] They have felt comfortable invading Jane's bedroom, examining her dreams, and studying her body, yet Jane has maintained the privacy from her "gentle reader"[3] that Brontë so carefully constructed for her. Jane's addiction to privacy is crucial to any understanding of the novel, for this marriage plot could only have been written without the husband's knowledge.

While feminist critics in particular have always noticed the vying for power between Jane and Rochester, they have seen the humbled and chastened husband and the sexually fulfilled and financially secure wife resolving all conflict in the novel's final pages. But the narration makes clear that the vying for power persists well after Jane's marriage. Jane is not completely satisfied with any of the benefits of marriage that she mentions – acting as Rochester's amanuensis, talking with him all day, caring for him, or raising his children. She must write. The act of writing itself belies her claims to ultimate happiness in marriage. For what Jane has written is a revenge novel, one that exposes Rochester's cruelty to Bertha, to Adèle, and especially to herself.

Critics have seldom focused on Jane's status as a writer, and those critics who have studied Jane's narration have seen her development as a narrator occurring simultaneously with her development as a character.[4] But because Jane's is a retrospective narrative, it demands to be read independently of the plot. Her carefully constructed narrative strategy is developed specifically in response to Rochester, but is in play from the first pages of the novel, and does not wait for his entrance to materialize. While nearly all discussions of Jane as narrator pay lip service to the fact that she should not be confused with Jane the character, critics who discuss Jane's narrative in terms of the plot have inevitably conflated the two. I would suggest that continued efforts to analyze the narration in terms of the plot will fail because the narration does not work in tandem with the plot but, instead, serves to undermine it.

In this chapter I hope to defamiliarize a heroine who has engendered a profound but false sense of intimacy with her reader. I will do this by concentrating on Jane's construction of the reader as confidante, a role modeled on her own position as confidante to Rochester. By remaining a silent confidante as a character, Jane is given a voice as a narrator. While tracing Jane's fascination with vengeance, I will show how her expressed desire for a close relationship with both Rochester and her reader is countered by the subterfuge of her narrative.

The first overt suggestion in *Jane Eyre* that the relationships between Jane and Rochester and between Jane and her reader are built on a series of parallel confidence games occurs in the first extended conversation between Jane and her future husband. Rochester says:

> 'Know, that in the course of your future life you will often find yourself elected the involuntary confidant of your acquaintances' secrets: people will instinctively find out, as I have done, that it is not your forte to talk of yourself, but to listen while others talk of themselves; they will feel, too, that you listen with no malevolent

scorn of their indiscretion, but with a kind of innate sympathy; not the less comforting and encouraging because it is very unobtrusive in its manifestations.'
'How do you know? – how can you guess all this, sir?'
 'I know it well; therefore I proceed almost as freely as if I were writing my thoughts in a diary.'

(pp. 166–7)

Rochester takes Jane into his confidence in order to lie to her; Jane masquerades as a confidante in order to obtain stories that she will later write about; and the gentle reader is made to overlook Rochester's miscalculation of Jane's unobtrusively innate sympathy while recognizing his misreading of her talents. For Rochester has, of course, misread Jane. He sees no novelist in his shy, unassuming governess. It is no mere accident that Rochester overlooks Jane's forte for telling of herself; it is the calculation of the character Jane and the basis of narrative design of the narrator Jane. Jane's novel develops out of the interplay between her voluntary role as confidante to Rochester and her part as "confessant" to her gentle reader. From Rochester she obtains information while masking her literary aspirations; to the reader she reveals her literary aspirations while imparting what may be unreliable information.[5]

Toying with us as she has been toyed with, the narrator convinces us that she is flattered by Rochester's attention: "'Strange that I should choose you for the confidant of all this ... [that I should] tell stories of [my] opera mistresses to a quaint, inexperienced girl like you! But ... you were made to be the recipient of secrets.'" (p. 176), and "The confidence he had thought fit to repose in me seemed a tribute to my discretion. I regarded and accepted it as such" (p. 180).

Soon after this encounter, Rochester is glad that it is Jane who finds him in his burning bed, for as he says to her "you are no talking fool: say nothing about it" (p. 186). After their engagement, Jane admits that she "would much rather have all [his] confidence" than his fortune, and Rochester responds: "you are welcome to all my confidence that is worth having" (p. 186). The night before their wedding Rochester urges Jane: "give me your confidence ... relieve your mind of any weight that oppresses it, by imparting it to me" (p. 353). Yet he deliberately misinterprets the stories she will tell him about Bertha. The following night Jane realizes that "never more could [she] turn to him; for faith was blighted – confidence destroyed!" (p. 374). Disguised as the gypsy, Rochester has admitted that it is in fact Grace Poole, not Jane, who is "close and quiet: any one may repose confidence in her" (p. 248). In his final extended confession the night after their aborted wedding, Rochester corroborates this position, for she and the surgeon Carter "are the only two I have ever admitted to my confidence" (p. 395). Conveniently forgetting how he has won Jane's love, Rochester apologizes for his long string of deceptions by claiming that "I wanted to have you safe before hazarding confidences" (p. 402).

Jane confides as comfortably in her reader as Rochester has confided in her. Brontë has written what is arguably the first important female *Bildungsroman* in English literature, and what is crucial to her novel of education is that the heroine learns to lie. Paradoxically, in order to argue that Jane is lying to us we must accept much of what she tells us as the truth. We must accept her version of Rochester's words so that we can see how her narrative style echoes his. We must notice that he has learned from his own family and Bertha's how to win and keep a spouse through lies. We must accept that Rochester is a liar in order to see how Jane beats him at his own game – how she is a better liar, for her narrative is able to expose all of his lies without revealing her own. The extraordinary power of Brontë's novel is that we are being seduced – as is Jane the character – by lies. Aware that she is being lied to, Jane is no less seduced by Rochester; we are still less resistant to seduction. Jane flees after learning the truth; we read on. I will show how Jane's narrative strategy belies the lessons learned by the character Jane, the moral messages with which the novel sums itself up. Generations of readers have been charmed by the prospect of a marriage of mutuality that the *narration* makes clear cannot be Jane and Rochester's.

*

In the opening chapters of *Jane Eyre* Jane must repeatedly defend herself against charges of duplicity and falsehood. But in the pivotal scene at Lowood she gains the confidence of Miss Temple and Helen Burns by learning to "[infuse] into the narrative [of her life at Gateshead] far less of gall and wormwood than ordinary" (p. 83). That is, she learns not to tell. Rosemarie Bodenheimer reads this scene as "the socialization of Jane's narrative style."[6] Bodenheimer finds a correlation between Jane's acquisition of speech and her development as the writer of her story. But I find this scene crucial in that just as Jane finally gains the confidence of others, she stops talking. Within the story of her life we do not see her developing as a storyteller. Instead, we watch a young girl who vents her anger verbally in the opening pages, retreating further and further into silence as the novel progresses. Jane's reluctance to communicate with other characters is not readily apparent to us, for the direct addresses to the reader occur more frequently in the latter half of the novel. Jane is most likely to share intimacies with her reader, however, when she is most loath to tell her story to anyone else in her narrative.

Although Jane has had no confidants, she refers to herself as a storyteller: "I told [Miss Temple] all the story of my sad childhood. Exhausted by emotion, my language was more subdued than it generally was when it developed that sad theme" (p. 82). Yet within several pages she has lost her gift. Her friend Mary Ann Wilson "had a turn for narrative, [Jane] for analysis; she liked to inform, [Jane] to question" (p. 91). She has gained Miss Temple's confidence by not telling. She will go on to gain Rochester's, Adèle's, Mrs. Fairfax's, and her cousins' by not telling. To mark the transition from her Lowood to Thornfield chapters Jane writes: "I now pass a space of eight years almost in silence" (p. 98). The bizarre syntax of this sentence suggests both that Jane omits eight years from her narrative and that the years themselves were spent almost in silence. In one of the only scenes that Jane gives us from this period she describes her annoyance with a roommate's "prolonged effusion of small talk" (p. 101), which keeps her from uninterrupted thought. After the death of Helen Burns, Jane is paired with chattering females such as Adèle and Georgiana Reed, with whom she is the silent listener. At Gateshead, Jane had remained silent until her anger toward Mrs. Reed could no longer be contained. Because of her outburst, she is banished to an inhospitable place where her bad reputation has preceded her. Jane's narrative does not trace the development of her voice, but rather the movement from her sulking, unproductive silences at Gateshead to her cultivated silences at Lowood and beyond.

While still at Gateshead, Jane's taste for vengeance is acute and overt. Questioned by Brocklehurst about her favorite books from the Bible, she names Daniel, Genesis, Samuel, Exodus, Kings and Chronicles, Job and Jonah. She finds precedence for her hatred of John Reed in the stories of Cain and Abel and Joseph and his brothers, and she finds hope in the tales from Exodus that the guilty will be punished, the oppressed rewarded. Young Jane likes only one book from the New Testament. Revelation, the first book that she mentions to Brocklehurst, and presumably her favorite, figures prominently in the novel.[7] Just before she leaves St. John, he reads to her from its twenty-first chapter:

> 'He that overcometh shall inherit all things; and I will be his God, and he shall be my son. But,' was slowly, distinctly read, 'the fearful, the unbelieving, &c., shall have their part in the lake which burneth with fire and brimstone, which is the second death.' Henceforward, I knew what fate St. John feared for me.[8]
>
> (p. 532)

The crucial words that "&c." replaces are "all liars." Like Brocklehurst, St. John appears in Jane's narrative to warn her against the dangers of deceit. But by refusing his hand and his diagnosis, by closing her story with a quotation from Revelation 22:20 and her own response to it, Jane celebrates her own achievement and triumphantly rejects any fear of being judged. As critics have noted, Jane figures her life story as a pilgrim's progress.[9] She ends her religious journey by placing herself in the site of Christ's last biblical appearance, in the position of judgment.

Revelation ends as the beast is defeated and the beast's city, Babylon, "the great whore," is destroyed. God judges the world; a new heaven and earth replace the old; the holy city, Jerusalem, the bride, comes down from God, and all of earth's splendor is gathered into it. *Jane Eyre* ends with the destruction of Thornfield and its would-be mistress, the "unchaste" (p. 391) Bertha – "what it was, whether beast or human being, one could not, at first sight, tell: it grovelled, seemingly, on all fours" (p. 370). Rochester is punished for his sins. His bride returns to him, and together they build what Jane describes as an idyllic life in their new home.

A biblical scholar describes Revelation, the Bible's most apocalyptic book in this way:

> The whole book purports to be what John has seen and heard, but it is clear that his visionary experience has been shaped both by canonical and apocalyptic writings .... Probably it is a mixture of genuine experience and literary elaboration. Biblical metaphors and images – dragon, lamb, harlot, bride – come to new life in his imagination. There are allusions to or echoes of practically every book in the Hebrew Bible. Daniel and Ezekiel are particularly formative; Isaiah, Jeremiah, Zechariah, and the Psalms are pervasive influences; so too are the stories of creation and Exodus.[10]

Like John's epistle, Jane's epistle to her reader purports throughout to be the truth, the exact rendering of the experience of her eyes and ears. But as Elaine Showalter writes, "Brontë ... expresses her heroine's consciousness through an extraordinary range of narrative devices. Psychological development and the dramas of the inner life are represented in dreams, hallucinations, visions, surrealistic paintings, and masquerades .... Jane's growth is further structured through a pattern of literary, biblical, and mythological allusion."[11] I am concerned, however, not with *Brontë's* but with *Jane's* decision to model the end of the novel on and to take its final lines from the Book of Revelation, the book that D.H. Lawrence claimed gives "the death-kiss to the Gospels."[12] As Carolyn Williams notes, "for Jane to end her story by quoting these last words of the book about last things, which is itself the last book of the Book of Books – this is having the last word, with a vengeance."[13]

Today the early reviews of *Jane Eyre* strike us as naive and misinformed: "Altogether the auto-biography of Jane Eyre is pre-eminently an anti-Christian composition," wrote Elizabeth Rigby.[14] "Never was there a better hater," the *Christian Remembrancer* said of Brontë; "All virtue is but well masked vice, all religious profession and conduct is but the whitening of the sepulchre, all self-denial is but deeper selfishness ... all Christian profession is bigotry and all Christian practice is hypocrisy."[15] Yet I would argue that these reviewers hit on an element of truth in the novel. For although the adult Jane comes to read the New Testament, she seems most attracted to, and to ally herself with, the Christ of Revelation rather than the Christ of the Gospels. Jane removes herself from the scene of destruction, from the death of Bertha, the ruin of Thornfield, and the maiming of Rochester, but the novel is not concerned with Bertha's anger and judgment, but with that of Jane – its moral center. Jane's anger does not manifest itself as Bertha's does, through fire and destruction, but through the act of writing a novel in which the heroine lives an irreproachably Christian life but in which the narrator is utterly unforgiving. Like the Christ of Revelation, Jane unleashes "the wrath of the Lamb" (Revelation 6:16).

Brontë was dissuaded from taking her own revenge against Elizabeth Rigby in the preface to *Shirley*. Yet her response to the *Christian Remembrancer*'s less pointed attack on *Villette* in 1853 shows again that lashing out was never Brontë's preferred method of dealing with an enemy. As Lyndall Gordon writes of her letter to W.S. Williams, "she pictured her opponent [whom Brontë mistakenly took to be a man] as a High-Church ecclesiastic, hating Currer Bell's latitudinarianism, yet feeling, in the very heat of resistance, the compulsion of the Reader:"[16]

> He snarls, but still he reads. The book gets hold of him he curls his lip, he shows his teeth, he would fain anathematize; excommunicate the author; but he reads on, yes – and as he reads – he is forced both to *feel* and to *like* some portion of what is driven into his hostile iron nature. Nor can he ... altogether hide the involuntary partiality; he does his best; he still speaks big and harsh, trying to inflict pain, striking at hazard, guessing at weak points, but hoping always to hit home. And that author reads *him* with composure, and lays down the review content and thankful – feeling that when an enemy is so influenced – he has not written in vain.[17]

Gordon describes Brontë's letter as "a bravura performance: Currer Bell in vigorous form, enjoying the battle in which she asserts all the composure of a David with a supreme power behind her."[18] But I do not see a David and Goliath at battle here. Brontë has no desire to wound her opponent. Nor does she wish to appeal immediately and unconditionally to her reader. Like Rochester with Jane and Jane with her reader, Brontë wants to get hold of her, to expose the "involuntary partiality," to seduce. I detect in Brontë's letter the delicious thrill that she experienced when watching her self-righteous reader undergo a kind of religious conversion.

Jane's own conversion apparently occurs at Lowood, where she is still plotting her revenge against Mrs. Reed: "When we are struck at without a reason, we should strike back again very hard; I am sure we should – so hard as to teach the person who struck us never to do it again" (p. 65). When Jane is finally reunited with Mrs. Reed, she has long since learned from Helen Burns how to turn the other cheek. Jane can now assure us that "time [has] quell[ed] the longings of vengeance and hushe[d] the promptings of rage and aversion" (p. 288). Jane's studied serenity convinces her readers of her deeply felt Christian forgiveness, but her desire for revenge is as acutely present here as it was in the novel's first chapter.

In a compelling argument Janet Gezari has shown that Eyre may be pronounced ire, or eyer rather than air.[19] Both the fact of Jane's ire and of her position as eyer are crucial to this encounter. Jane feels "ire" after succumbing to the icy stare of Mrs. Reed's "stony eye – opaque to tenderness, indissoluble to tears" (p. 289). Mrs. Reed explains that her hatred for her niece stems from Jane's "continual, unnatural watchings of one's movements!" (p. 290). Although Mrs. Reed is not blind, she has difficulty recognizing her niece, and just before her aunt's death Jane "gaze[s] awhile on her who could not now gaze on me" (p. 297). Mrs. Reed plies her with the same question – "Is this Jane Eyre? ... are you Jane Eyre?" – to which Jane continually replies, "I am Jane Eyre." Mrs. Reed seems unable to accept that Jane is alive: "The fever broke out [at Lowood] and many of the pupils died. She, however, did not die: but I said she did – I wish she had died!"(pp. 289–90).

The parallels between these scenes and Jane's final reconciliation with the blinded Rochester are striking. As with Mrs. Reed, the moment of recognition is delayed and must be reaffirmed repeatedly. "*Who* is it? *What* is it? ... Is it Jane? ... My living Jane? ... " she replies, "I am Jane Eyre" (pp. 554–5). Just before Mrs. Reed confesses her sin against Jane, she orders her to "bring me some water" (p. 300). Jane is reunited with Rochester as she brings him the water he has demanded of a servant. Early in the novel, Jane "long[s] for a power of vision which might overpass" (p. 132) the limits of Thornfield's estate, and by the end of the novel her painfully nearsighted creator grants her wish. It is no accident that Rochester and Mrs. Reed meet with similar fates, for Jane's ability to see long after Mrs. Reed's "eye of flint was covered with its cold lid" (p. 301), or Rochester's once brilliant eyes are blinded, cannot be divorced from her desire for revenge against both of them. Jane takes her revenge through the written word, and Brontë herself was all too familiar with the necessity of strong eyesight for a writer. Two years before beginning *Jane Eyre* she wrote: "once upon a time I used to spend whole days, weeks, complete months in writing ... but at present my sight is too weak for writing – if I wrote a lot I would become blind."[20]

Richard Chase's discussion of Rochester's blindness has remained largely unchallenged for fifty years: "Rochester's injuries are, I should think, a symbolic castration. The faculty of vision, the analysts have shown, is often identified in the unconscious with the energy of sex."[21] By emphasizing discussions of sex, the critical literature on *Jane Eyre* has ignored the importance to both Brontë and Jane of "the faculty of vision." For while looking affords Jane great erotic pleasure, not being seen is as crucial to her experience as is seeing itself. Here Jane describes sitting in the window-seat at Rochester's party:

> No sooner did I see that [Rochester's] attention was riveted on [the ladies], and that I might gaze without being observed, than my eyes

were drawn involuntarily to his face: I could not keep their lids under control: they would rise, and the irids would fix on him. I looked, and had an acute pleasure in looking, – a precious, yet poignant pleasure; pure gold, with a steely point of agony.

(p. 218)

Jane is ecstatic because she is not incriminated by her looking, as she had been in the place from which she chooses to begin her narrative, hiding in a window seat at Gateshead. Again, her acute pleasure in looking through the pages of Bewick's *History of British Birds* cannot be divorced from the experience of hiding. The novel suggests that it is for the crime of looking without being looked at that Jane is punished when John Reed discovers and then severely abuses her. In the later scene Jane is not punished for her looking, but she cannot actually keep it a secret. When Rochester, disguised as the gypsy, questions her about her master's interest in Blanche Ingram, Jane lets slip that "I cannot remember detecting gratitude in his face." "Detecting!You have analyzed, then," he counters (p. 250). And soon this eye that has taken on a life of its own comes under Rochester's keen scrutiny:

'The flame flickers in the eye, the eye shines like dew ... an unconscious lassitude weighs on the lid: that signifies melancholy resulting from loneliness. It turns from me; it will not suffer farther scrutiny; it seems to deny, by a mocking glance, the truth of the discoveries I have already made.'

(p. 251)

Because Jane's eye implicates her in her own crime, the narrator needs a blinded Rochester to carry out her project. Seeing without being seen is both crucial to writing her narrative about Rochester and a narrative technique, like winning a confessor's confidence and telling a tale in retrospect, whose importance she first learns from Rochester.

These lessons are made most manifest in Jane and Rochester's last conversation together at Thornfield. Rochester's lengthy story of his life before and after meeting Jane is meant as a heartfelt apology for hiding Bertha's existence. Yet his last narrative repeatedly undoes its own good intentions. It omits his false flirtation with Blanche and his crueler toying with Jane, makes no mention of his bizarre secrecy on the nights of the bed burning and of Mason's visit, and leaves out any reference to his game-playing and his gypsy disguise. His attempt to snare Jane into bigamy is forgotten in his retrospective rendering of history, for in retrospect facts can be put in their proper place. They need not interfere with seduction. At this moment in her narrative Jane is moved by her lover's words, but when, years later, she comes to write down her experience of him in her early days at Thornfield, he is once again represented as capricious and even cruel. Her narrative indicates that while here the character Jane is clearly taken in by Rochester, the narrator Jane will remain skeptical. From her master Jane will learn that it is easier to lie in retrospect. In one of the rare instances of Jane's telling a story within her story, she confides the mysteries of the night before her wedding night to her lover. Her artless, unthinking rendition leaves him many opportunities to correct her. The following night Rochester's story, told long after the events narrated, leaves Jane ill-prepared to confront him with her own version.

Although Jane does not counter Rochester's interpretation with her own, her narrative resists his version of their courtship by offering a calculatedly different one. Because Brontë fully digests the power of the tale told well after the fact, she rescues her heroine from Pamela's unguarded position. As Brontë indicates in the first chapter of her novel, Jane is enthralled by Pamela's story as a girl and becomes aware of its larger implications when she finally reads it as an adult. Bessie "fed our eager attention with passages of love and adventure taken from old fairy tales and older ballads; or (as at a later period I discovered) from the pages of *Pamela*" (p. 7). Pamela, whose immediate thoughts are known immediately, is necessarily in a less empowered position than Mr B. who saves his feelings for the appropriate moment. Because Pamela is in a less privileged position than her reader, because she cannot review her letters, she succumbs to Mr B.'s version of events. He tells a pretty tale and sweeps her off her feet. After their marriage, he tells a less pretty tale of his abandonment of a pregnant woman and their illegitimate child. But again, in retrospect, his tale wins the pity and devotion of his wife, not the scorn and disgust of his servant. Like Mr B., Rochester wants to buy time. He hopes that after a year of marriage that he can, without fear, tell his tale to his devoted mistress. Because Jane escapes this fate, because she is able to wait and marry legitimately, she is able to write the autobiography of a virtuous woman. More importantly, she, like Mr B., is able to buy time: she is able to construct the kind of narrative her master has taught her, not succumb to the narrative her master has told her.

So when we hear Rochester's version of their courtship, we can be sure that Jane's narrative has offered us a calculatedly different version.

Rochester remembers observing Jane the day after their first meeting until she was wakened by "the voice of Mrs. Fairfax": "you ran downstairs and demanded of Mrs. Fairfax some occupation: the weekly house accounts to make up, or something of that sort, I think it was. I was vexed with you for getting out of my sight" (pp. 399–400).

Yet in the story that Jane has already shared with us, Mrs. Fairfax interrupts Jane's solitude on orders from Rochester to bid her to take tea with him. Jane leaves the room on Mrs. Fairfax's recommendation that she change her dress before appearing before her master. Rochester's version shows his desire to absolve himself of some of his own whims. He hopes that Jane will show some of the same penchant for game playing that he exhibits. Rochester says to her, "I wished to see whether you would seek me if I shunned you" (pp. 400–1). Jane, however, tells the story of a servant in her master's house who comes when she is summoned and leaves when she is dismissed. By painting himself as a lovelorn, frustrated man Rochester does everything to pretend away the inherent inequality of their relationship and the inherent cruelty of his capricious behavior. Although Jane's version may also be inaccurate, her autobiography makes clear through these two distinctly different stories that Rochester's retrospective confession is intended to absolve himself while winning the reader's sympathy. Even while confessing, even while gaining our sympathy, Rochester cannot help using the diction of a charlatan. His motives were not simply those of a lover and a desperate husband but also those of a man who delights in playing games: "you did not know what my caprice might be – whether I was going to play the master and be stern, or the friend, and be benignant" (p. 401).[22]

Thus Jane's narrative is able to expose all of Rochester's lies while disallowing such exposure of her own. She covers herself beautifully, far better than Rochester ever could. When the plot doubles back upon itself, we accept Jane's version simply because the competitor's is so flawed. For example, at the end of the novel the innkeeper tells Jane the story of her life at Thornfield while explaining how Bertha has died. The innkeeper's overt condemnation of Jane involves a simultaneous elevation of Rochester: "'a more spirited, bolder, keener gentleman than he was before that midge of a governess crossed him, you never saw, ma'am ... for my part I have often wished that Miss Eyre had been sunk in the sea before she came to Thornfield Hall'" (p. 547). He becomes a gallant figure risking his own life to save Bertha and the servants. Such a figure we have found nowhere in Jane's narration. This is the same man who needs her help when he falls from his horse and is burned in his bed, who comes to her for assistance when Mason is bitten. His gallantry is also at odds with his cruelly false courtship of Blanche and Jane, his aversion to accepting Adèle as his own, and his attempt to entrap Jane in adultery or bigamy. The power of the written word is made manifest in this encounter with the innkeeper. Although the oral tradition of the town will remember Jane as the one who bewitches, distracts, and emasculates the spirited, keen, bold gentleman and Bertha as the one who blinds and cripples him, Jane's written account will redeem herself and implicate Rochester in Bertha's crime.

Salvaging the monstrous Bertha has become the emphasis of much feminist criticism of *Jane Eyre*. Sandra Gilbert reads Bertha as Jane's "truest and darkest double," the figure who, by biting Mason, tearing the wedding veil, crippling Rochester, and destroying Thornfield, acts out all of Jane's unexpressed resentment.[23] But by whose agency Bertha acts out these unarticulated fantasies, Gilbert does not say. She hints that it is by Brontë's design, yet her argument never makes clear how much, if at all, Brontë makes Jane responsible for Bertha's existence or actions. Mary Poovey's discussion of Bertha's agency is still more vague as it consistently relies on the passive voice:

> The 'blow' Jane's announcement delivers is then graphically acted out when Bertha, who is Jane's surrogate by virtue of her relation to Rochester, attacks Mason, whose textual connection to Rochester has already been established. As before, anger and violence are transferred from one set of characters to another, revenge is displaced from Jane's character, and agency is dispersed into the text.[24]

How does our reading of the novel change if we acknowledge *Jane* as the one who positions Bertha's violent responses alongside her own unexpressed emotions?

By reading Bertha as the instrument of Jane's suppressed anger, feminist critics have tended to neglect readings of the novel that allow for the actual expression of Jane's anger. By consistently referring to Bertha as a figure for Jane's subconscious or repressed desires, they erase Jane's narrative agency, her part in the creation and construction of Bertha. But I read Jane as actively and consciously using Bertha to draw attention away from her own act of revenge. Instead of looking at how Jane's unexpressed anger prefigures Bertha's violence, then, I want to consider how Bertha's demonic malignity is consistently followed by Jane's exaggerated benignity. Jane purposefully sets herself up in contrast to Bertha. Her description of the night of the "sharp,"

"shrilly" (p. 258) attack on Mason, for example, is replete with references to her own noiselessness – "[I] moved with little noise across the
carpet," (pp. 260–1) she assures us. Rochester is grateful that she is
"shod with velvet," (p. 268) and when he orders her to "make no
noise," she obeys, walking across "the matted floor as softly as a cat"
(p. 261). The silent cat spends the night listening for "a snarling,
snatching sound, almost like a dog quarrelling" (p. 262) and later hears
"a momentary renewal of the snarling, canine noise"(p. 264). A docile
carrier pigeon, Jane "flew thither and back" (p. 268) from Mason's to
Rochester's room while she likens "Grace" to "a carrion-seeking bird of
prey" (p. 264). Rochester himself calls Jane his "pet lamb" whom he
has left "near a wolf's den" (p. 271).

Jane's description of herself in this scene is a textbook example of a
virtuous Victorian woman – silent, obedient, content to know nothing.
When Jane arrives at Thornfield, her overactive and remarkably astute
imagination is still intact. Her immediate impression of Thornfield's
third story is of "a corridor in some Bluebeard's castle" (p. 129). And her
instant disappointment in Mrs. Fairfax is due to the fact that she seems

> to have no notion of sketching a character, or observing and
> describing salient points, either in persons or things ... my queries
> puzzled, but did not draw her out. Mr. Rochester was Mr. Rochester
> in her eyes; a gentleman, a landed proprietor – nothing more: she
> inquired and searched no further, and evidently wondered at my
> wish to gain a more definite notion of his identity.
>
> (p. 127)

And yet, after caring for the bleeding Mason, seeing him safely evicted
in the middle of the night, and obtaining no explanations about what
has transpired, Jane "supposing [Rochester] had done with [her], prepared to return to the house"(p. 270). Receiving unsatisfactory answers
to such calm, unintrusive questions as "[w]ill Grace Poole live here
still, sir?" Jane admits that "I like to serve you, sir, and to obey you in
all that is right" (pp. 271–2). Thus, Jane uses Bertha's attacks as opportunities to advertise her own utter harmlessness. Jane's victory over her
harsh upbringing never gives her reader cause to question her strength.
Yet when Bertha tears her wedding veil, Jane faints with terror, provid-
ing Rochester with the opportunity to treat her like the hothouse
flower that passed for the upper-class female of his day: "I must be
careful of you, my treasure: nerves like yours were not made for rough
handling" (p. 359).

Moreover, while Jane uses the biting scene to describe her silence and patience, she uses Bertha's first attack on Rochester to illustrate her own resourcefulness and efficiency, as she speedily douses the flames engulfing her master's bed. The contrast with Bertha is again explicit; hers is an incompetent beastliness. She is no Frankenstein's monster, for Shelley's creation, whether seen as a figure of Romantic excess or as a fantasy of female empowerment, is successfully, mortally dangerous. Bertha, however, bungles all of her attempts to kill and succeeds only at self-destruction. (Why have critics never questioned Bertha's ineptitude? She manages to set fire to Rochester's bed, but cannot find a way to escape from Thornfield. She tears Jane's veil and mysteriously ends up in her prison cell again.) Her pretensions to vampirism are beyond her own scope. In the only words she is reported to speak, she swears that, through sucking Mason's blood, she will "drain [his] heart" (p. 267). Through Bertha, Jane demonstrates a kind of revenge that does not work. Her own is successful because it is everything Bertha's is not – controlled, sustained, articulate, and, above all, disguised. Striking out, biting and burning are no match for obedience, silence and unquestioning contentment.

In recent years some critics have moved away from reading Bertha as Jane's dark double and see her instead as the racial other. Gayatri Spivak reads Jane as gaining her position as the first great heroine of the Victorian novel at the expense of the colonized Bertha.[25] Some critics have countered that in the figure of Bertha can be found Brontë's critique of imperialism. Jane takes her place in literary history, writes Jenny Sharpe, by displacing not a woman of color but a member of "an idle plantocracy in the state of decline."[26] Susan Meyer argues that Bertha sacrifices herself in order to "[burn] away Rochester's oppressive colonial wealth,"[27] but because Jane's fortune is also "tainted," she too is implicated in colonialism. Meyer says that Brontë acknowledges that

> creating one's own triumphant identity as a woman no longer oppressed by class or gender inequalities at home in England – or writing *Jane Eyre*, the fiction of a redistribution of wealth and of power between men and women – depends on a colonial ink.[28]

I take issue with much that is implicit in this debate. As these critics generally agree, Bertha's race is indeterminate. (Her brother's face is "sallow" [p. 192]; hers is "purple" [p. 296].) Her Creole heritage suggests to some that she represents the colonizers, to others, the colonized. What unites this criticism is the notion that Rochester's first wife must be destroyed because of her *birth*. Jane triumphs, however, as a result of her *education*. Even if we agree that Jane and Bertha are of different races, Jane never presents herself as racially superior. The qualities that distance her from Bertha are not innate to either woman. (Jane actually entertains the possibility that she too could be afflicted by Bertha's genetic inheritance – madness.) Instead, Jane takes great pains to show that her powerful innocuousness is learned. Her time at Lowood cures her tendencies toward monstrousness at Gateshead; her days at Thornfield test the resolve of this education.

Clearly Jane's innocuousness is a mask. At the end of Mason's visit Rochester and Jane engage in a typical confidence game. He tells her the story of his life while omitting all pertinent details, confesses he has made a serious error without ever naming it, and ends by extracting a promise from her that she will sit with him the night before his marriage to Blanche. Yet it is Jane who has drawn both of them into this game with the admission that "if you have no more to fear from Mr. Mason than you have from me, sir, you are very safe" (p. 219). Rochester immediately responds to this avowed benignity by inviting her to share a seat with him. Jane's calculated harmlessness thus serves both to shield her from his seduction and to excite his desire. As if this relationship needed stimulation!

Perhaps the most puzzling aspect of the criticism of *Jane Eyre* over the last fifty years is its reliance on psychoanalytic readings that find evidence of sexual disturbance and malfunction in the novel.[29] Rochester is reduced by the end of the novel, but why, if he is able to father children, have critics needed to view him as symbolically castrated? Does not Jane's rejection of St. John's sterile proposal indicate a healthy sexual appetite? And where is the evidence that what Jane lacks in her marriage is sexual fulfillment? In the most passionate of her thirty-five direct addresses to the reader Jane reveals the rich fantasy life that sustains her through her difficult days at Morton:

[R]eader, to tell you all, in the midst of this calm, this useful existence – after a day passed in honourable exertion amongst my scholars, an evening spent in drawing or reading contentedly alone – I used to rush into strange dreams at night: dreams many-coloured, agitated, full of the ideal, the stirring, the stormy – dreams where, amidst unusual scenes, charged with adventure, with agitating risk and romantic chance, I still again and again met Mr. Rochester, always at some exciting crisis; and then the sense of being in his arms, hearing his voice, meeting his eye, touching his hand and cheek, loving him, being loved by him – the hope of passing a lifetime at his side, would be renewed, with all its first force and fire. Then I awoke. Then I recalled where I was, and how situated. Then I rose up on my curtainless bed, trembling and quivering; and then the still, dark night witnessed the convulsion of despair, and heard the burst of passion. By nine o'clock the next morning, I was punctually opening the school; tranquil, settled, prepared for the steady duties of the day.

(p. 468)

The passage seems to have been lifted directly from Brontë's "Roe Head Journal."[30] But in her journal entry that begins "all this day I have been in a dream," Brontë's passion is not for a flesh and blood man but for writing and a life of the imagination:

Then came on me, rushing impetuously, all the mighty phantasm that this had conjured from nothing to a system strange as some religious creed. I felt as if I could have written gloriously. I longed to write. The spirit of all Verdopolis, of all the mountainous North, of all the woodland West, of all the river-watered East came crowding into my mind. If I had had time to indulge it, I felt that the vague sensations of that moment would have settled down into some narrative better at least than anything I ever produced before. But just then a dolt came up with a lesson. I thought I should have vomited.[31]

Christine Alexander has written that the Angria of the "Roe Head Journal" had

become 'an infernal world,' a 'world below,' to be expiated only in confession. But Brontë could not betray her secret. The nearest she came to revealing the truth to the unsuspecting Ellen Nussey was when she wrote: 'If you knew my thoughts; the dreams that absorb me; and the fiery imagination that at times eats me up and makes me feel Society as it is, wretchedly insipid, you would pity and I dare say despise me.'[32]

Are the secrets Brontë found too terrible to share with her dearest friend the same secrets Jane cannot articulate to her gentle reader? Quite possibly Brontë is using an obsession with writing to sublimate her sexual desires. Yet Jane appears to be doing exactly the opposite – freely describing her sexual frustration in order to sublimate still more unacceptable thoughts. While Jane's sexual feeling is a constant theme of the novel, her desire to write and the circumstances under which this novel was written, are secrets that are as closely held from the reader as is Jane's romantic past from the community at Morton.

As readers of the novel, however, we have an insight into Jane that Rochester is never allowed. While Jane never writes in front of us, her moments of greatest closeness with the reader are always when she is most invested in concealing her position as narrator from Rochester. For instance, as she hides in a window seat during Mr. Rochester's party she directly addresses the reader and moves immediately into the present tense: "You are not to suppose, reader, that Adèle has all this time been sitting motionless on the stool at my feet" (p. 216). It is one of the reader's most "intimate" moments with Jane, yet Rochester has no inkling of his governess's literary pretensions, for as he enters the room the book in her hands magically transforms itself into a set of netting-needles. Samuel Richardson had written that "the pen is almost as pretty an implement in a woman's fingers, as a needle,"[33] and Brontë latches onto all of the subversive implications of this association, for just when Jane should be seen with a pen, she finds a needle handy. Without ever revealing her passion for writing or letting us in on her surreptitious scribbling, she makes the reader aware of her position as author while simultaneously masking this effect to Rochester. Never does Jane write in Rochester's presence until, in the novel's final paragraphs, he gains partial vision (but not enough to "read or write much") as Jane is "writing a letter to his dictation"(p. 577). Like Pamela who, after marrying, insists that she must limit her writing to the household accounts, Jane becomes the first great female narrator of the Victorian novel by masquerading as an amanuensis.

It is impossible to know to what extent *we* do not "know" Jane, but it is possible to recognize the strategies by which she convinces us that we do. When she writes, "I had not intended to love him: the reader knows I had wrought hard to extirpate from my soul the germs of love there detected" (pp. 218–19), we remind ourselves of Jane's ugly crayon self-portrait and her ivory miniature of Blanche. If we begin to think her fickle, she chides us for our own disloyalty: "Perhaps you think I had forgotten Mr. Rochester, reader, amidst these changes of place and fortune. Not for a moment" (p. 509). She saves her fiercest challenge to the reader for the end of her novel: "And, reader, do you think I feared him in his blind ferocity? – if you do, you little know me" (p. 436). For

150 years romantic readers have reviewed the case Jane has made for herself as the soul of fidelity and devotion. The young girl who clings passionately to the neck of her dying friend, the discreet young woman sitting silently by the side of a bleeding man, the newly made heiress who shares her fortune with her cousins, could never turn away in disgust from the man she has loved. We have passed all of Jane's tests, and in these last chapters we are assured that we do know her, that the girl who has never tried to rise above her own physical and social inferiority has finally met her equal in the transformed Rochester.

The reader is repeatedly pitted against Rochester for Jane's affections. The narrator frequently moves into the present tense when addressing the reader, giving her the illusion of being on an equal footing with Jane's master: "Stay till he comes, reader; and, when I disclose my secret to him, you shall share the confidence" (p. 348). In the novel's last pages, after telling most of the tale of her life with the Riverses, Jane immediately adopts the mask of the silent confidante. Rochester describes hearing her voice in the middle of the night: "Reader, it was on Monday night – near midnight – that I too had received the mysterious summons .... I listened to Mr. Rochester's narrative; but made no disclosure in return" (p. 573). Her description of these events is couched between addresses to the reader: "'Shew me – shew me the path!' I entreated of Heaven. I was excited more than I had ever been; and whether what followed was the effect of excitement, the reader shall judge" (p. 535). So, in fact, her telepathic communication with Rochester is never communicated to him, but only to the reader: "that mind, yet from its sufferings too prone to gloom, needed not the deeper shade of the supernatural. I kept these things, then, and pondered them in my heart" (p. 573). This is Jane's most explicit confession that Rochester never has read and never will read the novel to which the reader is afforded such intimate access.

Yet as we are taken in by Jane's confidences, we must recognize that she woos her reader as Rochester has wooed her. He tries to shock her with stories of his mistresses; she titillates her reader with a tale of averted bigamy. He tests her loyalty each time Bertha menaces him; she proves her fidelity to him by questioning her reader's to her. Even the pace and frequency of Rochester's avowals of intimacy are echoed in Jane's direct addresses to the reader. While Rochester begins by playing the distant master in Hay Lane and at the party, he ends by demanding Jane's constant company. Jane, too, cautiously makes her reader's acquaintance, addressing her only twice in the novel's first one hundred pages, thirteen times in the last one hundred.

Most readers have abandoned themselves to the narrator's seduction, but there is certainly evidence that we should follow Jane's example and chasten ourselves against such temptation. In the final chapter of her novel she begins with her penultimate address to us: "Reader, I married him" (p. 574). This chapter, like those that conclude nearly every nineteenth-century novel written before or after *Jane Eyre*, describes marital bliss. Feminist critics have seldom challenged this description: the first wave of feminist critics forgave Brontë for her conventional ending. In 1977 Elaine Showalter wrote:

> Can we imagine an ending to *Jane Eyre* in which Jane and Bertha leave Rochester and go off together? Obviously such a conclusion would be unthinkable. Such possibilities and such solutions are beyond the boundaries of the feminine novel ... in feminine fiction men and women become equals by submitting to mutual limitation, not by allowing each other mutual growth.[34]

Feminist critics in the 1980s and 1990s have been more judgmental of Brontë's acquiescent ending. Steven Cohan and Linda Shires write:

> The discourse of revolution, which positions Jane as a subject of 'discord,' is [replaced by a] discourse of domesticity ... so as to position Jane as the subject of 'concord.' Once this happens, rebellion is drained of its political meaning and domesticity is likewise protected from any real politics by its simple equation with concord.[35]

Whether Brontë's novel is ideologically palatable or suspect, however, is impossible to determine until we decide if it is narratologically believable. Rochester and Jane have achieved "perfect concord" because "all my confidence is bestowed on him; all his confidence is devoted to me" (p. 576). Since Jane's first engagement, she has expressed the desire to have Rochester's confidence rather than his fortune. And yet it is in these last chapters that we learn most explicitly that whatever confidence Rochester has bestowed on her has not been reciprocated:

> I began the narrative of my experience for the last year. I softened considerably what related to the three days of wandering and starvation, because to have told him all would have been to inflict unnecessary pain: the little I did say lacerated his faithful heart deeper than I wished. I should not have left him thus, he said, without any

means of making my way: I should have told him my intention. I should have confided in him: he would never have forced me to be his mistress.

(p. 563)

Like a good Victorian housewife, Jane keeps her book out of her husband's hands ostensibly not to hurt but to protect him. Yet in this episode, the reverse of their early conversation about confidantes, Rochester, believing that Jane is fully confiding in him now, wishes that she had done the same earlier. Like Jane in the earlier scene, Rochester cannot distinguish the truth from its edited version. Like Rochester, under the guise of protecting his lover, Jane demonstrates her own fierce need for self-protection. Were this an unedited version of her story it would, nevertheless, reveal her strong resistance to confiding in her husband, for to confide is to relinquish an advantaged position. Jane does not seek comfort from Rochester; she seeks to comfort. Jane does not pour out her heart; she tests the waters. As Rochester assumed the more empowered position during their courtship, Jane will assume it during their marriage. By lacerating his heart *deeper than she wished* is Jane indicating that she fully intended to lacerate his heart, at least a little? Jane does not tame her man; she tortures him.

*

In writing these last pages Brontë proved to herself that she could successfully complete a novel without her blind father's knowledge. Only after receiving favorable reviews did she reveal her secret to Patrick Brontë. Her motivation does not seem to have been to punish him, but to protect him, as well as herself. She knew, then, that Jane could complete her novel without Rochester's knowledge. Moreover, she knew that it could not exist *with* his knowledge. Bertha blinds Rochester so that Jane can perpetrate a more damaging and permanent form of revenge. Jane does not submit to anything, least of all mutual limitation. Nor does she easily equate domestic bliss with the sharing of confidences. What she makes clear in these last pages is that there is little that is mutual or shared in this marriage. Jane has won the confidence game. Beginning her days at Thornfield as the silent listener to a great storyteller, she begins her marriage by "putting into words the effect of field, tree, town, river, cloud, sunbeam – of the landscape before us; of the weather round us – and impressing by sound on his ear what light could no longer stamp on his eye" (p. 577). Rochester is in a position of helpless dependence. His perception of their marriage cannot be hers; it is derived from what she deigns to tell him.

And our relationship with Jane, as well, is based on what she has seen fit to share with us. If we are reluctant to question our status as confidants, we might think of the readers of Brontë's novel *Villette*, who are denied crucial information about Lucy Snowe only to be taunted by their limited knowledge of this later first-person narrator:

> It will be conjectured that I was of course glad to return to the bosom of my kindred. Well! the amiable conjecture does no harm, and may therefore be safely left uncontradicted. Far from saying nay, indeed, I will permit the reader to picture me, for the next eight years, as a bark slumbering through halcyon weather, in a harbour still as glass.[36]

Lucy's vexed relationship with her reader reflects her inability to achieve intimacy. Writing as an old woman, she needs more than a blinded husband for her to narrate her story – she presumably needs the death of every other character in the novel. Rather than satisfying narrative curiosity, rather than telling the end of her sad tale, Lucy invites her reader to imagine a different one:

> Here pause: pause at once. There is enough said. Trouble no quiet, kind heart; leave sunny imaginations hope. Let it be theirs to conceive the delight of joy born again fresh out of great terror, the rapture of rescue from peril, the wondrous reprieve from dread, the fruition of return. Let them picture union and a happy succeeding life.
>
> (p. 715)

Lucy's cruel and capricious parting is from the reader she has held herself back from throughout her narrative, the romantic reader taken in by Jane Eyre.

This chapter was originally published © 1991 by The Regents of the University of California, in *Nineteenth Century Literature*, Vol. 53.4, and is reprinted by permission of University of California Press.

2
Nelly Dean: Changing Tactics

In one of the many stunning misreadings in her 1850 preface to her sister's novel, Charlotte Brontë writes: "For a specimen of true benevolence and homely fidelity, look at the character of Nelly Dean ... "[1] While critics have suspected Charlotte's other characterizations – "Heathcliff, indeed, stands unredeemed"[2] – they have too readily accepted this judgment of Nelly. Indeed, her apparent innocuousness has rendered her unworthy of much critical attention at all. But *Wuthering Heights* is as much the story of Nelly Dean as it is of Heathcliff. From chapters 4 through 34 Nelly appears in and plays a crucial part in virtually every scene of the novel. Why then do we not read her as a, possibly the, major character in *Wuthering Heights*? Perhaps it is because we open this novel to read a story of unbridled intensity and passion, not to learn about the life of an unemotional celibate. But if it is commonplace to ask how an awkward, painfully shy young woman who lived in a remote village and apparently never fell in love with anyone could have written *Wuthering Heights*, then it is time to consider how her chosen narrator, a sensible old maid, is responsible for much of the novel's passionate energy.

The relatively few critics who have written about Nelly have certainly not achieved consensus. James Hafley has read her as "one of the consummate villains in English literature."[3] Other critics have read her as merely ordinary, stable, and commonsensical.[4] Some critics have seen her as a product of a sexist class system. For Gilbert and Gubar she is "patriarchy's paradigmatic housekeeper."[5] For others she is more of a device than a character:

[O]ne senses that ... Isabella's writing to Nelly is unlikely or that Heathcliff's perennial willingness to reveal his feelings, actions and plans to Nelly is principally dictated by the technical needs of composition .... *In short, Nelly's formal function as narrator may have determined her problematical character.*[6]

I will be arguing precisely the opposite. I will be showing how Nelly's failings as a character determine the necessity of her narrative. The difficulty critics have had in assessing and agreeing upon Nelly lies in the doubleness of her role and her story. More overtly than in *Jane Eyre*, the distinctions between Nelly the character and Nelly the narrator, Nelly's life and Nelly's rendition of it call attention to themselves. My reading will show why Nelly has been seen as both the villain and the good angel, both the figure who prevents love and the woman who encourages it.

It is, and will probably remain, unclear how disingenuous Charlotte is being in her preface. J. Hillis Miller has demonstrated that Charlotte contradicts herself at least four times. She manages to claim that "the novel is not Emily speaking, but nature speaking through her," that "the novel is sociologically accurate," that "the novel is a religious allegory," and that "whatever the nature of the work, Emily is not to be blamed for it because ... she was the passive medium through which something or someone else spoke .... "[7] Yet Charlotte and Emily were clearly tackling similar narrative problems. Both sisters were interested in the reasons why women tell their own stories, why certain women are chosen to hear others' stories, and why the way women live their lives differs from the way in which they narrate them. If we are to believe Jane Eyre at all, she lives a virtuous life, gaining the trust and confidence of those around her so that she can betray that trust many years later in writing. If we are to believe Nelly Dean, she is a completely untrustworthy character, a sneak and a snitch, a spy and an eavesdropper, who is inexplicably chosen to receive everyone's confidences. Like Jane Eyre, she does not share her story with anyone while she is living it. But when it comes time for her to tell it many years later, she tells the truth, not to seek revenge, but to pay for her sins. If Jane uses her narrative as an opportunity to deceive, Nelly uses hers as a chance to confess. Jane's plot works toward marriage; her narration dismantles our romantic illusions. Nelly's plot prevents happiness and romantic fulfillment; her narration tries to bring about the union of two people. So while retrospection allows Jane the chance to reconstruct her past and put it in the best possible light for herself, retrospection allows Nelly, although always reluctantly, to come clean. Jane's narration, written ten years after the fact, does not affect her plot; Nelly's narrative, told in medias res, can, she hopes, create a different plot.

Nelly's confession is only partly motivated by a need to clear her conscience. She has a more pressing agenda, a new husband for Cathy, a new employer for herself. It will be obvious from many of the passages that I quote that Nelly's is an unwilling confession. Nelly is well-practiced at all forms of deceit. Honesty does not come naturally to her. Yet she knows that only as a narrator can she ameliorate the many years of damage she has caused. Lockwood (as well as many a reader of the novel) is able to overlook her small crimes and misdemeanors because they so frequently take the form of half-hearted admissions of guilt.

We may remember *Wuthering Heights* as one of the great love stories in the English language, but if we consider the plot closely, we may find that the impulse to avoid all romantic, indeed all personal experience is as profound as the pull toward passion and feeling. For if love leads to marriage and marriage to childbirth, then childbirth leads to death. "For the mothers die. *Wuthering Heights* is a landscape of childhood grief and loss; an orphaned earth where mother-love is nowhere to be found."[8] Stevie Davies has written particularly eloquently about the lack of mothers in the novel. Taking on Juliet Barker's contention that "the loss of the Brontë mother [was] a commonplace occurrence – much more commonplace than it is today – and therefore accepted more readily. In a more pious age, too, there was the comfort of knowing that she had gone to a better place .... " Davies replies:

> Mother-loss *cannot* be commonplace. We only have one each to lose. Nor do pious platitudes compensate for having the centre ripped out of your life. Charlotte and Anne were to undergo periods of doubt in the Christian God. Emily and Branwell viewed him with Byronic contempt for his execrable logic and malignity .... Common in eighteenth- and nineteenth- century England, mother-lessness in Emily Brontë's world is comprehensive. Her own experience of mother-loss is projected out upon the planet as universal catastrophe. Constantly, the novel reaches back to origins – and finds them in loss.[9]

Nelly's character is imbricated in this catastrophic motherlessness. For she is responsible at various times for six orphaned children – Heathcliff, Catherine, Hindley, Hareton, Cathy, and Linton. Yet Nelly is the only woman in the novel who successfully avoids motherhood. Because we tend to read the Victorian novel as the great age of the marriage plot and the birth of children as the most conventional of happy endings, we would not readily see spinsterhood, celibacy, and childlessness as achievements, but for Nelly this is clearly the case. By excluding herself from all the experiences most common to her sex, she becomes the only survivor of her generation. The plot of *Wuthering Heights* seems to validate Nelly's position. We can respect her decision to remain unmarried in a landscape littered with the bodies of young women. When romantic interaction means the infliction of pain, we might even admire her determination to remain unloved.

By all accounts Emily was raised by a very loving mother substitute, her beloved servant Tabby, clearly in part the inspiration for Nelly herself. (The sisters were so devoted to her that after she broke her leg in a fall on the ice, they went on a hunger strike until they were given permission to take care of her.) Like Nelly, Tabby was a great storyteller, enchanting the Brontë children with moorland folklore from the 1780s (the time of many of the events in *Wuthering Heights*). Winifred Gérin points to Tabby as quite possibly Brontë's most important literary influence: "To Tabby's doric parlance she owed the homeliness of her epithet in place of the laboured one. Thanks to Tabby's influence, unwitting as it was, Emily chose not to write a 'Gothic romance' about demon lovers,' but 'a cuckoo's tale.'[10] But Tabby and Nelly are also significantly different. She spoke in the thick Yorkshire dialect that Brontë reserves solely for Joseph. She entered the Brontë home in her fifties and was seventy-seven when Brontë wrote her novel. It is quite conceivable that Charlotte was thinking of Tabby while reading *Wuthering Heights*, hence her glowing portrait of a wholly benevolent figure. Gérin believes that "in her the children gained what no stepmother could ever have given them: disinterested devotion.... She became in the true primitive sense a member of the 'family,' and left it only for the grave."[11] Emily has a much more vexed relationship toward Nelly. She is not a quaint, grandmotherly figure but a young woman in her childbearing years for virtually all of the narrative. She is twenty-one when Hareton is born, twenty-seven when Cathy is born. She is in fact Emily's own age for much of the story. Nelly is not a wicked stepmother, but she perceives herself as a poor substitute for what has been lost as we see from the lullaby she sings to the infant Hareton:

> It was far in the night, and the bairnies grat,
> The mither beneath the mools heard that.[12]
> (It was far in the night, and the little ones wept
> The mother beneath the earth of a grave heard that.)

Brontë found this primitive Danish ballad, "The Ghaists Warning" in the appendix to Scott's *The Lady of the Lake*.

> A stepmother withdraws light, food, heat from a family of seven motherless children. The mother, dragged from her grave by her children's weeping, returns as a corpse, to comb, dress and dandle them, suckling the baby from her decayed breast .... The stepmother is terrified into doing her duty to her unwanted charges .... Nelly's macabre quotation over the sleeping Hareton speaks into a world whose children are rejects or orphans and get, at best, makeshift foster care.[13]

Is Nelly's story then a defense of the vicarious life, of a life lived on the safe margins of experience, or a bitter acknowledgment that being a stand-in is not the same as being the real thing?

To answer this question I believe that we need to return to a distinction between plot and narration, character and narrator. I will be reading the plot of *Wuthering Heights* not as the story of a man motivated by his passions to destroy lives and take over two houses, but as the tale of one woman who actively works against the romantic impulses of everyone around her, who tries in one form or another to prevent unions between Catherine and Heathcliff, Heathcliff and Isabella, Edgar and Catherine, and Cathy and Linton. If we see this as the plot, then we can begin to recognize the brilliance of the narration. For Brontë chooses the character most immune to feeling to try to induce feeling in another. The same character who creates so much pain by forbidding passion and obstructing desire must tell a narrative of seduction. The product she presents Lockwood with, her own story of how love, marriage, and childbirth are all the most dangerous of occupations is unraveled by the process of telling it.

Once we read Nelly as the main character, we can see most of the other characters operating as her foil. Nelly is the same age as Hindley. The narrative even hints that she may have had romantic feelings for him, but Nelly follows exactly the opposite trajectory. While he begins at the center of the family with money and status and ends in penury and depravity, a victim of his former servant, Nelly begins as kitchen help and ends as a member of the family.

Two of the women of her generation, Frances and Catherine, die in childbirth. Nelly, however, accumulates and abandons children without any harm to herself. While Catherine's and Isabella's passions destroy them, Nelly survives by allowing herself no fervent attachments. The only other major character who, like Nelly, is not ruled by his passions (and not coincidentally singled out for unequivocal praise by Charlotte Brontë) is Edgar Linton. But while both take full advantage of the library at Thrushcross Grange, Edgar uses it to retreat from a world he cannot comprehend, Nelly to "cultivate her reflective faculties," (p. 48) to negotiate her way through a world she cannot afford but to understand, to go further than one could "expect of a poor man's daughter" (p. 49). By transcending the circumstances of her birth through self-education Nelly earns the reader's respect. Her fellow servant, Joseph, is a parodic figure whose laughable religiosity and impenetrable dialect ensure his social stasis. And, of course as I will discuss in greater detail later, Nelly is Lockwood's foil. Her fellow narrator tries to penetrate the mystery of *Wuthering Heights* to no avail. He longs for a connection to the place through friendship with Heathcliff and marriage to Cathy. He narrates the book without understanding its implications about himself, Heathcliff, and especially Nelly.

For now the central character whom we must read against Nelly is Heathcliff. She works for the Earnshaws and Lintons; Heathcliff works against them. She lives a contentedly celibate life; he sets out to rape one woman and to devote his soul to another. She blithely takes on the care of whichever child is dropped in her lap; he participates in killing his own son. She moves easily between the two worlds of the Grange and the Heights; he takes them by storm. Yet Nelly's story finally justifies Heathcliff's for it points to the reality that class distinctions are random and insupportable. If anything, Nelly's story proves that she is of better stock than her employers. Nelly is as bright and articulate as any of her peers. She is also clearly stronger and healthier. The chronological story of *Wuthering Heights* begins with six children – Hindley, Catherine, Heathcliff, Edgar, Isabella, and Nelly. They are all born within eight years of each other, but while Isabella is having her hair done, Nelly is nursing the sick. While Hindley is going off to university, Nelly is cleaning the kitchen. While Catherine is playing on the moors, Nelly is tending a baby. Nelly is a servant, but not unsurprisingly a discontented one. She is unable to be dutiful, discreet, honest, obedient, to be like a good Victorian lady. Wedded to the security of a home and job, she still has difficulty obeying orders, sustaining loyalties, minding her own business, or thinking herself less than the people who employ her. She is, in short, as unsuited to be a servant as Heathcliff. And it is she unsurprisingly who first plants the idea in his head that he is destined for better things: "You're fit for a prince in disguise. Who knows but your father was Emperor of China, and your mother an Indian queen, each of them able to buy up, with one week's income, Wuthering Heights and Thrushcross Grange together? And you were kidnapped by wicked sailors, and brought to England. Were I in your place, I would frame high notions of my birth ... "(pp. 44–5). Before this encounter, Nelly has described Heathcliff as "a sullen, patient child, hardened, perhaps, to ill-treatment: he could stand Hindley's blows without winking or shedding a tear, and my pinches moved him only to draw in a breath, and open his eyes as if he had hurt himself by accident, and nobody was to blame" (p. 30). Immediately after this encounter, he throws a tureen of hot apple sauce at Edgar's face. Nelly claims that Heathcliff's "violent nature was not prepared to endure the appearance of impertinence from one whom he seemed to hate" (p. 45). Since when, we must ask, does Heathcliff have "a violent nature?" Nelly takes this opportunity to distance herself from the boy whose head she has just turned, but we should read this instead as the first of many signs of the profound identification between the two characters.

For they are the two liminal figures in the novel, neither insiders nor outsiders, neither servants nor members of the family. Much work has been done on the liminality of Heathcliff's character. Both Marxist and post-colonial critics have seen him as the outsider trying to gain a foothold in a community which resents him because of his class, race, or ethnic identity.[14] Soon into her narrative Nelly establishes herself as an insider, telling Lockwood that "we don't in general take to foreigners here ... unless they take to us first" (p. 35). But Nelly often stumbles over her family status: "Hareton is the last of [the Earnshaws] as our Miss Cathy is of us – I mean of the Lintons" (p. 27). For she is actually in as precarious a position as Heathcliff, and she is finally equally responsible for the destruction of the Earnshaw and Linton families.

Towards the end of her narrative, locked into a bedroom at Wuthering Heights while Heathcliff is forcing Cathy to marry Linton, Nelly "pass[es] harsh judgment on my derelictions of duty; from which, it struck me then, all the misfortunes of all my employers sprang. It was not the case in reality, I am aware; but it was, in my imagination, that dismal night, and I thought Heathcliff himself less guilty than I" (p. 210). In fact, very little happens in *Wuthering Heights* for which Nelly cannot be blamed. She validates Heathcliff's position as an outsider in the Earnshaw home by abandoning him on the stairs the night he arrives. She allows him to run away for several years by not telling Catherine that he has overheard her say that marriage to him would degrade her. She incites a violent encounter between Edgar and Heathcliff that leads Catherine to lock herself in her room. After three days without food or water, Catherine announces she is dying – Nelly sees fit to keep the report to herself. Her neglect leads to Catherine's death and many years later to the younger Cathy's discovery of the Heights. She obeys orders that allow Hareton, Linton, and Cathy to be abandoned. She fuels Cathy's love for Linton by burning his letters. In fact, by actively resisting passion throughout the novel she merely inflames it. Like Heathcliff, Nelly always behaves impulsively. While Heathcliff's impulse is to act out of passion, anger, and unceasing devotion, Nelly's is always to act against passion and feeling. While Heathcliff does everything to resist servitude, to become the master himself and oppress others as he was oppressed, Nelly does everything not to get fired. Heathcliff is hell-bent on self-destruction, Nelly committed to her self-preservation. What Brontë makes clear is that the impulses of each are equally dangerous and equally at fault in the destruction of the two families. And just as importantly Nelly herself understands this. She sees the results of her negligence and interference wherever she turns. After provoking a violent encounter between Edgar and Heathcliff, she confesses that Catherine "did not know my share in contributing to the disturbance, and I was anxious to keep her in ignorance" (p. 90). After ignoring the signs of danger in Catherine's bedroom, she admits that "I should not have spoken so, if I had known her true condition, but I could not get rid of the notion that she acted a part of her disorder" (p. 94). When she visits Edgar on his deathbed, she assures him that Catherine was kidnapped because "Heathcliff forced me to go in, which was not quite true" (p. 214). And when the doctor is "perplexed to pronounce of what disorder [Heathcliff] died ... I concealed the fact of his having swallowed nothing for four days, fearing it might lead to trouble" (p. 254).

The prosaic story of a servant trying to keep her job coincides with the tale of passion we remember as *Wuthering Heights*. Nearly every major event in Heathcliff's life provokes a corresponding crisis in Nelly's. As a child she is banished from the Heights for leaving him on the stairs overnight. When she snitches to Catherine about Heathcliff "wooing" Isabella, she is warned that "To hear you, people might think *you* were the mistress! ... You want setting down in your right place!" (p. 86). When Heathcliff entices Cathy to visit the Heights for the first time, Nelly insists that Edgar not be told, for "if she revealed my negligence of his orders, he would perhaps be so angry that I should have to leave ... " (p. 153). Nelly can never get it right. When she fails to tell Edgar about Catherine's self-starvation, he threatens her, "You shall account more clearly for keeping me ignorant of this!" (p. 99). But when she squeals on Heathcliff and Catherine, her mistress realizes that "Nelly has played traitor; Nelly is my hidden enemy" (p. 100), and Edgar warns, "the next time you bring a tale to me, you shall quit my service, Ellen Dean!" (p. 100).

By the time Lockwood meets her, Nelly's incompetence as a plotter has made her success as a narrator absolutely crucial. Through her lack of feeling she has helped to antagonize Heathcliff and kill Catherine. Her motherless charge has been lured to her doom because of Nelly's inability to tolerate teenage infatuation. The task of Nelly's narrative is to write a new plot, but in order to do so she must tell her story to the spouse she has chosen for Cathy. Although they approach their narratives differently, Charlotte and Emily begin with the same problem. What is a woman to do when a man doesn't want to hear her story? Defoe and Richardson wrote novels in which men desperately want to get their hands on women's words, but the reticent Brontë sisters never *assumed* that anyone would want to hear their own or their heroines' stories. Thus, Rochester begins by talking at Jane, and Lockwood longs to be entertained by any story not about Nelly herself.

We enter *Wuthering Heights* with Lockwood, a born misreader, as our guide. After mistaking dead rabbits for puppies, Heathcliff for a considerate landlord and Cathy for Heathcliff's wife, he returns to Thrushcross Grange to introduce us to Nelly – "the housekeeper, a matronly lady taken as a fixture along with the house, *could not or would not* comprehend my request that I might be served by five" (p. 7, emphasis added). In this innocuous description he has already begun to form our misimpression. Nelly is not a "fixture" (like Joseph) but the most mobile character in the novel, the only figure capable of moving between the two worlds of the Heights and the Grange. And if by matronly Lockwood means a wifely or maternal woman, then he has clearly misunderstood the spinster who abandons (willingly or unwillingly) at least five children left in her charge. Even in this first description of Nelly we are able to see evidence of a woman uncomfortable with simply following orders. Yet the ignorant Lockwood has no cause to suspect her of intrigue, and goes on to advise his readers of her dullness and marginality to the plot. When he returns from his unhappy visit to the Heights to be greeted by "my human fixture and her satellites" (p. 25), he finds himself in need of company and

under pretence of gaining information concerning the necessities of my establishment, I desired Mrs. Dean, when she brought in supper, to sit down while I ate it, hoping sincerely she would prove a regular gossip, and either rouse me to animation, or lull me to sleep by her talk .... She was not a gossip, I feared, unless about her own affairs, and those could hardly interest me.

(p. 26).

Thinking himself in control of the narrative – "Oh, I'll turn the talk on my landlord's family! ... A good subject to start ... " (p. 26) – Lockwood allows her to proceed. Each time he reenters the narrative he reassures himself and us that he is not listening to Nelly Dean's "affairs." "Now continue the history of Mr. Heathcliff," he instructs her after one narrative break (p. 70). At another he writes that

I have now heard all my neighbour's history, at different sittings, as the housekeeper could spare time from more important occupations. I'll continue it in her own words, only a little condensed. She is, on the whole, a very fair narrator and I don't think I could improve her style.

(p. 120)

Still misreading Nelly's centrality to the plot, Lockwood reminds us that she is "the housekeeper" who has more crucial responsibilities than gossiping about other people. Still convinced that he has heard the story of a disinterested narrator, he feels as qualified as his servant to take over the narrative.

Lockwood condescends to praise Nelly's narrative powers, but does not notice that she has previously been denied the opportunity to be a storyteller. He takes her to be a regular gossip and does not see how her need to tell her story rivals his desire to hear it. He is able to value the story she tells without recognizing her place in it. (Just as Rochester will never know that Jane is a storyteller, Lockwood will never realize that Nelly is a fascinating character.) The bed-ridden auditor using Nelly to pass the time cannot see the urgency of her participation. But this unfeeling spinster must quickly learn how to seduce.

Because of Nelly's apparent lack of interest in all things sexual, many critics have insisted that she does not "get" the story she is telling. Like Robert Browning's Duke of Ferrara or Ford Madox Ford's John Dowell, she is read as an inadvertently unreliable narrator, a narrator unaware of her own sexual and emotional limitations and her author's ability to communicate passion and feeling through her and despite her. I would like to give Nelly more credit. We do not understand a story apart from the one the narrator has told; we remember this as one of the great passions in literature because of, not in spite of, Nelly's presentation. Nelly is not an obstacle to our understanding; she creates the obstacles around which the novel is structured. She does not rein in anarchy; she creates desire. Her narration does not control passion; it fosters it. As a character she has experienced this story with judgment and lack of emotion; as a narrator she is able to convey the intensity of feeling that motivates nearly all her acquaintance. Nelly's narration and Lockwood's response to it ultimately suggest that there is no set and determined content in this novel, but only their and our experience of it.

Nelly's passionate narration is aided by an extraordinary memory for her interactions with Heathcliff, Catherine, and Isabella. And although told under great pressure and urgency, what critics have termed her "largely unscripted narrative"[15] reveals an incredible sense of structure and design as well. Certainly I am not the first to recognize how tightly constructed this novel is. A. Stuart Daley has shown how the novel is organized around the cycles of the moon.[16] Charles Percy Sanger has shown how the family pedigree "is a remarkable piece of symmetry in a tempestuous book."[17] After dating many of the novel's events and demonstrating Brontë's knowledge of arcane English property laws, Sanger concludes that "there is, so far as I know, no other novel in the world which it is possible to subject to an analysis of the kind I have tried to make .... Did the authoress carry all the dates in her head, or did she work with a calendar?"[18] I am interested in how Brontë has Nelly herself carry around these dates in her head, how conscious she makes her of the patterns and structures which lend meaning to her tale.

In particular Nelly is aided by the use of the threshold. She situates nearly every scene at a window or in a doorway. Catherine and Heathcliff stare in the windows of Thrushcross Grange until they are attacked by the Lintons' dogs. Unobserved, Heathcliff goes out the door while Catherine explains why she cannot marry him. Catherine locks the doors of Thrushcross Grange against Edgar's men as they try to bar Heathcliff from the house. Catherine locks her bedroom door against the meals and help which might have saved her life. Catherine gazes longingly at the entrance to her bedroom as Heathcliff finds her door and strides in to embrace her. Edgar expels Joseph from the house when he comes to claim Linton for Heathcliff. Nelly remembers how "the latch was raised and fell" (p. 161) as she abandons Linton at Wuthering Heights. Heathcliff seduces Cathy back to the Heights as Nelly is trapped on the other side of a locked roadside door. Nelly is locked behind another door as Heathcliff forces Cathy and Linton to wed. Joseph bars Nelly from entering the Heights after Cathy's marriage. As Heathcliff realizes his impending death he notes that he has moved from "the threshold of hell" to "within sight of my heaven" (p. 249). After locking himself into his room, he is discovered by Nelly who first closes his window then tries unsuccessfully to close his eyes and mouth. These are only a handful of the examples of how Nelly uses the threshold.[19] Through her extensive use of this device Nelly creates distance between the lover and the beloved. The novel's famous sexual tension is engendered by countless frustrated attempts to penetrate various entrances.

Thus, far from misunderstanding the sexual implications of her story, Nelly deliberately sets out to titillate her auditor and, playing on his own desire and liminality, to draw him into her community's propensity for irresistible passion. Her narrative's agenda is the transformation of Lockwood from "misanthropist" to lover, from outsider to family member. Although Lockwood never articulates his desire for Cathy to her, Nelly proves herself a more astute reader:

> "[W]ho knows how long you'll be a stranger? You're too young to rest always contented, living by yourself; and I some way fancy no one could see Catherine Linton, and not love her. You smile; but why do you look so lively and interested, when I talk about her? and why have you asked me to hang her picture over your fireplace?"
>
> (pp. 194–5)

Nelly has learned the lesson of her own narrative. She is finally trying to bring two people together rather than to drive them apart. Yet in the last words Nelly utters before Lockwood leaves for the first time, we see that her confession has allowed her to remain as duplicitous as ever: "I can see no remedy [for Cathy], at present, unless she could marry again; and that scheme, it does not come within my province to arrange" (p. 226).

Nelly's passionate narrative has clearly worked on generations of readers. Why does it not work on Lockwood? I would suggest two possible answers. The first is that Nelly's parting words are accurate. Her schemes have prevented and destroyed marriages, but she does not have the agency to create them. Only when the plot is taken out of her hands can it realize its ultimate potential. Only then can the unfulfilled tragedy of Catherine Earnshaw Heathcliff Linton reverse itself in the marital happiness of her daugher, Catherine Linton Heathcliff Earnshaw. The second is that Lockwood has heard the wrong story. Lockwood introduces himself as a man "perfectly un-worthy" of "a comfortable home," a man who has gained a reputation for "deliberate heartlessness" (p. 5). As he asks for the latest installment of Heathcliff's violent history, he fails to hear that he is listening to the story of a woman like himself, a woman characterized by her "deliber-ate heartlessness." Lockwood, who immediately and throughout identifies with Heathcliff, believes that Nelly's narrative is teaching him why not to love. He'll "extract wholesome medicines from Mrs Dean's bitter herbs" by learning to "beware of the fascination that lurks in Catherine Heathcliff's brilliant eyes" (p. 120). Lockwood hears an indictment of Heathcliff, not a confession by Nelly. He hears a warning against too much feeling; Nelly is in fact warning him against too little.

Thus, unlike Defoe's or Richardson's novels, *Wuthering Heights* is not a struggle for narrative control, for Lockwood has no reason to alter or reinterpret Nelly's narrative. That would require him to understand what he has in his hands. Wilkie Collins must certainly have looked back to *Wuthering Heights* when designing his complicated narrative structure. In the next chapter I will discuss his "master" narrator's mis-interpretation of the narrative of the great Marian Halcombe, another old maid with much to teach men about love.

3
Marian Halcombe: Appropriating an Identity

In my chapters on *Jane Eyre* and *Wuthering Heights* I have tried to show how narration works against plot; in my analysis of *Bleak House* I will argue that the mode of narration mirrors the plot. In none of these novels is the narrative project made explicit. Wilkie Collins's *The Woman in White,* however, begins with a self-conscious statement of intent, to use a method of narration that will arrive at the truth by exposing the lies of the plot. This plot is about the appropriation of identity. Briefly Percival Glyde appropriates the identity of a baronet. In order to keep his crime hidden he institutionalizes Anne Catherick, the woman he erroneously believes knows his secret. Then, with the help of the Count and Countess Fosco, he appropriates Anne's identity and gives it to his wife, Laura Fairlie. In turn, he appropriates his wife's identity and gives it to the dead Anne Catherick. In order to live safely in England Count Fosco has appropriated a false identity; in order to return to the continent after committing his crimes, he appropriates yet another one. The narration of the novel, designed to expose the truth, to right the wrongs perpetrated by the villains, actually commits the same "crime," for the heroes of *The Woman in White* (Walter Hartright and Marian Halcombe) are using the same techniques to narrate as the villains are to commit crimes.

In this chapter I will show how Walter Hartright appropriates others' identities in order to arrive at the "truth" and in the process how he counters Count Fosco's sensation plot with his own conventional Victorian marriage plot. But I will not be arguing, as many critics have, that Marian is an apologist for this marriage plot or, as Walter himself believes, that she is furthering his cause. Instead, I will show how Marian, through the process of narrating, appropriates a sexual identity that challenges the truths Walter has collected and the inevitability of

52

the story he tells. I will spend the first part of this chapter discussing Walter's project and how my reading of it departs from previous criticism. In the latter part of the chapter I will show how Marian is modeled on Marian Evans and how both women threaten male plots of sexual attraction and domestic fulfillment.

*

In the last chapter of *Jane Eyre* Brontë holds out the tantalizing possibility of a sequel to the novel in which Rochester completely regains his vision and reads the novel composed in secrecy by his wife. Brontë never wrote a novel about male anxiety inspired by female narrative and sexual authority, but Wilkie Collins did. Unlike *Jane Eyre*, in which writing takes place outside the confines of the story and away from the penetrating eyes of internal or external readers, *The Woman in White* is constructed around continual, often illicit acts of reading and writing. When Jane addresses her gentle reader, she is speaking to a figure whom she has inscribed into her text, whose process of reading she has anticipated and accounted for. When Walter Hartright addresses his reader, he does so first and foremost as a reader himself, seeking confirmation of his interpretation of the pages confronting him. What Walter reads, reconstructs, and writes, we read as a chronological series of events. This chronology creates the suspense that unnerves the reader; the process of reconstructing this chronology engenders Walter's own anxiety. For his first experience of the story that he will finally claim as his own is his actual absence from it. His own narrative registers the shock and disorientation of reading competing narratives in which his character is marginalized, his narrative authority questioned, his ideology devalued, and his sexual preferences challenged. Thus, while critics have consistently read *The Woman in White* as product, as individual narratives merging "into texts that are ultimately unified, fictions that seem fully explicated,"[1] I will read the novel as process, as competing narratives vying for authority. The pretense of Walter's narrative authority rests on his misinterpretation of the documents he has collected.

The narrative of *The Woman in White*, writes Jan-Melissa Schramm, is "indebted to the techniques of the court-room" but "the plot is generated by its very dissimilarity to a trial; the conception of law as foil in turn liberates fiction to pursue its own idea of justice."[2] In her fascinating discussion of the relationship between nineteenth-century law and literature Schramm goes on to illustrate that

What fiction sought to claim as its own, what it saw as marginalised by the post-enlightenment, scientific language of the common law was emotion, the discourse of passion and of bodily sensation. Time and again in Victorian fiction we see the law ridiculed for its reductionism, for its legalese, for its callous failure to acknowledge that behind the language of rights, duties, and sanctions lies a seething world of emotional turmoil and physical experience which defies easy categorisation or description.[3]

While this is certainly a compelling description of *our* experience of reading *The Woman in White*, it does not capture Walter's experience of his own text. For Walter simultaneously depends upon legal language and evidence while repudiating its callousness and reductionism. More importantly Walter is exclusively interested in his own passions and physical sensations. His project can only succeed by denying the seething world of emotional turmoil and physical experience which challenges him at every turn.

The first evidence of Walter's protracted misreading is the first sentence of *The Woman in White:* "This is the story of what a Woman's patience can endure and of what a Man's resolution can achieve."[4] What will become by the last words of the novel "our Story" now masquerades as a parable on the sexes. Walter's desire to read the novel as a lesson in gender stereotypes is his most consistent and overt response to narratives that debunk such categories. His opening sentence is a misappropriation and vulgarization of the rhetoric used throughout Marian's narrative in particular. Referring repeatedly to her own "resolution"(pp. 253, 289, 312, 357), she eschews the patience, propriety and petticoats to which she has been condemned for life (p. 221) and warns her sister that "our endurance must end, and our resistance must begin" (p. 321). In her most daring act of resistance she crawls out onto the roof in time to hear Fosco assert that "quiet resolution is the one quality the animals, the children, and the women all fail in …. Where are your eyes? Can you look at Miss Halcombe, and not see that she has the foresight and the resolution of a man?" (p. 346). These words, I will argue, are addressed less to Percival Glyde than to Walter Hartright, whose blindness to Marian's virtues is crucial to the construction of his conventional narrative. While Fosco finds Marian's "masculine resolution" intoxicating, Walter finds it merely threatening to his fixed notions of what Man and Woman are.

In the famous scene in which Walter first meets the woman in white, Anne Catherick lays her hand on Hartright's bosom: "Remember that I was young; remember that the hand which touched me was a woman's," he reminds the reader (p. 50). From this moment on Hartright drives home the notion of himself as a "normal" man, highly susceptible to the attractions of the opposite sex. We pity his frustrations, as he has trained himself "to leave all the sympathies natural to my age in my employer's outer hall, as coolly as I left my umbrella there before I went upstairs .... I was admitted among beautiful and captivating women, much as a harmless domestic animal is admitted among them" (p. 89). But his long apprenticeship in repression is for nothing at Limmeridge House. He first allows himself to linger over the body of Marian Halcombe ("her waist, perfection in the eyes of a man"[p. 58]) and then falls madly in love with her younger sister. (It is worth noting here that Walter takes up pages of his narrative recording his first conversation with the exhilaratingly verbal Marian. He does not, however, find "the few kind words of welcome" [p. 77] which Laura utters worth quoting.) His portrait of Laura is his clearest identification of a sympathetic, heterosexual male reader of his text:

> Think of her as you thought of the first woman who quickened the pulses within you that the rest of her sex had no art to stir. Let the kind candid blue eyes meet yours, as they met mine, with the one matchless look which we both remember so well. Let her voice speak the music that you once loved best, attuned as sweetly to your ear as to mine. Let her footstep, as she comes and goes, in these pages, be like that other footstep to whose airy fall your own heart once beat time. Take her as the visionary nursling of your own fancy; and she will grow upon you, all the more clearly, as the living woman who dwells in mine.
>
> (p. 76)

Hartright can never speak of his desire in personal, only in universal terms. Anne's touch thrills him because he is a young man; Marian's waist is perfection, not in his own eyes, but in the eyes of man, the sexual feelings he has are natural to his age, and the passion he has for Laura must be expressed as the passion each man has for his first love. He can only express Laura's effect on himself by making her sexually desirable to other men. Yet Walter's persistent attempts to underline the naturalness and normality of both his heterosexuality and his desire for Laura clearly refute the evidence he has spent pages compiling. The "normal" male reader whom Hartright addresses exists nowhere in the pages of his document. Fosco is as sexually indifferent to Laura as Percival is actively repulsed by her. Like Mr. Gilmore and Pesca, Percival betrays no heterosexual predilections. Percival's passion seems exclusively for money, Gilmore's singular interest the law, and Pesca's attachment solely to Walter. Mr. Fairlie is an effeminate male, if not an explicit homosexual, who is utterly repulsed by the female form: "What have I to do with her bosom?" (p. 363) he complains of an irritating servant.

The only other distinctly heterosexual male in the novel is Fosco, but in stark contrast with Hartright's hyper-masculine, often legalistic and businesslike self-presentation, Fosco's is sentimental and flamboyant. As Marian notices, he is as comfortable with his effeminacy as Hartright is uncomfortable with his masculinity:

> He puts the rudest remarks Sir Percival can make on his effeminate tastes and amusements, always calling the baronet by his Christian name; smiling at him with the calmest superiority; patting him on the shoulder; and bearing with him benignantly, as a good-humored father bears with a wayward son.
>
> (p. 245)

Hartright's construction of a sympathetic heterosexual male reader deliberately pits his narrative against his competitors'. Fairlie addresses a neurotic of his own class who shares his contempt for servants, foreigners, the female body and "that extremely troublesome person, Mr. Walter Hartright" (p. 369). Fosco, who writes at Hartright's demand under threat of death, invokes (among others) the lovestruck youth of England: "Behold the cause, in my Heart – behold, in the image of Marian Halcombe, the first and last weakness of Fosco's life! ... Youths! I invoke your sympathy. Maidens! I claim your tears" (p. 631). Ignoring his jailer's artistic pretensions, he claims an audience all his own: "A word more – and the attention of the reader (concentrated breathlessly on myself) shall be released" (p. 631). When a narrator assumes the unusual stance of actually addressing Hartright, our master-narrator is repulsed by her acknowledgment of his oft-mentioned heterosexuality. He considers the contents of Mrs. Catherick's letter – "If I was a young woman still, I might say, 'Come! put your arm around my waist, and kiss me, if you like.' – 'shamelessly depraved'" (p. 548).

It is Walter's conceit that each of the narrators is contributing his smaller narrative to the larger project, but much of the most delicious writing in the novel jettisons Hartright's agenda. The more self-serving the observations in Mr. Fairlie's hypochondriacal litany, the more extraneous the points in Fosco's flamboyant rantings, the more inappropriate the innuendos in Mrs. Catherick's confession, the more the humorless earnestness of Hartright's carefully detailed project stands in sharp relief.

But the goals of this project are already suspect. Despite its main objective – "to present the truth always in its most direct and most intelligible form" (p. 33) – the novel is filled with lies, not the least of which are Walter's own. He describes the drawing room of Limmeridge House as one "which after this last night, I was never to see again" (p. 144). Yet, of course, the narrative is being written from Limmeridge House, his now permanent residence. Much later in the novel he writes: "My first and last concealments from the reader are those which caution renders absolutely necessary in this portion of the narrative" (p. 594). Yet several chapters earlier he confesses that he is writing this story with "feigned names" (p. 563).[5] The only other character more invested in "the truth" is Mrs. Michelson who, "as the widow of a clergyman of the Church of England" has "been taught to place the claims of truth above all other considerations" (p. 379). Her invariable misreadings singlehandedly challenge the efficacy of Hartright's enterprise:

> A nobleman [Count Fosco] who can respect a lady in distressed circumstances, and can take a fatherly interest in the fortunes of an humble servant girl, shows principles and feelings of too high an order to be lightly called in question. I advance no opinions – I offer facts only.
>
> (p. 381)

Hartright takes pains to obtain and to explain to his reader the process of procuring the written testimonies of Mrs. Michelson, Jane Gould, Hester Pinhorn, and Dr. Goodricke. He risks his life to obtain Count Fosco's written testimony. Yet Countess Fosco's written testimony, the evidence of the medical certificate, and the assertion of the inscription on the tomb are legal proof against Marian's recognition of her sister. Laura herself begins to doubt her identity when she finds "in good marking-ink ... as plain as print" (p. 448) Anne Catherick's name on each article of her clothing. Although Walter insists on written proof of the fact that Percival's parents were never married, it is a forged marriage record that he is determined to invalidate in writing.

Thus, when Collins significantly gives its own chapter and title to "The Narrative of the Tombstone" (p. 426), he allows the novel's shortest chapter to undercut most pointedly Hartright's stated purpose. For the novel's falsest narrative ("Sacred to the memory of Laura, Lady Glyde") is written not merely on paper but engraved in stone (p. 426).

Rather than establishing faith in the written word, then, *The Woman in White* questions the legitimacy of any piece of writing. The only narrative whose legitimacy Walter does not take pains to prove is Marian's. Yet neither the reader nor Hartright has access to Marian's diary. He takes her word that what she reads aloud to him over the course of three late-night tête-à-têtes (omitting those passages "relating to myself, which she thought it best that I should not see" (p. 456)) is the "truth" he records in *The Woman in White*. The implications of this arrangement may be lost on Walter, but they should not be on us. Once we recognize that Marian's is a retrospective and calculated narrative, and not necessarily the contents of her diary, we must question its intended effect, not on the male reader assumed by Walter, but on its sole intended recipient, Walter himself.

The contents of Marian's narrative have generated little critical discussion. Instead, much attention has been focused on Fosco's act of writing in Marian's diary. Indeed, his inscription is read as the climactic moment of the novel. Peter Brooks describes our state of shock at Fosco's inscription thus: "Our readerly intimacy with Marian is violated, our act of reading adulterated by profane eyes, made secondary to the villain's reading and indeed dependent on his permission."[6] D. A. Miller suggests further that

> it is not only, then, that Marian has been 'raped' as both the Count's amorous flourish ('Admirable woman!') and her subsequent powerless rage against him are meant to suggest. We are 'taken', too, taken by surprise, which is itself an overtaking.[7]

These readings have elevated the status of writing in the novel and generated similar readings in which Marian wields the phallus until first Fosco and finally Hartright force her to relinquish it.[8] But if Marian's narrative is not *written* for us, but *read* to Walter, we must re-examine how much power Marian wields with pen in hand and how little Walter's narrative silences her. Miller would have us the witnesses to or the victims of rape, but we are incidental to Marian's narrative. The intimacy which Fosco violates is that which Marian has established between herself and Walter. It is Walter who must experience the shock of Fosco's intervention. Why is Marian so interested in attracting Walter's attention?

In order to entertain the possibility of Marian's using her diary and Fosco's words to further her own (versus Laura and Walter's) interests, we must abandon the notion of this scene as a rape and her diary as a "violated textual body."[9] By conflating Marian's diary and virginal body, assumptions, whether intentional or unintentional, have been perpetuated about its contents, assumptions which must remain unproven as the diary is never given to us. The *purity* of Marian's narrative is the unspoken implication of the attention paid to the white pages upon which Fosco spills his ink. We are in danger of reading Marian's narrative as Walter hears it, as above suspicion, as reflecting her selflessness, disinterested motives, and pure thoughts. But if the circumstances of her writing – a spinster, closeted in her sister's home for hours with only a pen and paper for companionship – and of her narrating – the mistress of a desirable man's home in which her enfeebled sister is closeted with her sketchpad – differ, could not her motives as well?

Marian uses her narrative as an opportunity not, as Walter would have it, to convey the facts in the crime against Laura Fairlie, but to reinvent herself. Rather than conflating her narrative and her body, Collins compensates Marian within her narrative for the attractions and sexuality she denies herself outside of it. Marian introduces herself to Walter (in his narrative) thus:

> I have got nothing, and she is an heiress. I am dark and ugly, and she is fair and pretty. Everybody thinks me crabbed and odd (with perfect justice); and everybody thinks her sweet-tempered and charming (with more justice still).
>
> (pp. 60–1)

Her extravagant self-deprecation destroys any possibility of romance between herself and her drawing-master within the first pages of his narrative. For as Walter notes, "her lively familiarity" paradoxically ensures that it is "impossible to take the faintest vestige of a liberty with her, even in thought" (p. 60). Critics have agreed with Walter. Even Nina Auerbach who champions her Pre-Raphaelite beauty, finds that "Marian has no personal interest in love."[10]

But Walter's remarkable description of his first glimpse of Marian would have alerted any knowledgeable reader of 1860 to the fact that his heroine is modeled after a woman with strong personal desires, Marian Evans (George Eliot), Collins's friend since 1858:

> The easy elegance of every movement of her limbs and body as soon as she began to advance from the far end of the room, set me in a flutter of expectation to see her face clearly …. She approached nearer – and I said to myself (with a sense of surprise which words

fail me to express), The lady is ugly! Never was the old conventional maxim, that Nature cannot err, more flatly contradicted – never was the fair promise of a lovely figure more strangely and startlingly belied by the face and head that crowned it. The lady's complexion was almost swarthy, and the dark down on her upper lip was almost a moustache. She had a large firm, masculine mouth and jaw. To see such a face as this set on shoulders that a sculptor would have longed to model ... was to feel a sensation oddly akin to the helpless discomfort familiar to us all in sleep, when we recognise yet reconcile the anomalies and contradictions of a dream.

(p. 58)

Changing her hair and eye color, Collins retained Eliot's "heavy masculine jaw, charm of expression, beautiful speaking voice and good figure." While Catherine Peters notes that Hartright's description echoes both Henry James's and Bessie Parkes's memories of Eliot: "She is magnificently ugly – deliciously hideous".... her figure was "remarkably supple; at moments it had an almost serpentine grace,"[11] neither Peters nor any other critic has made much of Marian's relationship to Eliot. I would like to suggest that the story of Eliot's life and work in the 1850s can help us to understand Collins's ugly, brilliant, accomplished, self-sacrificing heroine.

In the early 1850s Eliot was in love with Herbert Spencer, a writer with whose work Collins would surely have been familiar as both were simultaneously writing for *The Leader* (the journal founded and published by Eliot's soon-to-be lover, George Henry Lewes). In these years before the publication of *Origin of Species*, Spencer was publishing his own evolutionary theories and basing these on his own tastes in women. Spencer's attempt to essentialize desire must have been anathema to Collins. For what is most strikingly comparable in the self-certainty of both Spencer's and Hartright's rhetoric is how all physical sensation is reserved for the male lover. The undesired does not herself experience desire, or more simply, desire is a masculine prerogative. In "Personal Beauty" Spencer argues that "the connexion between organic ugliness and mental inferiority, and the converse connexion between organic beauty and comparative perfection of mind, are distinctly traceable."[12] Features "which are by general consent called ugly" include a large mouth and prominent jaw, Marian Evans's and Marian Halcombe's most notable traits. That these ugly features bespeak an inferior moral and intellectual nature is proven by the fact that what the European cuts with a knife and fork, the Papuan tears with his jaws.[13] Several years later in "Physical Training" Spencer addresses himself specifically to feminine beauty, which he now argues has nothing to do with intellectual superiority:

> The truth is that, out of the many elements uniting in various proportions to produce in a man's breast that complex emotion which we call love, the strongest are those produced by the physical attractions; the weakest are those produced by intellectual attractions. As far as posterity is concerned, a cultivated intelligence based upon a bad physique is of little worth, seeing that its descendants will die out in a generation or two.[14]

Arguing that "humans are compelled by the same evolutionary forces which operate among all lower forms of life, uncontrolled by commands, traditions, or creeds," Spencer, writes Nancy Paxton, "was unable to see how 'commands, traditions, or creeds' shaped his own assessment of the compelling power of 'physical sensations' in human sexual selection."[15]

Spencer and Evans spent a great deal of time together and enjoyed each other's company, but Spencer was physically repulsed by his friend. Gordon Haight notes that "as her intimacy with Spencer deepened, GE's consciousness of her want of beauty increased." When she wrote to her friend Cara Bray of her "deliciously calm *new* friendship" with Spencer, she reported that "I look like one of those old hags we used to see by the wayside in Italy – only a little worse, for want of the dark eyes and dark hair in contrast with the parchment."[16] When her new friend warned her that he could not love her, she responded: "I felt disappointed rather than 'hurt' that you should not have sufficiently divined my character to perceive how remote it is from my habitual state of mind to imagine that any one is falling in love with me."[17]

By 1858 Eliot had recovered from the suffering of this painful, unrequited love and had found finally in her mid-thirties a man who did not deem her "fatally unattractive." She and Spencer remained friends, but she was increasingly critical of his "scientific" theories and while writing her first novel, *Adam Bede*, she took on Spencer's science of physiognomy. As Nancy Paxton writes: "Eliot questions Spencer's unexamined assumption that perfect beauty reflects … moral virtue in women. Hetty's beauty, [as described below] indeed, disguises the private and various secrets of her limited inner life."[18]

> Ah, what a prize the man gets who wins a sweet bride like Hetty!
> ….The dear, young, round, soft, flexible thing! Her heart must be

just as soft, her temper just as free from angles, her character just as pliant .... Every man under such circumstances is conscious of being a great physiognomist. Nature, he knows, has a language of her own, which she uses with strict veracity, and he considers himself an adept in the language. Nature has written out his bride's character for him in those exquisite lines of cheek and lip and chin .... I find it impossible not to expect some depth of soul behind a deep grey eye with a long dark eyelash, in spite of an experience which has shown me that they may go along with deceit, peculation, and stupidity .... One begins to suspect at length that there is no direct correlation between eyelashes and morals ....[19]

A great deal had happened to the Marian Evans so resigned to her own undesirability that she had prostrated herself enough to write these words to Spencer:

If you become too attached to someone else, then I must die, but until then I could gather courage to work and make life valuable, if only I had you near me. I do not ask you to sacrifice anything – I would be very good and cheerful and never annoy you. But I find it impossible to contemplate life under any other conditions .... You will find that I can be satisfied with very little, if I am delivered from the dread of losing it.[20]

George Eliot was now unwilling to support a correlation between looks and destiny; she was now able to write: "Human feeling does not wait for beauty – it flows with resistless force and brings beauty with it."[21]

By the time Collins met her, the homely spinster was living in sin with the married George Henry Lewes and at the center of one of the most notorious sex scandals of the century. But she and Lewes were devoted to each other and remained so through the many years of being ostracized by her family and polite society. While she had no children of her own, she was called *Mutter* by Lewes's three children and was more of a mother to them than their natural one.[22] (Lewes himself had been a father to the three illegitimate children of his wife and her lover.) When Lewes failed to acquire a European divorce, Eliot was not sorry:

I prefer excommunication. I have no earthly thing that I care for, to gain by being brought within the pale of people's personal attention, and I have many things to care for that I would lose – my freedom from petty worldly torments, commonly called pleasures, and that isolation which really keeps my charity warm instead of chilling it, as much contact with frivolous women would do.[23]

As Phyllis Rose writes: "If ever a couple was united in purpose it was Marian Evans and George Henry Lewes, dedicated to Duty, to Work, to Love, spreading warmth and light from their domestic hearth in the most approved style of Victorian domestic fiction. They were the perfect married couple. Only – they weren't married."[24] Strangely, though Walter seems not to notice, the same might be said of his relationship to Marian. The novel ends with Marian assuming the role of Walter's primary companion, helpmate and confidante. Like most Victorian domestic fiction *The Woman in White* ends with the birth of a child. But it is Marian, not his natural mother, who holds Walter's son in his only appearance in the novel. Marian continues the tradition of surrogate motherhood in the novel. Both Mrs. Fairlie and Mrs. Clements act as mothers to Anne Catherick when Mrs. Catherick has no natural feeling for her daughter. Legitimate family connections, as I will discuss later, appear to have been meaningless to Collins.

Although Collins and Eliot grew to be good friends (he was a frequent guest at the Leweses' Saturday evenings),[25] it is not clear how much he knew of Eliot's personal history. What is clear is that in 1860 Eliot was a figure of derision – denounced by Victorian prudes for her unlicensed sexuality or mocked by those who saw a homely woman desperately and neurotically in need of male love.[26] So common was it to lampoon Eliot that one biographer, Frederick Karl, lists Marian Halcombe among a number of unfavorable portraits of Eliot.[27] But we are certainly not meant to poke fun at Marian Halcombe. What Collins has achieved in Marian is a sympathetic portrait of a woman who, like the writer who inspired her, has little regard or patience for the rules of Victorian femininity. Of a letter in which Eliot invites the chilly Spencer (while fully aware of her limited powers to seduce) to leave hot London and visit her in Broadstairs – "No credit to me for my virtues as a refrigerant. I owe them all to a few lumps of ice which I carried away with me from that tremendous glacier of yours"[28] – her biographer Rosemary Ashton asks: "Was ever another letter written by a woman to a man showing such frankness, pride, humility, vulnerability, commanding power, and wit?"[29] We may justifiably ask the same question of Marian's lengthy "epistle" to Walter. Marian may know that Hartright will reject her, but she is unwilling to surrender so easily. Her sister may have his eyes, but while she has Walter alone for a few nights, Marian will own his ears.

Although George Eliot longed to be seen as a sexually desirable woman, she thrived on men's regard for her "masculine" intellect. She would have welcomed Spencer's posthumous description of her:

> I have known but few men with whom I could discuss a question in philosophy with more satisfaction. Capacity for abstract thinking is rarely found along with capacity for concrete representation, even in men: and among women, such a union as existed in her, has, I should think, never been paralleled.[30]

Marian Halcombe repeatedly longs for "the privileges of a man" and knows that she must act against her own nature by "compos[ing] [her]self in some feeble and feminine way" (p. 221). Fosco blinds her to his faults and wins her over by "flatter[ing] my vanity, by talking to me as seriously and sensibly as if I was a man" (p. 245).

Yet, like the "unwomanly" Eliot, Marian is motivated finally by her own desires. Because they are not expressed overtly, because they are not easily understood, Marian's desires are the novel's most compelling mystery. So unlike Pamela's seamless series of letters, Marian's diary has large gaps in it (for example, during the six months of Laura's honeymoon) which she acknowledges, and many about which we can only guess. Unlike Richardson, Collins is admitting that there are secrets in a woman's diary to which he would not be privy, which he would not dare to ventriloquize.

It is the *indeterminacy* of Marian's sexuality which has confounded critics and challenged Hartright's definitions of masculinity, femininity, and desire. For in the trajectory of her narrative she positions herself as first Percival's sexual rival, then Countess Fosco's and finally and inevitably Laura's. Marian's narrative is threatening to Walter because it allows her a sexual identity which his own has immediately denied her. Walter's narrative project requires him to wrap up every detail of his story neatly. But this means that his own sexual desires must remain expressed and unchanging long after the fulfillment of these desires makes any narrative sense. In her narrative Marian *appropriates* a personal and sexual identity for herself. Walter writes about his own sexuality as something his employers try to suppress artificially, but something of which he is always aware. Marian, however, sees herself as lacking a sexual identity and comes to acquire one not through the process of writing, but through the act of sharing her narrative with Walter.

As she begins her narrative, she describes her role in Laura's sexual initiation. Although a virgin as well, Marian portrays herself in sexually aggressive and knowledgeable terms. While the critical literature perpetuates the notion of Marian as rape victim, Marian figures herself as her sister's unwilling initiator:

> Drop by drop, I poured the profaning bitterness of this world's wisdom into that pure heart and that innocent mind, while every higher and better feeling within me recoiled from my miserable task. It is over now. She has learnt her hard, her inevitable lesson. The simple illusions of her girlhood are gone; and my hand has stripped them off. Better mine than his – that is all my consolation – better mine than his.
>
> (p. 208)

Falling early in Marian's narrative, this passage allows her to introduce her own sexuality to Walter while simultaneously infantilizing the sister he believes he loves. Like a mother tucking in a small child, she visits her maiden sister each night before going to bed:

> In stooping over to kiss her, I saw the little book of Hartright's drawings half hidden under her pillow, just in the place where she used to hide her favourite toys when she was a child. I could not find it in my heart to say anything; but I pointed to the book and shook my head.
>
> (p. 188)

Throughout her narrative, Marian refers to the "childish restlessness" with which Laura twines her hair around her fingers, a habit which her governess still "tries so patiently and so vainly to cure her of" (p. 187) or to her dependence, her "unwillingness ever to be left alone." Laura is "almost happy at the prospect of seeing the wonders of Florence and Rome and Naples.... in the full conviction, that I should be with her, wherever she went, the poor child – for a child she is still in many things .... " (p. 207)

We must wonder what, out of a sense of female propriety, Marian omits from her narrative when she contrasts Laura's sexual incuriosity with her own intense scrutiny of the Foscos' relationship:

> His management of the Countess (in public) is a sight to see. He bows to her; he habitually addresses her as 'my angel' .... The rod of iron with which he rules her never appears in company – it is a private rod, and is always kept upstairs.
>
> (p. 244)

Marian's interest in Fosco is immediately reciprocated, and he corners her in conversations the language of which is as uncomfortably sexually charged as her own: "Surely you like this modest, trembling English twilight? ... Does it penetrate your heart, as it penetrates mine?" (p. 309). As Marian gradually turns herself into a sexual object for Walter's benefit, she simultaneously begins to express her own desires. While Walter will clearly not share his own narrative with Marian, a narrative in which she is introduced as a freak of nature, Marian needs Walter to hear her own story, to hear how his own charms fade in the presence of Fosco. She needs to make him jealous. Fosco, she tells Walter,

> has interested me, has attracted me, has forced me to like him .... It absolutely startles me, now he is in my mind, to find how plainly I see him! – how much more plainly than I see Sir Percival, or Mr. Fairlie, or Walter Hartright, or any other absent person of whom I think, with the one exception of Laura herself! ... He has the quiet deference, that look of pleased, attentive interest, in listening to a woman, and that secret gentleness in his voice, in speaking to a woman, which, say what we may we can none of us resist.
>
> (p. 240)

As Laura returns from her honeymoon so "changed in person [that] ... I can only say that she is less beautiful to *me*" (p. 233), Marian becomes the sole object of male desire. Both Percival and Fosco remain indifferent to Laura's charms and even Walter, Marian reminds him, would have to re-evaluate the power of his art to capture her essence:

> There was, in the old times, a freshness, a softness, an ever-varying and ever-remaining tenderness of beauty in her face, the charm of which it is not possible to express in words – or, as poor Hartright used often to say, in painting either. This is gone.
>
> (p. 234)

That Fosco enters and latches onto Marian as Laura returns a faded image of her former self is consistent with the narrative Walter has constructed. Within the first forty pages of his document, Walter moves from desiring the touch of Anne Catherick to the body of Marian Halcombe to the face of Laura Fairlie. It is he who first notes the interchangeability of women in the novel when he remarks that "in her attitude, in the turn of her head, in her complexion, in the shape of her face [Laura was] the living image ... of the woman in white!" (p. 86). Yet despite the evidence of his own experience and narrative, Walter is unwilling to entertain the possibility of the fickleness of desire and the instability of identity. Fosco and Percival can as easily deprive both Laura and Anne of their identities as they have appropriated false identities for themselves. Marian does not wait for Walter to transfer his desire yet again. She acts on her own desire for self-transformation, appropriating the identity she has been denied.

Just before Marian narrates her tale to him, Walter describes their living arrangements:

> Our poor place of abode, our humble calling, our assumed relationship, and our assumed name, are all used alike as a means of hiding us in the house-forest of London .... I am an obscure unnoticed man, without patron or friend to help me. Marian Halcombe is nothing now, but my eldest sister, who provides for our household wants by the toil of her own hands.
>
> (pp. 433–4)

The description is remarkably like Laura's dream of happiness with Walter which Marian relates:

> 'Oh Marian ... thank God for your poverty – it has made you your own mistress, and has saved you from the lot that has fallen on *me* .... I used to fancy what I might have been, if it had pleased God to bless me with poverty, and if I had been his wife. I used to see myself in my neat cheap gown, sitting at home and waiting for him, while he was earning our bread – sitting at home and working for him, and loving him all the better because I *had* to work for him – seeing him come in tired, and taking off his hat and coat for him – and, Marian, pleasing him with little dishes at dinner that I had learnt to make for his sake.'
>
> (pp. 280–1)

As Laura envies Marian her poverty, Marian envies Laura's fantasy, a fantasy which she herself has stepped into, greeting Walter at the door each night and keeping his humble home for him. The timing of Marian's narrative is crucial. She tells her story while her sister is still lacking an identity. Living under an assumed name, she is recognized as neither Frederick Fairlie's niece nor yet Walter Hartright's wife. Had Walter and Marian loved her less, even they, he admits, might not have known her. As Laura is able to do nothing beyond play children's card games, the housework is *"taken as her own right* by Marian Halcombe"(p. 453, emphasis added). Marian has arrogated to herself the identity which Laura sought. As readers we must doubt Laura's sexual claim to Walter at this point. Indeed, we may be appalled when he later chooses to marry the child-woman. This is an appropriate time for Marian to stake out her own claim, to use her narrative as a weapon of seduction. If Walter has failed to be captivated by her sexual knowledge, curiosity, and attractiveness, he cannot fail to be moved by her greatest scene, which non-coincidentally is replete with impropriety and immodesty.

It begins by Marian taking off her silk gown and next removing the white and cumbersome parts of her underclothing in order to crawl out onto the roof and eavesdrop on Fosco and Percival. While much has been written about Marian masculinizing herself in this scene in order to penetrate a forbidden space, I am more concerned with the immediate effect of her narrative, to draw Walter into this scene and excite his curiosity by describing to him how she has undressed in order to go to work. From Marian's precarious position she hears the conversation crucial to the understanding of the conspiracy against Laura Fairlie, but even more central to an understanding of Marian's desires. She quotes Fosco as saying about her:

> 'This grand creature – I drink her health in my sugar and water – this grand creature, who stands in the strength of her love and her courage, firm as a rock between us two, and that poor flimsy pretty blonde wife of yours – this magnificent woman, whom I admire with all my soul ... you drive to extremities, as if she was no sharper and no bolder than the rest of her sex.'

> (p. 346)

Within a few pages Fosco will take Marian's diary, but in this scene Marian reveals how crucial it has been to her narrative all along to appropriate Fosco's words. Through Fosco she is allowed to remind Walter of Laura's inferior intellect. (When Laura recites platitudes, Fosco counters with "those are admirable sentiments; and I have seen them stated at the tops of copy-books" (p. 254).) Through Fosco's cruel insinuations she can question Laura's marital motives:

> 'You marry the poor man whom you love ... and one half your friends pity, and the other half blame you. And, now, on the contrary, you sell yourself for gold to a man you don't care for; and all

your friends rejoice over you; and a minister of public worship sanctions the base horror of the vilest of all human bargains.'

(pp. 258–9)

By ventriloquizing Fosco Marian is able finally to articulate an accurate comparison between herself and her "poor, flimsy pretty blonde sister." No longer "ugly and crabbed and odd," she is a grand and magnificent woman, superior to any other. Yet, as is characteristic with Marian, she is as vigilant about disowning unflattering opinions of Laura as she is at recording details of conversations. Her immodesty is always qualified by a mask of virtuousness. She has recorded Fosco's words, she insists, not to benefit herself, but to fuel her anger against him.

Yet Fosco's inscription *does* benefit Marian. He writes:

Yes! These pages are amazing. The tact which I find here, the discretion, the rare courage, the wonderful power of memory, the accurate observation of character, the easy grace of style, the charming outbursts of womanly feeling, have all inexpressibly increased my admiration of this sublime creature, of this magnificent Marian. The presentation of my own character is masterly in the extreme. I certify, with my whole heart, to the fidelity of the portrait, I feel how vivid an impression I must have produced to have been painted in such strong, such rich, such massive colours as these.

(pp. 358–9)

One critic has written that "Fosco's critique echoes Victorian literary reviewers who, though often complimentary, established both condescending and constraining standards for evaluating female writers."[31] Yet by praising Marian's masterly portrait, Fosco is in fact complimenting Collins or is it that Collins is complimenting Marian? As the identities of Anne, Laura, and Marian are continually in flux, so too is Fosco's identity frequently indistinguishable from Collins's. Fosco's hyperbole, upon finishing reading Marian's or writing his own narrative, may strike us as insincere, yet it does not differ substantially from Collins's own tone when finishing a novel. Responding, as he often did, to his own creation as if it were the work of another hand, he wrote after the completion of *Armadale*: "I was never so excited myself when finishing a story as I was this time. Miss Gwilt's death quite upset me."[32] Like Lydia Gwilt, the problematic villain of *Armadale* with whom Collins consistently identifies himself, Fosco is an obsessive writer:

One o'clock struck, two, three, four – and still the slips flew about all round him; still the untiring pen scraped its way ceaselessly from top to bottom of the page; still the white chaos of paper rose higher and higher all round his chair.

(pp. 552–3)

"The untiring pen scraped its way ceaselessly" as it will again in *Armadale* and as it had earlier in Collins's composition of *The Woman in White*. While describing how he has drugged Laura and destroyed Anne, Fosco interrupts himself to say "what a situation! I suggest it to the rising romance writers of England. I offer it, as totally new, to the worn-out dramatists of France" (p. 630). If Fosco is profiting from this exploitation of women, Collins is as well. As a rising English writer, who, in *The Woman in White*, created the first sensation novel, Collins, as well as Fosco, is proposing taboo plots as the proper subject of literature. The writer who made insane asylums, drug abuse, arson, adultery, bigamy and divorce the standard fare of novels hides again behind Count Fosco's persona: "Ah, I am a bad man, Lady Glyde, am I not? I say what other people only think; and when all the rest of the world is in a conspiracy to accept the mask for the true face, mine the rash hand that tears off the plump pasteboard, and shows the bare bones beneath" (p. 259).

Thus, the inscription in Marian's diary represents a fascinating conflation of identities. Collins, in the guise of Fosco, comments on the writing of Marian, i.e. Collins. Collins implicitly equates the commission of crime and the creation of art. He enters his text each time in the guise of a criminal, first advocating, then perpetrating, then praising his own crime. Walter's limited vision, his quest for legal truths, blinds him to what Fosco sees in Marian, a "person of similar sensibility," an *artist* who, by painting in such strong, rich, massive colours has awakened his finest sensibilities.[33]

What was Collins's vision of the artist? In one of the many stories of his opium addiction Collins would tell how, as an old man, he would work late into the night and another Wilkie Collins would appear:

[T]he second Wilkie Collins sat at the same table with him and tried to monopolise the writing pad. Then there was a struggle ... when the true Wilkie awoke, the inkstand had been upset and the ink was running over the writing table.[34]

The anecdote does not mention what, if anything, is written on the page, but the implication is clear that no matter which Wilkie gained narrative control, the "true" Wilkie would claim authorship. This story echoes not only the scene of the usurpation of Marian's diary, but the entire structure of *The Woman in White* in which narrative control is always hotly contested and in which authorship is claimed by the victor, not necessarily the writer. In his later novel *The Moonstone* Blake decides that the story should be written by each character involved "in turn – as far as his own personal experience extends, and no farther."[35] Yet the two most climactic points in Blake's own narrative are the narratives of other characters. The first is a letter from Rosanna Spearman, informing him that he has stolen the diamond; the second is the garbled message of Mr. Candy, hinting at how this may have happened. Blake's narrative of his "own personal experience" is no more valuable than any other disinterested party's, since he has no first-hand knowledge or memory of it.

The Woman in White, then, is not only about the appropriation of identity, but Collins defines authorship itself, his own position, as the appropriation of both. Indeed, for Collins the ability to take on new identities is the true mark of the artist. What he must have admired in Eliot was her power to transform herself, to take on new identities and not to settle for those imposed upon her. He allowed his heroine the same power and gave her a similar story.

Personal identity for Collins was always problematic. As a young man he spent his days haunted by a double, convinced that "someone was standing behind him."[36] Collins consistently equated identity with legitimacy in his novels. ("He was not Sir Percival Glyde at all" (p. 529), Walter writes after discovering Percival's forgery. In *No Name* Norah and Magdalen learn of their illegitimacy as young women and immediately refer to themselves as "Nobody's Children.") Yet he defined legitimacy as a false status imposed on paper. As a father he used aliases on the birth certificates of his three illegitimate children. *The Woman in White* ends in a final conflation of identity and legitimacy when Walter fails at first to recognize his son as the Heir of Limmeridge. "I think I can still answer for knowing my own child" (p. 646), he exclaims at the sight of the boy seated on his aunt's lap. Is this moment a final ironic reminder that our identity to those who know and love us and our identity as recorded on legal documents are mutually exclusive or that the quest to pinpoint identity will continue to elude Walter?

Walter's quest to claim a legal identity for Laura, his son, and especially himself eventually renders his narrative the most conventional of Victorian marriage plots. While Collins clearly delights in reading the competing plots, those which constitute the first work of sensation fiction ever written, we need not guess what effect a reading of Walter's plot has on Collins, for he has read it many times before. In his satirical piece of 1856, "A Petition to the Novel Writers" Collins derides the convention that

> when two sisters are presented in a novel, one must be tall and dark, and the other short and light. I know that five-feet-eight of female flesh and blood, when accompanied by an olive complexion, black eyes, and raven hair, is synonymous with strong passions, and an unfortunate destiny. I know that five feet nothing, golden ringlets, soft blue eyes, and a lily-brow, cannot possibly be associated by any well-constituted novelist, with anything but matrimonial happiness. Would any bold innovator run all risks, and make them both alike in complexion and in stature? Or would any desperate man effect an entire alteration, by making the two sisters change characters?[37]

Yet these characteristics are closely borne out by the tall, dark-eyed Marian with her "almost swarthy complexion" and "coal-black hair" and the fair-haired, blue-eyed, delicate Laura. Perhaps Marian does not meet with the "unfortunate destiny" to which Collins refers here, but her overwrought feeling for her sister does result in her near-death. Laura, however, is even duller than the woman described here, for by the time Hartright and she embark on marital happiness she has long since lost all appeal. Would Collins so easily resort to the stereotypes he had earlier blasted?

Collins's own disgust for marriage was expressed most eloquently in his 1856 piece for *Household Words*, "Bold Words by a Bachelor" in which he argues that marriage, as commonly practiced, is a narrowing and selfish institution,[38] and most overtly in his relations with women. He refused to marry both Caroline Graves, the woman he lived with for most of his life, and Martha Rudd, the woman who bore him three children. After leaving him for several years to marry and gain respectability, Caroline moved back in with Collins as he was busily fathering children with Martha. He named the first of these illegitimate children Marian after his own clearly-favored Fairlie sister.

It is unfortunately impossible to imagine that *All the Year Round*, which serialized *The Woman in White*, would have allowed Marian Halcombe Marian Evans's happy, unconventional marital arrangement. But Collins still managed to voice his aversion to marriage in each of the competing narratives. Gilmore's chapter emphasizes that marriage is a financial and legal agreement which cannot benefit a woman of independent means. Mrs. Catherick's letter implies that a marriage of convenience will ultimately break down in scandal and shame. And Frederick Fairlie's defense of bachelorhood can only make us grateful that certain men choose not to marry:

> When you have once shown yourself too considerate and self-denying to add a family of your own to an already overcrowded population, you are vindictively marked out, by your married friends, who have no similar consideration and no similar self-denial, as the recipient of half their conjugal troubles, and the born friend of all their children. Husbands and wives *talk* of the cares of matrimony; and bachelors and spinsters bear them.
>
> (p. 367)

"The Narrative of the Tombstone" defines marriage as loss of identity and burial, just as Collins's friend W.H. Wills had during their apprenticeship at *Household Words*: "When she marries, she dies; being handed over to be buried in her husband's arms, or pounded and pummelled into the grave with his arms ... a wife – like a convict – cannot have or hold one iota of anything that has value."[39] The competing narratives trace the decline of Countess Fosco through her years of marriage. "Mr Philip Fairlie had lived on excellent terms with his sister Eleanor, as long as she remained a single woman" (p. 172), writes Gilmore. Remarking on the amazing transformation of the loquacious, troublesome Eleanor into the silent, submissive Countess, Marian ends by unwittingly prophesying her aunt's part in the crimes against Laura, crimes of which Eleanor Fairlie could not have been capable:

> I have once or twice seen sudden changes of expression on her pinched lips, and heard sudden inflexions of tone in her calm voice, which have led me to suspect that her present state of suppression may have sealed up something dangerous in her nature, which used to evaporate harmlessly in the freedom of her former life.
>
> (p. 239)

Finally, in words which surely echo Collins's own disdain for monogamy, Fosco writes of how little his wife's compliance and obedience have earned her:

I learnt to adore Marian. At sixty, I worshipped her with the vol-
canic ardour of eighteen. All the gold of my rich nature was poured
hopelessly at her feet. My wife – poor angel – my wife, who adores
me, got nothing but the shillings and the pennies. Such is the
World, such Man, such Love.

(p. 619)

Walter has written not just any marriage plot, but the very one against
which Collins wrote. Were Walter determined to ignore the abundant
evidence against making a legal contract with a woman, he might still
have opted for the correct choice, the choice evident to every other
reader of the novel. Even the oblivious Laura notes that "I am so
useless – I am such a burden on both of you. You will end in liking
Marian better than you like me" (p. 499). Early reviewers of the novel
found that "Laura Fairlie fails to inspire us even with the gentlest sort
of interest,"[40] while its earliest male readers wrote Collins asking for
Marian's address in order to propose to her.[41] Today's literary critics
have too readily accepted Walter's vision. If he teaches us how to look
at the novel's women, Marian forces us to look again. It is not simply
because of Marian's clearly superior intellect, wit, courage, or strength
that the reader anticipates a different outcome in this marriage plot,
but that the individual supporting documents prepare us for a resolution in which Marian takes over Laura's identity altogether. The plot
Walter insists on writing is one which ignores the appropriations of
identity. In order to construct his marriage plot Marian must remain
the "crabbed and odd" spinster, Laura the first and last woman who
"quickened the pulses" within him. The construction of his own story
rests on his misreading of every other.

4
Esther Summerson: Looking Twice

Marian Halcombe is considered one of fiction's first female detectives. Although *Bleak House*, which predates *The Woman in White* by seven years, has been called the first detective novel, Esther Summerson has not been placed in Marian's company. Instead, in a novel in which many characters including Richard, Tulkinghorn, Lady Dedlock, and especially Inspector Bucket, are seeking knowledge, Esther appears reluctant to know anything. Her "mode," writes Gordon Hirsch, "is the repression of active curiosity, desire, and hostility."[1] In particular, notes Audrey Jaffe, she "block[s] curiosity about her mother."[2] Esther makes it difficult for critics to credit her in the investigation and resolution of the novel's mysteries. When, at the end of the eighteenth installment (Chap. 59), she finds her mother's dead body, we can thank the omniscient narrator, Tulkinghorn, Inspector Bucket, Lady Dedlock herself, even the illiterate Jo for helping us to understand what has occurred. Indeed, we may comprehend before Esther who is busy reminding herself that "she had not the least idea what it meant," that there was some connection she "could not follow," that she "saw but did not comprehend," that her "understanding for all this was gone."[3] Esther moves from touching her mother's dead body in the last line of the eighteenth installment to "proceed[ing] to other passages of her narrative" (p. 869) in the first line of the nineteenth. But is this in fact more evidence of her naïveté, incuriosity, and fear of sexual knowledge? Or does that enormous gap between the two installments indicate that Esther has been actively engaged all along in solving the mysteries of her parents and her parentage?

One of the few defenses and to my mind the most impressive analysis of Esther's narrative is Audrey Jaffe's. Jaffe uses Freud's discussion of negation, "a characteristic structure whereby unconscious material emerges into discourse" to explain Esther's peculiar rhetoric.

> Freud claims that ... statements of negation – what Lacan, combining the terms 'denial' and 'negation,' calls 'denegations' derive from judgments about what the ego wishes to take into itself and what it wishes to reject .... It is through her denegations that readers gain the sense that they know more about Esther than she knows about herself. When Esther says ... 'They said I was so gentle, but I am sure *they* were!' we 'emend,' as Freud does with his patient: so she *is* the subject. Esther's denegations signal her otherness to herself – the presence of material she wishes to distance herself from – and even as they efface her, they constitute her, marking her for us as a distinctive personality whose most prominent feature is a very loud insistence on her own insignificance. But they also comprise a narrative strategy that enables Esther to construct her identity while – and by – constructing herself as a reflection of the gazes of others.... Presenting herself as alienated from her own knowledge, Esther cannot be held responsible for what she knows or says. Her denials are essential to the sense we have of her as a passive construction, a character who is not responsible for what she knows.[4]

I too will argue that Esther's self-effacement constitutes a narrative strategy, one that allows her to accept and reject her parentage simultaneously. But I will depart from Jaffe's Freudian model by insisting on Esther's as a *conscious* and *retrospective* strategy, one that acknowledges without articulating desire. Marian's narrative strategy demands that she foreground her role as investigator; Esther's that she downplay her own. None of Esther's many desires – to know, to punish, to reject, to fulfill herself in marriage, to move on with her own life unburdened by her parents – is expressed overtly. But we can unravel the mysteries of Esther's apparently repressed, naive, incurious personality, we can discover her desires, by examining the relationship between her own and the omniscient narrator's narratives.

That narrator has always been preferred by critics. Many readers of *Bleak House* have considered Esther's narrative a failure and Dickens's decision to have her tell her own story a mistake.[5] Yet while many have dismissed Esther's narrative, few have tried to see what it is doing in *Bleak House*. The conventional reading of the double narrative has largely remained unchallenged: the omniscient narrator's account is objective, his domain the world of the law and politics. Esther's story is personal, her domain the home. But such a dichotomy is severely limited. We are as likely to find the narrator in a bedroom as Esther in Chancery. We are more likely to know the opinions and interpretations of the "objective" narrator than those of the reticent, coy Esther. This chapter will try to answer some of the most nagging questions about this most anomalous of narrative constructions. Why does *Bleak House* have two narrators? Why do they write in different tenses? Why do they scarcely acknowledge each other? Why is a skilled narrator paired with a hesitant one? And finally how does Esther's relationship to her companion narrator allow us to understand the difference between Dickens's only female narrator and his more popular men, David Copperfield and Pip?

Great Expectations opens in a graveyard with Pip studying the tombstones of his parents. David Copperfield, recording the circumstances of his birth, remembers the "white gravestone in the churchyard" of his unfortunate father who died six months before his own arrival: "I used to feel for it lying out alone there in the dark night, when our little parlour was warm and bright with fire and candle, and the doors of our house were – almost cruelly, it seemed to me sometimes – bolted and locked against it."[6] In the first chapter of her narrative, Esther buries her "dear old doll" (p. 70), but her father's body is not so easily done away with. Not only does Captain Hawdon die over and over again during the course of *Bleak House* but his unburied, rotting corpse takes on a life of its own as it transmits disease to Lady Dedlock, Jo, Charley, and Esther. Despite their unhappy childhoods, David and Pip are able to move forward in their stories because they can leave their parents behind. Pip explains the circumstances of his birth in several sentences, David in several pages, but the omnipresence of Hawdon's body prevents Esther from moving forward; she spends the five hundred pages of her narrative justifying her own existence. Yet Esther's need to maneuver her way around the bodies and legacies of her parents manifests itself both in her underconfident narrative voice and in the complex relationship between her narrative and that of the third-person omniscient narrator.

As popular as *David Copperfield* was in its own time, it did little to change Dickens's reputation for excessive sentimentality and caricaturization. Several critics reviewed it alongside Thackeray's *Pendennis*. David Masson's article in the *North British Review* is a representative comparison. While he applauds Thackeray for "a knowingness, an air of general ability and scholarship, that suggests that the man who wrote it, could take an influential place, if he chose, either in an assembly of critics, or in a committee of men of business," he praises Dickens for "the keen and feminine sensibility of a fine genius, whose instinct is always for the pure and beautiful, [rather] than from the self-possession of a mind correct under any circumstances, by discipline and sure habit."[7] F.S. Schwarzbach has noted that by the mid-1850s many reviewers including Fitzjames Stephen, Walter Bagehot, R.H. Hutton, George Lewes, and George Eliot had concluded that Dickens's was a *feminine* genius.[8]

But if Dickens's favorite male character and narrator was not able to convince the critics of his author's "masculine" genius, the omniscient narrator of *Bleak House* should have dispelled all doubts. The unidentified narrator is indisputably male, uncannily exemplifying the very qualities Masson used to define Thackeray's masculine style. To my knowledge no critic has tried to prove the omniscient narrator's maleness; his self-assurance bordering on arrogance speaks for itself. Dickens's double narrative seems to be an overt response to his critics. If you want to see masculine writing, I'll show you masculine writing; if you want to see feminine writing, I can do that as well. But it is crucial that Esther's narrative only *appear* to satisfy the requirements of feminine writing. She triumphs finally not because of her sentimentality and naïveté, but because of her insight, because of what Masson might call her "knowingness."

*

Our primary experience of reading *Bleak House*'s double narrative is of living in the present and past simultaneously. The novel's characters routinely experience this as *déjà vu*. Jo upon meeting Esther asks, "If she ain't the t'other one, she ain't the forrenner. Is there three of 'em then?" (p. 488). Esther upon first seeing Lady Dedlock wonders: "But why her face should be, in a confused way, like a broken glass to me, in which I saw scraps of old remembrances; and why I should be so fluttered and troubled (for I was still), by having casually met her eyes; I could not think" (p. 304). But as Robert Newsom writes:

it is finally we, the readers, for whom the experience of déjà vu is most persistent .... There are in *Bleak House* about a hundred characters .... Of these, thirty or so ... figure in both narratives. Now what this means is that we are introduced to all of these characters, as though for the first time twice .... We are continually being led to believe that we are meeting people, or entering places, or witnessing events, that are new and unfamiliar to us, only to discover that what we are seeing as though for the first time is nothing new at all, but something old and familiar.[9]

Using Freud's definition of the *unheimlich* [uncanny] as "what was once *heimisch* [homey], familiar"[10] Newsom argues that many of the most uncanny moments in *Bleak House* are strange because they are so familiar. Yet, beyond acknowledging Dickens's interest in the "romantic side of familiar things" (p. 43), he does not consider why Dickens has created such an uncanny narrative. In other nineteenth-century novels that employ more than one narrator, the relationship between the narrators is explicit. Lockwood leaves off his account in *Wuthering Heights* when it makes sense for Nelly Dean to pick up the story. Walter Hartright knows each of *The Woman in White's* disparate narrators and compiles and organizes all of the testimony. There is no intermediary figure in *Bleak House* to explain to us the relationship between these two narratives or, as in *The Woman in White*, to explain to the narrators themselves what information is required of them. The two narratives are clearly related to each other. There are familiar elements in each. Yet they cannot recognize and acknowledge what is familiar – they are estranged from one another. Thus, in trying to understand the relationship between Esther's and the companion narrative, it is fruitful to consider how it reflects the *unheimlich* family life seen everywhere in the novel.

Bleak House is first and foremost about bad parenting and familial estrangement. The dreadful parents and surrogate parents include the Jellybys, Pardiggles, Skimpoles, and Smallweeds, Mr Turveydrop, Miss Barbary, and Mrs Chadband. The neglected, abused, orphaned, or abandoned children (some now grown) include Jo, Charley, Tom, Emma, Prince, Richard, Ada, Guster, Judy, Bart, Phil, the Jellybys, Pardiggles, and Skimpoles. George is estranged from the Rouncewell family, Krook from the Smallweeds, Miss Barbary from her sister, and, of course, in the main plot of the novel Esther discovers that neither of her parents knows of her existence. I read the novel's third-person account as the parent narrative, Esther's as its offspring. I am not arguing that the third-person narrator is a character in the novel or that he is in fact Esther's father, but that her relationship to this unidentifiable figure is modeled on the relationships between parents and children in the novel. Esther overtly discusses the relationships between dozens of parents and children. By examining her relation-ship to the parent narrator, we can come to some understanding of the parent-child relationship she never mentions – that between herself and her own father. Thus, while I will discuss Lady Dedlock, my analy-sis will depart from most feminist criticism that has focused almost exclusively on Esther's relationship to her mother.

Bleak House overtly links the abuse, exploitation, and neglect of chil-dren with writing and literacy. Jo is introduced to the reader as an illit-erate and an orphan. Indeed, from Jo's limited perspective, the two seem synonymous:

> Name, Jo. Nothing else that he knows on. Don't know that every-body has two names. Never heerd of sich a think. Don't know that Jo is short for a longer name. Thinks it long enough for him. He don't find no fault with it. Spell it? No. He can't spell it. No father, no mother, no friends.

> (p. 199)

The orphaned Charley, who as a child has managed to raise her brother and sister and who according to Esther, "was uncommonly expert at other things and had as nimble little fingers as I ever watched"

> seemed to have no natural power over a pen, but in [her] hand every pen appeared to become perversely animated, and to go wrong and crooked, and to stop, and splash, and sidle into corners, like a saddle-donkey. It was very odd, to see what old letters Charley's young hand had made; they so wrinkled, and shrivelled, and tottering; it, so plump and round.

> (p. 482)

Prince Turveydrop's "education had been so neglected, that it was not always easy to read his notes ... he put so many unnecessary letters into short words, that they sometimes quite lost their English appear-ance" (p. 249). Caddy Jellyby's indentured servitude to her mother is in the form of an amanuensis. While she has learned to write and will do so for both herself and her husband, she considers herself as unedu-cated as he: " 'Besides, it's not as if I was an accomplished girl, who had any right to give herself airs ... I know little enough, I am sure, thanks to Ma!' " (p. 249). Dickens finally renders Mrs. Jellyby's particular form of exploitation as Caddy's genetic inheritance when her daughter is born with "curious little dark veins in its face, and curious little dark marks under its eyes, like faint remembrances of poor Caddy's inky days; and altogether, to those who were not used to it, it was quite a piteous little sight" (p. 736). (That Caddy's baby is also born deaf, however, ensures that she can be neither her mother's amanuensis nor her father's dancing mistress.)

Esther, then, is one of the few neglected though literate offspring in the novel who appear to enjoy writing. As a representative of the many abused, orphaned, or abandoned children in *Bleak House*, however, she cannot be expected to perform the literary gymnastics of the third-person narrator. Her narrative justifiably shows the tentativeness of a novice trying to get on her own feet without anyone's help. Like Charley trying to get a firm grip on a pen, like Krook chalking his wall with letters, Esther must teach herself how to write. At the beginning of the novel we may be convinced that she will fail, that she will relate the minor points she knows and hand the role of narrator over to a more qualified subject. The novel cannot be about Esther for as she repeatedly reminds us:

> I don't know how it is, I seem to be always writing about myself. I mean all the time to write about other people, and I try to think about myself as little as possible, and I am sure, when I find myself coming into the story again, I am really vexed and say, 'Dear, dear, you tiresome little creature, I wish you wouldn't!'.
>
> (pp. 162–3)

Without making personal references to himself, the third-person narrator, in contrast, writes with the most unapologetic self-confidence. His role in the novel will clearly not be usurped.

While her parents' writing plays a tremendous role in the plot – her father's handwriting is probably its single most important catalyst; her mother's letters to her father the most sought after possession in the novel – Esther's own writing seems insignificant to the *plot*. Of all the narrators in this study, Esther is certainly the most benign. She need not write surreptitiously as Pamela, Jane and Marian Halcombe do. She need not confess her sins to a perfect stranger as Nelly does. Her writing seems to pose no threat to anyone. Getting his hands on Pamela's letters is Mr B's main pursuit, getting his own pen between the pages of Marian's diary the consummation of Count Fosco's fantasy. Jane Eyre (as well as Charlotte Brontë) writes only when the man she lives with is blind; Molly Bloom narrates only after her husband is asleep. But Esther appears to be writing quite openly. She leaves us in her final chapter "looking up from my desk as I write, early in the morning at my summer window ... " (p. 933). Throughout the novel she refers to the process of writing by reminding herself that she should rub out lines or by self-consciously repeating herself. There is no need for Esther to write in privacy for her contribution to the novel is so consistently *overlooked* by her companion narrator.

In *Bleak House* children look while parents overlook. Mrs Jellyby

> would come occasionally with her usual distraught manner, and sit calmly looking miles beyond her grandchild, as if her attention were absorbed by a young Borrioboolan on its native shores. As bright-eyed as ever, as serene, and as untidy, she would say, 'Well, Caddy, child, and how do you do today?' And then would sit amiably smiling, and taking no notice of the reply; or would sweetly glide off into a calculation of the number of letters she had lately received and answered, or of the coffee-bearing power of Borrioboola-Gha. This she would always do with a serene contempt for our limited sphere of action, not to be disguised.
>
> (pp. 739–40)

Mrs Pardiggle is so indifferent to her immediate surroundings that she knocks over any furniture in her path. Marching forward – her eyes always on her next charitable project – her back is turned to her five sons who are busy pinching and stomping on Esther whose eyes are always firmly focused on what is before her. Her immediate self-description is of having "always rather a noticing way – not a quick way, O no! – a silent way of noticing what passed before me, and thinking I should like to understand it better" (pp. 62–3). Her understanding is understated but no less acute than the narrator's. In her first visit to the Neckett family she sums up in one simple sentence the focus of Dickens's massive social canvas. Bowled over by the image of three orphaned children caring for each other, Esther laments,

> '*It was a thing to look at.* The three children close together, and two of them relying solely on the third, and the third so young and yet with an air of age and steadiness that sat so strangely on the childish figure.'
>
> (p. 262, emphasis added)

This horrifying scene is being taken in simultaneously by arguably the worst parent in the novel, Harold Skimpole. Skimpole has brought

Esther and her guardian to this home, for Neckett (Coavinses), before dying and leaving these three orphans, had been sent after Skimpole for the collection of debts. Skimpole is cheered by this sight for he

> had sometimes repined at the existence of Coavinses. He had found Coavinses in his way. He could had dispensed with Coavinses. There had been times when, if he had been a Sultan, and his Grand Vizier had said one morning, 'What does the Commander of the Faithful require at the hands of his slave?' he might have even gone so far as to reply, 'The head of Coavinses!' But what turned out to be the case? That, all that time, he had been giving employment to a most deserving man; that he had been a benefactor to Coavinses; that he had actually been enabling Coavinses to bring up these charming children in this agreeable way, developing these social virtues! Insomuch that his heart had just now swelled, and the tears had come into his eyes, when he had looked round the room, and thought, 'I was the great patron of Coavinses, and his little comforts were my work!'
>
> (p. 270)

Esther will become increasingly disillusioned by Skimpole's immaturity, but in this early scene she responds with her characteristic sense of forgiveness: "There was something so captivating in his light way of touching these fantastic strings, and he was such a mirthful child by the side of the graver childhood we had seen, that he made my guardian smile ... " (p. 270). And indeed what is so striking about this passage is its rendering of the fantastical, of Skimpole's ability to transcend this appalling scene and project himself into a dream of himself as a Sultan attended by an overly obsequious servant. The rhetorical "if I had been" is so markedly absent from Esther's own narrative. Esther is only able to see herself as what she has actually been to others. Although a married woman when she writes her story, she can never even admit that she has been loved by Woodcourt. She is slow to admit to her many virtues. Skimpole, however, turns his vices into a cause for celebration. He too looks around the room, but sees not what is before him, but a mirror of his own conceit.

The most visionary "parent" in the novel, able to see behind closed doors and into the hearts of his subjects, to predict the future and accurately detail the past, the third-person narrator is extraordinarily dimsighted when it comes to seeing his child. Like Mrs Jellyby who fails to notice ink stains on her daughter or "notched memoranda" on the

limbs of her son, the narrator is expert at overlooking Esther's narrative. We read so much of the novel twice because information provided
by Esther is given again in the narrator's account as if he had no knowledge of a companion narrator. Thus, Esther visits Krook's shop with his
female tenant and six chapters later the narrator writes "'Run, Flite,
run! The nearest doctor! Run!' So Mr Krook addresses a crazy little
woman who is his female lodger" (p. 190). We move immediately from
Esther's lengthy description of Gridley's tale of woe to the narrator's
off-handed treatment of Gridley as "a disappointed suitor, [who] has
been here today, and has been alarming" (p. 276). But, of course, the
omniscient narrator is fully aware of Esther's narrative. When she ends
the first section of her narrative by going to bed, he begins his next
chapter with "While Esther sleeps, and while Esther wakes, it is still wet
weather down at the place in Lincolnshire" (p. 131). While he will
occasionally mention Esther herself as the novel progresses, he will
never again allude to her narrative or to her role as a narrator.
Moreover, although Dickens has him function as the novel's progenitor, as the figure who gives life to the narrative and to Esther as well,
the narrator's account is incomplete and utterly dependent on Esther's
to supply content and meaning. For instance, when he begins the
novel in Chancery with the Lord High Chancellor placing a girl and
boy in the custody of their cousin, he gives no information as to who
any of these three are. Instead, he relies on Esther's account two chapters later of watching the Lord High Chancellor turning Ada and
Richard over to John Jarndyce. By simultaneously ignoring and depending upon Esther's narrative, the narrator relates to his companion narrative as Mrs Jellyby does her daughter or Mr Turveydrop does his son.

Like the parent narrator, Esther will allude to a companion narrator
only once. Her first words acknowledge his presence: "I have a great
deal of difficulty in beginning to write my portion of these pages ... "
(p. 62). Yet while both narrators are aware of writing a portion of a
greater whole, Esther *seems* to be entirely ignorant of the contents of
the other narrative. Each of her sections picks up where the last ended.
So when chapter 6 ends with her going to bed, chapter 8 opens with
her waking before daylight. Chapter 15 ends with her visiting London
and chapter 17 begins with Richard visiting them often in London.
Chapter 18 ends with a visit to Mr Boythorn's; chapter 23 begins with
their coming home after six weeks at Mr Boythorn's. The other narrator's sense of continuity is quite different. Chapters 7 and 16 end with
the sound of footsteps on the Ghost's Walk at Chesney Wold and
chapters 10 and 19 open in Chancery Lane. The omniscient narrator

moves more freely through the text. Esther is limited to moving from point A to point B. She cannot rely on the parent narrative. When the narrator repeats information from Esther's account, he is willfully ignoring it. When Esther repeats information from his, she simply appears ignorant of it. After we have witnessed Nemo's death and Miss Flite's reaction to it, Esther must be told three chapters later that "there had been a sudden death there, and an inquest; and that our little friend had been ill of the fright" (p. 250). Many chapters after we have met Sir Leicester, he is still a stranger to Esther who introduces us to him as "a great Sir Leicester Dedlock" (p. 164). This becomes our experience of reading the novel. We accept the fact that information from the parent narrative will be withheld from Esther as she herself grows over the course of the novel to accept that her parents and surrogate parents will withhold information from her.

The first parent-child encounter we witness is that between Esther's "godmother" and herself.

> 'O, dear godmother, tell me, pray do tell me, did mama die on my birthday?' 'No,' she returned. "Ask me no more, child!' 'O, do pray tell me something of her. Do now, at last, dear godmother, if you please! What did I do to her? How did I lose her? Why am I so different from other children, and why is it my fault, dear godmother? No, no, no, don't go away. O, speak to me!' I was in a kind of fright beyond my grief; and I caught hold of her dress, and was kneeling to her. She had been saying all the while, 'Let me go!' But now she stood still .... 'Your mother, Esther, is your disgrace, and you were hers. The time will come – and soon enough – when you will understand this better, and will feel it too, as no one save a woman can.'
>
> (pp. 64-5)

The hunger Esther feels for answers, for connection to another human being, will never again be so fully expressed. Never again will we see Esther in such a state of grief and despair. Never again will she plead with anyone, least of all a parent, for information, recognition and love. When she finally meets her mother, it is Lady Dedlock who assumes Esther's former position and Esther who must "beseech her not to stoop before me in such affliction and humiliation" (p. 565). Without questioning or challenging her mother's decision she agrees that they "never could associate, never could communicate, never probably from that time forth could interchange another word, on earth" (p. 566). She burns her mother's letter as asked and avoids Lady

Dedlock until the night of her death. While neither cruel nor unforgiving, John Jarndyce, like Miss Barbary, provides Esther with only enough information to make her suffer, withholds as much information as possible and teases her by only hinting at the truth. When he brings her to Yorkshire on mysterious business, Esther does not blame Jarndyce for the capriciousness of his action. When she learns the truth about the house she has been brought to see, she does not complain that she has been lied to and toyed with, for Jarndyce has simply been exhibiting parental behavior: "'I am your guardian and your father now,'" he assures her (p. 913). Esther's behavior throughout the novel, her increasing sense of duty and responsibility to her parents' needs before her own, is also reflected in her relationship to the parent narrator's account, of which she seems to know nothing and of which she overtly expresses no desire to know.

Yet while Esther fills most of her narrative by contentedly jingling her housekeeping keys or rhapsodizing about the love which sustains her in her relationships with Ada, Charley, Caddy, and Jarndyce, she will occasionally besiege the reader with an uncharacteristic outpouring of emotion, with a profound longing for reconciliation with her mother:

> It matters little now how often I recalled the tones of my mother's voice, wondered whether I should ever hear it again as I so longed to do, and thought how strange and desolate it was that it should be so new to me. It matters little that I watched for every public mention of my mother's name; that I passed and repassed the door of her house in town, loving it, but afraid to look at it; that I once sat in the theatre when my mother was there and saw me, and when we were so wide asunder, before the great company of all degrees, that any link or confidence between us seemed a dream.
>
> (p. 647)

This image of Esther and her mother occupying the same space but existing in separate, irreconcilable spheres mirrors the dynamic between the two narratives which are always poised on the verge of interconnection but never manage to merge. Esther's desire that the connection between herself and her mother be made manifest echoes the omniscient narrator's central question:

> What connexion can there be, between the place in Lincolnshire, the house in town, the Mercury in powder, and the whereabouts of Jo the outlaw with the broom, who had that distant ray of light

upon him when he swept the churchyard-step? What connexion can there be between many people in the innumerable histories of this world, who, from opposite sides of great gulfs, have nevertheless, been very curiously brought together!

(p. 272)

The narrator recognizes here the reader's desire for *relationships* to be established among the novel's various, *unrelated* elements. Yet his question does not go far enough. For certainly when reading the chapter, "Tom-All-Alone's," we wonder at the connection between Lady Dedlock's visiting a slum and Esther's visit to one in the previous chapter. We wonder at the "great gulfs" in this narrative, both those that the narrator is and is not willing to acknowledge. Thus, our narrative desire parallels Esther's own desire. As Esther's would be fulfilled by the bridging of that gap at the theater, ours would be satisfied by connections being made between the two narratives. When Esther longs for reconciliation, she has moved (if only temporarily) beyond a desire for self-erasure. Her longing for a relationship to her mother overwhelms her fear of shaming the great Lady Dedlock. So, too, when we desire narrative reconciliation, we do not want Esther's voice to be lost, to be subsumed by the narrator's more forceful presence. Instead, we want the narratives to be in communication so that our understanding of the novel is improved. But long before Esther spies her mother at the theater, long before she knows who her mother is, the reader learns the connection between them. So that by the end of the ninth book we know far more than Esther and we long for narrative reconciliation not to remedy our own ignorance, but Esther's.

As the ninth book ends Lady Dedlock learns that she has a child named Esther Summerson, and we learn the extent to which the narrator knows about Esther. If we have managed to overlook the vacuum in which Esther writes her narrative, we cannot do so after seeing the transition from the previous chapter which ends with Lady Dedlock on her knees crying "O my child, O my child!" to her own which begins: "Richard had been gone away some time, when a visitor came to pass a few days with us. It was an elderly lady. It was Mrs Woodcourt .... " (p. 467). The disjunction between these two chapters (29 and 30) and between the two narratives is quite startling. Chapter 30 details Esther's relationship to Mrs Woodcourt. The snobbish old lady convinces Esther that she stands no chance with her son because of his "aristocratic" lineage. Esther, unaware of both her illegitimacy and her relationship to a more prestigious family than the MacCoorts, agrees with her that "it was a great thing to be so highly connected" (p. 468). But rather than repairing the rifts between the narratives as his revelation of Esther's parenthood would seem to promise, the narrator becomes increasingly estranged from Esther's narrative. In Chapter 31, one of the most poignant in the novel, Charley nurses Jo and catches smallpox from him. In turn, Esther nurses Charley and catches the disease as well. As soon as Charley is out of her sickbed she once again plays nursemaid, this time to Esther. Throughout Ada is begging to be let into the sickroom while Jarndyce is curiously absent from the scene. Harold Skimpole, a man with medical training, recommends that Jo be turned out in the streets and amuses himself outside the sickroom by "playing snatches of pathetic airs, and sometimes singing to them" (p. 492). Esther never comments on the cruelty of this sickroom arrangement yet the chapter echoes her first impression of Charley's family – that it is a sight worthy of mention, one orphan nursing another orphan who in turn nurses another orphan. When the chapter ends with Esther's shocking revelation "I am blind," it is clear that she is writing an orphaned narrative, for the novel picks up immediately with the other narrator's report that "It is night in Lincoln's Inn .... " (p. 498). When we last heard from the narrator, he was describing a distraught Lady Dedlock. When he resumes his narration without reference to either her or Esther, he is, like Captain Hawdon, abandoning both the mother and the daughter.

At this point we realize that Esther is the heroine and main subject of the novel. She herself has begun to understand this by writing more about herself without comment or apology. The only one who seems not to understand that the novel is about Esther is the other narrator, the parent who can never see his child's value or significance. Esther is literally abandoned by the narrative for the next three chapters. We understand at this point that the narrator knows of Esther's existence, condition and narrative. For whereas Esther's account always picks up oblivious to that which precedes it, chapter thirty-two begins by clearly referring to the last line of Esther's chapter. In its opening paragraph he writes: "From tiers of staircase windows, clogged lamps like the eyes of Equity, bleared Argus with a fathomless pocket for every eye and an eye upon it, dimly blink at the stars" (p. 498). Leaving blind Esther, we are met with the image of hundred-eyed Argus – clearly a mirror image of the omniscient narrator himself. As he moves the novel further away from Esther's sickroom into "the neighbouring court, where [Krook] the Lord Chancellor of the Rag and Bottle shop dwells," we should remember Esther's impression of the Lord High Chancellor as

Ada and Richard are handed over to Jarndyce: "at his best [he] appeared so poor a substitute for the love and pride of parents" (p. 78). We might find that the double narrative here serves to heighten the suspense. The original readers of *Bleak House* had to wait for the next installment to hear of Esther's condition. But I find that this chronology instead makes us question our own interest in Esther in light of the narrator's clear indifference to her. If Esther was accidentally lost to her mother as he concludes at the end of Chapter 29, she has been purposefully dropped by the narrator at this juncture. For with the loss of Esther's keen vision and "noticing way" she no longer poses a narrative challenge to her many-eyed "parent."

Once Esther has regained her eyesight and her health, however, the two narratives are temporarily reconciled as she helps Inspector Bucket navigate his way to her mother. As Chapter 56 ends, the narrator leaves Bucket at Mr Jarndyce's as her guardian goes to wake Esther. For the first time in the novel, with only a slight overlap, Esther's narrative will follow directly from the narrator's as Jarndyce knocks at her door and begs her to get up. Like Bucket, the narrator cannot go on without Esther. And Esther cannot move forward without first revisiting many of the novel's earlier scenes. "We appeared to retrace the way we had come," she writes. "After a while, I recognized the familiar way to Saint Albans" or as Mr Bucket calls it "an old acquaintance of yours, this road ... " (pp. 828–9). In these chapters Esther learns the truth about Jo's disappearance and returns to the scene of the death of Jenny's baby. Although Esther has largely managed to suppress mention of and repress feelings for her mother since their meeting at Chesney Wold, her fantasy of reconciliation with her mother is revealed through Lady Dedlock's connection to Jenny. When Jenny's child dies, Esther covers it with a handkerchief. She returns a week later and is told by Jenny's friend Liz that "She's scarcely had the child off her lap, poor thing, these seven days and nights, except when I've been able to take it for a minute or two" (p. 162). Esther describes lifting the handkerchief from the dead child: "how little I thought in whose unquiet bosom that handkerchief would come to lie, after covering the motionless and peaceful breast!" (p 162). The unquiet bosom is that of Lady Dedlock, who will show Esther the handkerchief at their reconciliation and who will leave it behind as a clue for Inspector Bucket to find when she flees her husband. It is crucial that this information is given to us in a rare moment of informed retrospection. Through this unusual narrative maneuver, Esther is able to connect Jenny and Lady Dedlock while simultaneously pretending not to. For, of course, Lady Dedlock does not hold her "dead" child in her lap for seven days. Esther is easily lost to her mother for only her aunt *"discover[s] signs of life in [her] when [she] had been laid aside as dead"* (p. 569, emphasis added). Esther's fantasy that her mother is alive when she sees her dead body at the gates of the cemetery is part of her fantasy that her pursuit of Lady Dedlock will lead to the reconciliation she has hungered for since childhood, that her mother is, like the woman with whom she has exchanged clothes, maternal:

> I saw, with a cry of pity and horror, a woman lying – Jenny, the mother of the dead child .... She lay there, a distressed, unsheltered, senseless creature. She who had brought my mother's letter, who could give me the only clue to where my mother was; she, who was to guide us to rescue and save her whom we had sought so far, who had come to this condition by some means connected with my mother that I could not follow, and might be passing beyond our reach and help at that moment; she lay there, and they stopped me!
>
> (p. 868)

After the discovery of her mother's body, Esther will no longer strike the reader as an ignorant, uninformed narrator. She will no longer be kept in the dark as the narrative proceeds. She and her companion narrator are finally working with the same set of circumstances, the same group of characters. But this reconciliation, as one critic reminds us, like all crucial events in the novel, occurs too late:

> The suit of Jarndyce vs. Jarndyce ends only after Richard Carstone has been irretrievably lost in the false hopes and expectations it spawns. Sir Leicester forgives Lady Dedlock her secret past only after she has already set out on her fatal flight .... Inspector Bucket arrests Hortense and brings her to justice, but as Hortense herself defiantly says, he cannot repair the damage she has already done.[11]

While Esther, along with Bucket, will pursue Lady Dedlock through the streets of London in chapter 57 and discover her body in chapter 59, the narrator will remain behind hovering over the prostrate body of Sir Leicester. The narrator who has been god-like, intangible and unreachable throughout, suddenly reveals his own mortality and humanity. In the only personal reference he makes to himself in the novel he writes: "As all partings foreshadow the great final one – so, empty rooms, bereft of a familiar presence, mournfully whisper what your room and what *mine* must one day be" (p. 845, emphasis added). After hinting at his own death and foreshadowing Lady Dedlock's, he leaves Esther in the next chapter to describe the reconciliation with her parents, both dead bodies. Esther's will become the dominant narrative voice, taking over six of the last eight chapters while the narrator moves further into the background.

But if reconciliation with the parent narrator is short-lived and with her parents too late, if the two narratives never again come together, if the narrator calls attention to himself as he senses his own narrative and narrative powers coming to an end, it is not too late for Esther to live her life. The force and determination with which Esther moves from the last line of the eighteenth book – "And it was my mother, cold and dead" (p. 869) – to the first line of the nineteenth – "I proceed to other passages of my narrative" – is comparable to the other radical transitions in the novel: from the revelation of Esther's birth to her own unknowing perspective, from the announcement of Esther's blindness to the narrator's shocking indifference to her affliction. Throughout the novel Esther has sought love, affirmation, and an identity. She has seen herself as inferior to others because of her illegitimacy. Pained at thinking herself an orphan, she wonders if this would not be better than being abandoned by living parents. Grateful to be alive, she half-believes her aunt's curse that she should never have been born. Her long movement into the past ends at the cemetery gate. She can only move into the future. In a rare moment in her narrative she begins her chapter in the present tense. In a few words she mentions her sorrow and illness, but never again does she mention either of her parents. With her typical propensity for repeating herself she ends her brief discussion of her unhappiness with the same words, "I proceed to other passages of my narrative" (p. 869). The first time she writes this line it seems too sudden and cruel. We are sure she will do what she has done before, backtrack, rub out lines, reverse her decision. The second time she writes it we believe her. We are seeing a new Esther.

While it is Esther who has attempted to redeem Lady Dedlock, Esther who has pursued Lady Dedlock, it is Esther's prerogative to drop Lady Dedlock. The woman is never again mentioned by her daughter after her dead body is found at the end of the eighteenth book. But the narrator who ends his account and apparently his days "Down in Lincolnshire" with an "invalided, bent, and almost blind" Sir Leicester visiting the mausoleum of his wife and the other dead Dedlocks, who introduced us to Lady Dedlock as a spoiled, pampered child, who never alluded to her remorseful reconciliation with her child, who through time, change, and crisis continued to paint her as haughty, proud, indifferent, and bored, has the final word on Lady Dedlock and it is apparently a word of sympathy:

> Some of her old friends ... did once occasionally say, when the Wold assembled together, that they wondered the ashes of the Dedlocks, entombed in the mausoleum, never rose against the profanation of her company. But the dead-and-gone Dedlocks take it very calmly, and have never been known to object.
>
> (p. 928)

*

So far, I have read *Bleak House* progressively, as a novel in which the parent narrative (as well as his present-tense account) dominates, in which it has been his prerogative to overlook and abandon his "child." I have seen Esther profoundly desiring reconciliation with her mother. As she comes close to realizing this possibility, the two narratives approach synchronicity as well. But just as Esther's dream is never fulfilled, narrative reconciliation is finally unrealized as well. Yet a novel written by two narrators in two tenses demands to be read both progressively and retrospectively. A retrospective reading makes us question whether narrative reconciliation and reconciliation with her parents are what Esther truly desires. Esther's extraordinary response to being held by her mother for the first and only time is to protect her parent before herself. She allows her mother what she needs, and agrees that familial estrangement is safer and more satisfactory than familial connection. She feels through all her "tumult of emotion, a burst of gratitude to the providence of God that I was so changed as that I never could disgrace her by any trace of likeness; as that nobody could ever now look at me, and look at her, and remotely think of any near tie between us" (p. 565). More than one critic has read Esther's response as immediate relief that she can disassociate herself from her mother and her sexual taint.[12] The desire for disassociation from her parents as an adult is as profound an impulse as reconciliation with them as a child. Thus, after the near-reconciliation of the narratives, the concluding chapters of the novel force us to reread Esther's relationship to the other narrator and to see that in an effort to distance herself from her genetic inheritance she has deliberately distanced herself from the parent narrative as well. As I now read the novel retrospectively we will see what we have seen before but with a difference –

this *déjà vu* will leave us with the unsettling impression that *Bleak House* has not one, but two omniscient narrators, that Esther is both a reader and a writer of the novel – fully aware of the content of both narratives. Thus, like Jane's performance of dutifulness or Molly Bloom's of naturalness, Esther's narrative is performed ignorance.

What critics have derided as coyness, belabored artlessness, or irritating self-consciousness, may be seen as her acknowledgment of the falsity of uninformed retrospection. In a passage such as the following she is daring us to question the naïveté of her narrative stance:

> [Mrs Woodcourt] was such a sharp little lady, and used to sit with her hands folded in each other, looking so very watchful while she talked to me, that perhaps I found that rather irksome. Or perhaps it was her being so upright and trim; though I don't think it was that, because I thought that quaintly pleasant. Nor can it have been the general expression of her face, which was very sparkling and pretty for an old lady. I don't know what it was. Or at least if I do, now, I thought I did not then. Or at least – but it don't matter.
>
> (p. 467)

Through her greatest "failing" as a writer, her tendency to repeat herself, she is continually calling attention to the doubleness of her narrative and the necessity of our reading twice what she has written twice. Her narrative starts with a preponderance of doubles. She begins her new life at Greenleaf with "two Miss Donnys, twins" (p. 73). "Six quiet years (I find I am saying it for the second time) I had passed at Greenleaf, seeing in those around me, as it might be in a looking-glass, every stage of my own growth and change there ..." (p. 74). Esther finally leaves Greenleaf crying " 'O, I am so thankful, I am so thankful' many times over!" (p. 75). She will meet Ada and refer to her as "my darling – it is so natural to me now, that I can't help writing it" (p. 78), and a page later as "my pet (it is so natural to me that again I can't help it!)" (p. 79).

Written in retrospect, Esther's narrative already doubles back on itself. But through her peculiar narrative technique she consistently doubles back on what has been doubled back on already and ends up saying everything twice.

> I have omitted to mention in its place, that there was some one else at the family dinner party. It was not a lady. It was a gentleman. It was a gentleman of a dark complexion – a young surgeon. He was

rather reserved, but I thought him very sensible and agreeable. At least, Ada asked me if I did not, and I said yes.

(p. 233)

Woodcourt is not a lady. Therefore, he is a gentleman. He is a gentleman of a dark complexion. Ada finds him sensible and agreeable. Esther finds him sensible and agreeable as well. Those critics who find Esther's narrative a failure can easily point to the above passage as evidence of either the overly simplistic or overly complex nature of her writing. (If Prince adds too many letters to his words, Esther adds too many words to her sentences.)

Yet Esther's narrative style is consistent with a novel in which we can expect to see things happening "over and over again." Richard, Ada, and Esther anticipate their first meeting with Jarndyce, "what he would say to us, and what we should say to him, all of which we wondered about, over and over again" (p. 111). Jarndyce and Jarndyce is "a monument of Chancery practice in which ... every difficulty, every contingency, every masterly fiction, every form of procedure known in that court, is represented over and over again" (p. 68). "All through the deplorable cause, everybody must have copies, over and over again, of everything that has accumulated about it in the way of cartloads of papers" (p. 145). "And thus, through years and years, and lives and lives, everything goes on, constantly beginning over and over again, and nothing ever ends" (p. 146). "Innumerable children have been born into the cause; innumerable young people have married into it; innumerable old people have died out of it" (p. 52). But they are as unable to escape it as Miss Flite's caged birds:

'I began to keep the little creatures ... with the intention of restoring them to liberty. When my judgment should be given. Ye-es! They die in prison, though. Their lives, poor silly things, are so short in comparison with Chancery proceedings, that, one by one, the whole collection has died over and over again. I doubt, do you know, whether one of these, though they are all young, will live to be free!'

(p. 104)

Because of the double narrative, Jo and Tulkinghorn seem to die over and over again. Captain Hawdon literally dies over and over again. Thus, retrospection also has a dual role in *Bleak House*. It liberates Esther to tell her story in her own way, but traps her in this pattern of retracing, doubling back, not moving forward.

When change in *Bleak House* can only be effected through spontaneous combustion, there seems little possibility that Esther can avoid
making, or suffering as a result of, the mistakes her parents have made.
The "sins of the fathers" is an oft-repeated phrase in the novel, and
Bleak House's children are routinely punished for their parents' behavior. Because Charley was the daughter of a debt collector, "some people
won't employ her ...; some people that do employ her, cast it at her;
some make a merit of having her to work for them, with that and all
her drawbacks upon her: and perhaps pay her less and put upon her
more" (p. 265). Mr Boythorn's antipathy to Sir Leicester seems to have
as much to do with his forebears as with himself:

> 'That fellow is, and his father was, and his grandfather was, the
> most stiff-necked, arrogant imbecile, pig-headed numskull, ever, by
> some inexplicable mistake of Nature, born in any station of life but
> a walking-stick's! The whole of that family are the most solemnly
> conceited and consummate blockheads!'
>
> (p. 170)

Because Sir Morbury crippled his wife, she curses his family by contin-
uing to be heard on the Ghost's Walk centuries after her death. After
the revelations of her birth, Esther too haunts the Ghost's Walk: "My
echoing footsteps brought it suddenly into my mind that there was a
dreadful truth in the legend of the Ghost's Walk; that it was I who was
to bring calamity upon the stately house .... " (p. 571). Racing home to
loving letters from Jarndyce and Ada, she returns to her senses:

> If the sins of the fathers were sometimes visited upon the children,
> the phrase did not mean what I had in the morning feared it meant.
> I knew I was as innocent of my birth as a queen of hers; and that
> before my Heavenly Father I should not be punished for birth, nor a
> queen rewarded for it.
>
> (p. 571)

Along with these references in the chapter "Chesney Wold" to the sins
of the fathers and the heavenly Father, comes Esther's assurance to her
mother that Jarndyce "had been the best of fathers to me" (p. 568). The
father who is conspicuously absent from the chapter is Captain Hawdon.

Dickens suggests an association between the anonymous narrator
and Esther's father by naming the latter Nemo – Nobody. (When
George writes Esther about him, within the parent narrative, he refers

to him as "a certain person" and "a certain unfortunate gentleman" (p. 907).) Nemo is one of many characters who has lost a name along the way. Jo may be told that everybody has two names, but George has abandoned Rouncewell, Krook appears to have no first name and Guster no last. Esther herself is nameless. She happily becomes Old Woman, Little Old Woman, Cobweb, Mrs Shipton, Mother Hubbard, and Dame Durden, until her "own name soon became quite lost among them" (p. 148). Her own name is, of course, no more legitimate than Dame Durden. She ends the novel's first installment with the declaration, "I was no one" (p. 94). She begins the second installment with a visit to Krook's Rag and Bottle Shop where she will walk past the room of No one – her father. It is crucial to Esther's narrative that her father remain no one to her. Given the one opportunity to ask her mother questions, Esther never broaches the subject of her father. He is mentioned only once in the closing pages of her narrative when Jarndyce hands her over to Woodcourt saying – he "stood beside your father when he lay dead – stood beside your mother" (p. 914). How would a reader understand Jarndyce's reference to her father without having read the other half of the novel? References to Esther frequently occur in the parent narrative. Each relies on her narrative to be explicable. For instance, the narrator never mentions Esther's smallpox, but when he tells of Liz's finding Jo, he knows that we will understand her accusation: "And that young lady that was such a pretty dear, caught his illness, lost her beautiful looks, and wouldn't hardly be known for the same young lady now, if it wasn't for her angel temper, and her pretty shape, and her sweet voice" (p. 688). Conversely, when her father finally enters her narrative, Esther is relying wholly on the reader's knowledge of the parent narrative, a narrative she pretends not to have read.

Shortly before the discovery of Lady Dedlock's body, we experience our last (chronological) bout with *déjà vu* as Bucket recapitulates *Bleak House*'s subplots to cure Mrs Snagsby's jealousy:

'You recollect where you saw me last, and what was talked of in that circle. Don't you? Yes! Very well. This young lady is that young lady.' Mrs Snagsby appeared to understand the reference better than I did at the time. 'And Toughey – him as you call Jo – was mixed up in the same business, and no other; and the law-writer that you know of, was mixed up in the same business, and no other; and your husband, with no more knowledge of it than your great-grandfather, was mixed up (by Mr Tulkinghorn deceased, his best customer) in the same business, and no other; and the whole bileing of people was mixed up in the same business, and no other.'

(p. 863)

Everything that Esther writes here would be pure gibberish to us if we had only been reading her narrative. We would have no idea what business has connected Tulkinghorn, Jo, the Snagsbys, etc. We would have no sense of why Bucket has discussed Esther with Mrs Snagsby earlier. The passage would seem more familiar in the parent narrator's account. For, as one critic writes of him, he is omniscient but never dependable. He offers us "little help with the mysteries, suspicions, guesses, and secrets which fill his narrative."[13] (He also has a fondness for the ridiculous, absent from Esther's narrative, as when he invites everyone from Lord Boodle to Lord Quoodle to Sir Leicester's dinner party.) Esther never presents us with such impenetrable dialogue. So that although Esther hears this conversation as nothing but gibberish – "Mrs Snagsby appeared to understand the reference better than I did at the time" – she records it conscientiously for her readers knowing that it makes sense to them. She knows that she is helping to piece together the various strands of the narrator's massive, disjointed account. In other words, she has known all along the contents of the other narrative.

Thus, when pages later she arrives at the cemetery gate and sees "Jenny" "with one arm creeping round a bar of the iron gate, and seeming to embrace it" (p. 868), she can leave her mother's body there without retracing the route it has taken from a handwriting sample, to a crossing sweeper, to a disguised woman recoiling in horror at the resting place of her lover. She understands her mother's story, but feels no compulsion to revisit it. Finally relying on the parent narrative, she can move forward in her own without doubling back and filling in the gaps. (All of this information could have been in Lady Dedlock's letter to her daughter, but after sharing with us the circumstances of her birth, she burns it, promising to tell us the rest later. No mention is ever again made of it.) The parent narrator has penetrated the cemetery gate; in Lady Dedlock's last gesture she reaches through its bars, but Esther remains outside. Neither she nor her narrative ever attempts to "embrace" her father. To reach this place in the narrative Esther has literally had to follow in her mother's footsteps. She proves here that she is not insipid and naive; she is not oblivious to the sexual choices made by her mother; she actively rejects her mother's path, a path that leads to the wrong choice of sexual partner, Esther's father. She makes no effort to learn more about him, and we are left with the narrator's amorphous portrait of a man believed drowned who mysteriously lived, an opium addict who is remembered by one child as "wery good" to him (p. 200), and by other children as having "sold himself to the devil" (p. 106) without, however, having any money left to show for it.

Hawdon, like the parent narrator, remains a shadowy figure, but by the terms of Dickens's novel, he has clearly sinned. First, like so many of the novel's parents, he destroys his family's lives through his attraction to the foreign over the domestic. Surely the novel's implication is that he and Esther's mother would have married if he had been in England when she discovered her pregnancy. Secondly, he ends his days through his own self-neglect and iniquity where the poor are condemned to live their lives. Lastly he is employed by Chancery as a law copyist. He supports his addiction by contributing to all that waste of paper and life. Jarndyce and Jarndyce is clearly massive enough to pay for what opium he needs. Like Richard, Hawdon is killed by the case. As Hawdon has sinned sexually and spiritually, Esther must wear the mark of his transgressions on her face. During Lady Dedlock's assignation with her dead lover outside the cemetery gate, she contracts the disease which will eventually kill her from deadly stains which contaminate her dress, and from his reaction to returning to the spot, presumably the place where Jo too contracts his disease: "'I won't go to the berryin ground. I don't like the name on it. She might go a-berryin me.' His shivering came on again, and as he leaned against the wall, he shook the hovel" (p. 485). The novel's implication is, then, that Esther's smallpox is transmitted from her father's body to Jo, Charley and finally herself. Like the inky stains under Caddy's baby's eyes, Esther's ruined face is her genetic inheritance. Her father's face is, like her own ruined one, indescribable: "You might as well ask me to describe the ladies whose heads of hair I have got in sacks downstairs," says his landlord (p. 191).

Faces are figured throughout the novel as mirrors. Even before she is scarred, Esther shies away from looking-glasses. Instead, she learns at an early age to use others' faces as mirrors. After the unhappy time with her aunt, she spends six years at Greenleaf where she "never saw in any face there, thank Heaven, on my birthday, that it would have been better if I had never been born" (p. 73). She describes her time there as "seeing in those around me, as it might be in a looking-glass, every stage of my own growth and change there" (p. 74). Guppy's response to her disfigurement can be seen in his red face; Woodcourt's silent sympathy Esther deduces from his face as well – "I saw that he was very sorry for me" (p. 680). It is crucial that faces act as mirrors for

Esther's is in a double bind and has finally a double meaning. While Esther is grateful that her ruined face will destroy any visible connection to her mother, her narrative is, of course, re-establishing that connection while simultaneously disguising the link to her father which her disfigurement has made manifest.

By refusing to acknowledge her father and by relying on a parent narrative that has consistently relied on hers, Esther is remedying the problem of male-female dependency in the novel. She will choose neither her mother's fatal path nor make the same mistakes as her best friends. Ada allows her engagement to be called off when Richard is still a viable man. Once he is a helpless invalid, she marries him. Impoverished and over-worked, Caddy spends her married life lying to and catering to the needs of her deluded father-in-law. She has already learned to treat her father as a child, and Harold Skimpole never refers to himself as anything but a child. Lady Dedlock is married to a man old enough to be her father and keeps her secret not because of fear of being punished by her husband, but because his name must be protected. Cornered by Tulkinghorn, she thinks first of how to spare her husband. We see woman after woman in *Bleak House* caring for and protecting men while Liz's husband beats her and Grandfather Smallweed throws sharp objects at his aged wife's head. Esther's story promises to reverse this course. For Esther, by Dickens's terms, makes the healthy sexual choice by denying herself any morbid attachment to her *fathers*, by marrying someone who will care for her and her daughters, a doctor.

Relatively little of Esther's narrative is taken up with discussion of Allan Woodcourt, but as I began this chapter by suggesting, for Esther to define herself sexually, to acknowledge herself as desirable, she must do in five hundred pages what David Copperfield and Pip are allowed to do in several sentences – she must justify her own existence. As she always couples references to her birth with references to her lost beauty – "my disfigurement, and my inheritance of shame," "the deep traces of my illness, and the circumstances of my birth"[14] – she can only imagine her lost face returning to her after she has moved beyond all of her parents, including Jarndyce. The night before she learns that Jarndyce is giving her to Woodcourt, not keeping her for himself, Esther writes: "I am bound to confess that I cried; but I hope it was with pleasure, though I am not quite sure it was with pleasure" (p. 911). Dickens is not validating the sacrificial sexuality of Caddy and Ada; he is deeming incredibly healthy the sexuality of a woman who does not want to marry her father. Critics may continue to read Esther as having no sexual desire, but we must not expect to find her desire expressed in positive terms, such as Jane Eyre uses, but always as a rejection of the parent in all his guises.

David Copperfield's and particularly Pip's are narratives of regret. In them grown men use retrospection to grapple with their younger selves. David must punish himself for his reckless infatuation with Dora; Pip must flagellate himself for his treatment of Joe and Magwitch. In his brilliant reading of *Great Expectations* Jack Rawlins argues that Pip should not be experiencing guilt, that he is justified in distancing himself from his sister, Joe, and Magwitch – his abusive, ineffectual, and manipulative parents. Dickens creates a compelling child hero who can see the truth in a world of adult lies, and then he reneges on the early promise of the novel by lying to himself about Pip's superiority to the novel's other characters. The clear-eyed child must, because of what Rawlins views as Dickens's own cowardice and dishonesty, learn to see the error of his ways.[15] None of Dickens's first-person narrators accuse their parents directly. *We* may recognize Mrs. Copperfield's weakness and disloyalty; *we* may regret Joe's implicit countenancing of abuse; *we* may shudder at Jarndyce's flirtation with incest, but Dickens's narrators forgive. Esther's narrative style lacks David's confidence or Pip's humor, but its complex relationship to that of the companion narrator allows Esther to use retrospection for entirely different ends. For her narrative is not motivated by regret – and Dickens need not pretend it is.

I have argued in Chapter 1 that Jane Eyre uses what the Victorians would have recognized as feminine virtues – obedience, silence, and unquestioning contentment – as narrative strategies. That is, she shows how revenge is best exacted without all "the gall and wormwood." The narrator who uses virtue wisely will have both the opportunity and credibility necessary to tell her subversive story. Dickens and Brontë place different values on feminine virtue. Brontë sees it as something possibly hateful yet potentially useful that is imposed on women; Dickens views it as something irrefutably desirable in women (and despite plenty of his own personal experience to the contrary) fantasizes that it is inherent in women. And yet in *Bleak House* Dickens uses feminine virtue, as Brontë does, as a narrative strategy. It is *only* as an innocuous angel in the house that Esther can perform the complicated narrative maneuver of complaining without bitterness, of critiquing while remaining loyal. As Brontë proves that neither unimpeachable virtue (such as Helen Burns's) nor monstrousness (such as Bertha's) is a compelling quality in a narrator, Dickens allows Esther to be more calculating than her fellow angels (Little

Dorrit, Agnes Wickfield, Florence Dombey, and the like who are more memorable for keeping silent than for speaking – remember Agnes's extraordinary means of wordlessly telling David his wife is dead) while eliciting all the sympathy denied his vitriolic harridans (Edith Dombey, Alice Brown, Miss Wade, and their like, who voice their complaints to their own shame and regret.) Thus, while remaining sentimental, "good," and apparently faithful, Esther is able to use retrospection not to grapple with her own past wrongs but with her parents'.

Fighting a morbid attachment to his own father, Dickens began writing *Bleak House* several months after the death of John Dickens. Dickens's biographer, Peter Ackroyd, describes Dickens wandering the London streets in the sleepless nights after his father's death:

> but long before that time it is clear that the image of his father haunted him in some generalised and unspecified way. He is even mentioned in his first published story .... It has been said that his father then reappears everywhere after this; in William Dorrit, in Wilkins Micawber, in Joey Bagstock (originally christened "John" by Dickens) and in that succession of false fathers and social parasites who sometimes bear the name "John" but who can be recognised in any case as images of that father who haunted him .... If he admired him he despised him, too, but he also recognised the presence of his father within himself so that, at times of great distress, his own self-pity spilled over into pity for the man who had begotten him. He was forever accusing him during his life of rapacity and ingratitude but, after his death, his constant refrain was "my poor father."[16]

Indeed, Dickens was no model parent himself. His relationship to his sons was particularly vexed. "In his accounts of his own children there are constant intimations of his disappointment and even on occasions hostility ... the boys realised that they were all 'failures' in their father's eyes."[17] But his girls were a different matter. His daughter Mamie was so attached to him that she never married. When his favorite, Kate, was married, Mamie found him after the wedding "upon his knees with his head buried in Katie's wedding gown, sobbing." It was an unwise marriage, one that Dickens strongly opposed, for he knew Kate was marrying only to get away from what she would describe as her "unhappy home." He blamed himself, telling Mamie, "But for me, Katie would not have left home."[18]

The father-daughter relationship is central to Dickens's novels. While he sometimes idealized such relationships as that between Doctor Manette and Lucie, he more frequently showed fathers depending on

(William Dorrit and Amy), exploiting (Gaffer Hexam and Lizzie), or neglecting (Paul Dombey Sr. and Florence) their daughters. Whatever cruelty the child endures in Dickens's early novels, we can expect to find him or her reconciled with a parent or parent figure in the closing chapters. Thus, one of the cruelest fathers in Dickens, Paul Dombey Sr., is reformed beyond recognition:

> The voices in the waves ... speak to him of Florence and his altered heart; of Florence and their ceaseless murmuring to her of the love, eternal and illimitable, extending still, beyond the sea, beyond the sky, to the invisible country far away. Never from the mighty sea may voices rise too late, to come between us and the unseen region on the other shore![19]

Such hopefulness is absent from *Bleak House* and the novels which follow it. Reconciliation with and understanding of his own father were now impossibilities. *Bleak House*'s conclusion is a radical departure from *Dombey and Son*'s Romantic ending in which nothing can happen "too late." None of the novel's fathers – Skimpole, Turveydrop, Jellyby – is reformed, and the only hope for Esther as a wife is to reject one father and as a mother to disavow the genetic inheritance of another. Esther, as a character, has been damaged by Chancery, by urban squalor, by false religiosity, by bad parenting, and no amount of marital love can fully compensate her for her losses.

Yet through her simple, unaffected style Esther, the narrator, outlives the flamboyant parent whose flame sputters out before her own. His last chapters and his last lines – "passion and pride, even to the stranger's eye, have died away from the place in Lincolnshire, and yielded it to dull repose" (p. 932) – are consumed with death while to Esther is left the happier task of describing marriages and births. After her mother's death, Esther's becomes the novel's dominant voice. In the final chapters her voice becomes emboldened. We hear traces of the venom, audacity, and irony of the parent narrator.

> [Mr Vholes] stood behind me, with his long black figure reaching nearly to the ceiling of those low rooms; feeling the pimples on his face as if they were ornaments, and speaking inwardly and evenly as though there were not a human passion or emotion in his nature .... [Richard and I] talked of the old times pleasantly. These did not appear to be interesting to Mr Vholes, though he occasionally made a gasp which I believe was his smile.

(p. 878)

But the narrator's imaginative capacity, which may have been her genetic inheritance, is never hers to own:

> Through some of the fiery windows, beautiful from without, and set, at this sunset hour, not in dull-grey stone but in a glorious house of gold, the light excluded at other windows pours in, rich, lavish, overflowing like the summer plenty in the land. Then do the frozen Dedlocks thaw. Strange movements come upon their features, as the shadows of leaves play there. A dense Justice in a corner is beguiled into a wink. A staring Baronet, with a truncheon, gets a dimple in his chin. Down into the bosom of a stony shepherdess there steals a fleck of light and warmth, that would have done it good, a hundred years ago .... Now, the moon is high; and the great house, needing habitation more than ever, is like a body without life. Now it is even awful, stealing through it, to think of the live people who have slept in the solitary bedrooms; to say nothing of the dead. Now is the time for shadow, when every corner is a cavern, and every downward step a pit, when the stained glass is reflected in pale and faded hues upon the floors, when anything and everything can be made of the heavy staircase beams excepting their own proper shapes ....
>
> (pp. 620–1)

It is impossible to imagine Esther writing anything so fantastical. By writing in the present tense the parent narrator literally creates the scene: by writing in the past, Esther limits herself to reporting on a scene. An imaginative life, a power of vision to transcend and transform the familiar, is a luxury afforded the parents of *Bleak House*, never the children. They inherit a world they must learn to live in.

> Judy [Smallweed] never owned a doll, never heard of Cinderella, never played at any game .... And her twin brother couldn't wind up a top for his life. He knows no more of Jack the Giant Killer, or of Sinbad the Sailor, than he knows of the people in the stars. He could as soon play at leap-frog or at cricket, as change into a cricket or a frog himself.
>
> (p. 342)

Esther, of course, did own a doll. So guilty does she feel about her imaginary life that she buries her only childhood friend before setting out for Greenleaf. (Ashamed of her own fantasy life, she is, nonetheless, as virtually the novel's only good mother, able to regale

Mrs Jellyby's children with Little Red Riding Hood and Puss in Boots, apparently the first fairy tales they have ever heard.) Like the parent narrator, Esther has extraordinary powers of description. But while she is brilliant at capturing the details of anything she sees, she is limited by an attachment to the factual and the realistic, and an incapacity to interpret and create:

> To see everything going on so smoothly, and to think of the rough-ness of the suitors' lives and deaths; to see all that full dress and ceremony, and to think of the waste, and want, and beggared misery it represented; to consider that, while the sickness of hope deferred was raging in so many hearts, this polite show went calmly on from day to day, and year to year, in such good order and com-posure; to behold the Lord Chancellor, and the whole array of prac-titioners under him, looking at one another and at the spectators, as if nobody had ever heard that all over England the name in which they were assembled was a bitter jest: was held in universal horror, contempt, and indignation; was known for something so flagrant and bad, that little short of a miracle could bring any good out of it to any one: this was so curious and self-contradictory to me, who had no experience of it, that it was at first incredible, and I could not comprehend it. I sat where Richard put me, and tried to listen, and looked about me; but there seemed to be no reality in the whole scene, except poor little Miss Flite, the madwoman, standing on a bench, and nodding at it.
>
> (pp. 399-400)

*

After a day of dutifully caring for her charge, Jane Eyre goes up to the roof of Thornfield and looks out at the distant view, and then she

> longed for a power of vision which might overpass that limit; which might reach the busy world, towns, regions full of life I had heard of but never seen .... I valued what was good in Mrs Fairfax, and what was good in Adèle; but I believed in the existence of other and more vivid kinds of goodness, and what I believed in I wished to behold.
>
> (p. 109)

Brontë allows Jane such a power of vision, I have argued, through Rochester's blindness and the liberating potential of retrospection. Her imagination is free to construct a narrative that transcends the limits of her narrow experience. Without fear of repercussions she is able to be artful and inventive. Like her drawings of places she has never seen, her story may be fantastical and imaginary or it may simply report her version of the truth. But Esther is confined by the pages of *Bleak House* and the walls of Bleak House. She can look behind herself, but not beyond herself. There are still too many parentless children who require her undivided attention. There is still too much housekeeping which only she can be counted on to do. And so in her greatest moment of health and imaginative transcendence – sensing that she is ready to reclaim the beauty which connects her to her mother's youth and to lose the scars which betray her father's transgressions – Esther cuts herself short. "Even supposing" must be the starting point of a different narrative.

*

Although I will now move on to the twentieth century and Joyce, I am not yet done with the nineteenth century or Dickens. In a postscript to my Molly Bloom chapter I will consider the influence of *Little Dorrit* (and particularly its great talker, Flora Finching) on *Ulysses*'s final chapter. Joyce's modernist breakthrough owes much to the Victorian novel.

5
Molly Bloom: Acting Natural

Perhaps no female narrative has divided feminist critics more than Molly Bloom's soliloquy. Joyce's ventriloquy has been read alternatively as mindless misogyny and as "one of the most tremendous summations of life that [has] ever been caught in the net of art."[1] Yet the approaches taken to Molly's text by both its detractors and proponents are strangely similar. The central "event" of the narrative for both is Molly's menstruation, and both find that for Molly "thinking and menstruating are similar and concomitant processes. She can no more govern the first, by sentence structure or punctuation, than she can the second."[2] The conflation of the mouth and vagina was read as patriarchal "linguistic *puissance*"[3] by the first wave of feminist critics, as "linguistic *jouissance*" by those inspired by French psychoanalytic theory. Thus, Gilbert and Gubar find Molly's narrative obscene, evidence that "for Joyce, woman's scattered logos is a scatologos"[4] while Christine van Boheemen sees Molly's blood as "the flow of the fertility of life which is obliquely seen as a symbol for a language, a textuality and a perverse form of writing against the grain."[5] Molly's narrative, although authored by a man, is now commonly read as a rare example of *écriture feminine*, woman writing her own body.

This insistence on Molly's artlessness is curious in light of Molly's progenitor – Penelope, one of the greatest artificers in Western literature. Even those critics who have taken Homer's weaver into account agree that "Joyce's use of the Penelope figure is, in the first place, ironic."[6] For if Penelope is faithful and chaste for nineteen years of waiting, Molly can scarcely contain herself until she next meets her current lover. If Penelope proves herself her husband's intellectual equal through the cunning with which she fends off her suitors, Molly makes Leopold look a genius with her relative ignorance of philosophy, language, and punctuation. But such comparisons are based on the false assumption that we can ever determine what Molly *is*. As James Van Dyck Card has argued so persuasively, "any discussion of Molly had best be careful in an analysis of her character, her habits, or her opinions ...." Molly is both amoral and fiercely religious. She alternately likes and despises her bed, other women, and the male body.[7] Like Card, I can find little value in any discussion of Molly which finds her "merely crude, sluttish, unmaternal, narcissistic, an Earth Goddess [or] the symbol of the eternal feminine."[8] While Card, however, is content to leave Molly as a mass of unresolved contradictions, I will use these contradictions to argue not for who Molly *is*, but for *how* her project echoes Penelope's. I will read her soliloquy as the textual performance of Penelope's "off-stage" activity of weaving in order to unweave, of doing in order to undo. Penelope's four-year ruse is reflected in the *artifice* of both the language and structure of Molly's narrative. Even the experiences of orgasm and menstruation are unwoven and revealed as pretense.

Although we tend to remember Penelope as faithful and cunning, there have been through the centuries as many interpretations of her conduct as there have been of Molly's. In some versions of the myth, Penelope, after prostituting herself to her suitors and giving birth to the monstrous god Pan, is banished by her husband. As Philip Herring has argued, Joyce's Zürich notebooks show that he was familiar with these alternative interpretations. The notations he made about Penelope from a lexicon of Greek and Roman mythology include "banished by U to Sparta", "what kind of child can much fucked whore have", and "sits smutty talking amg the Freiers."[9] If classical scholars differ, the modernists were no less divided as to Penelope's character. On the wall beside Joyce's desk hung

> a photograph of a Greek statue of Penelope, seated and looking at her raised forefinger. 'What is she thinking about?' Joyce asked. 'She is weighing up her wooers,' Budgen suggested, 'trying to decide which one of them will make the most manageable husband.' 'To me,' said Paul [Suter], 'she seems to be saying: "I'll give him just one week more."' 'My own idea,' said Joyce, 'is that she is trying to recollect what Ulysses looks like. You, see, he has been away many years, and they had no photographs in those days.'[10]

Rather than an "ironized" Penelope, Molly is one of many versions. If we take Joyce at his word, her narrative is neither about choosing between many men nor giving one man an ultimatum. It is about holding onto and reclaiming memory in order to sustain her marriage.

Without pursuing Molly's connection to Penelope, some feminist critics have begun to read Molly's narrative as performance. Cheryl Herr reads Molly not as a "character but rather as a role to be enacted by this or that major artiste" of Joyce's era – Molly may be a drag queen.[11] Kimberly Devlin reads Molly not as a single role, but as "an elaborate series of 'star turns' that undermines the notion of womanliness as it displays it."[12] Devlin is working with a notion of female mimicry, "the masquerade of (woman's) nature as nature, as what precedes cultural construction. She 'does' ideology in order to undo it."[13] Thus, Devlin has rejected the prominent readings of Joyce as a misogynist or Molly as the eternal feminine and sees her dismantling and de-signifying gender "through parody and critique. Molly is the poseur who nonetheless sees through all poses – actress, stage director, and critic of the gender theater itself."[14] While I read Molly dismantling her own text, I do not give Joyce credit for tearing down patriarchal ideology in the process. Rather, I see Joyce's radical form of writing as a conservative gesture, one which weaves and unweaves language in order to preserve marriage. Joyce does not give Molly the *time* to deconstruct gender. Her language does not reveal the thoughtfulness and insight of Devlin's social critic, but the desperation and urgency of a woman hanging onto a most tenuous "role," that of Bloom's wife.

Joyce's own interpretation of Penelope was in part influenced by Samuel Butler's, who, in *The Authoress of the Odyssey* claimed that a woman, not Homer, had written the epic, for what else would explain the whitewashing of Penelope?[15] Butler posited Nausicaa as the authoress, but perhaps Joyce had Penelope herself in mind when he gave Molly the last word and the opportunity to ameliorate a reputation damaged by fourteen of the previous episodes. "Penelope" provides more of an overview of the novel than any other episode. Here we revisit the bedroom encounter of "Calypso," the Ben Howth of "Lestrygonians," the scene of charity to a beggar in "Wandering Rocks," the jingling bed of "Sirens." We hear again about Stephen's dead mother, Josie Breen, and Milly. The episode which particularly haunts Molly's, however, is "Hades." From a newspaper photograph brought her by Boylan, Molly recapitulates an episode she cannot have read:

L Boom and Tom Kernan that drunken little barrelly man that bit his tongue off falling down the mens W C drunk in some place or other and Martin Cunningham and the two Dedaluses and Fanny MCoys

husband white head of cabbage skinny thing with a turn in her eye
trying to sing my songs shed want to be born all over again and her
old green dress with the lowneck as she cant attract them any other
way like dabbling on a rainy day I see it all now plainly and they call
that friendship killing and then burying one another and they all
with their wives and families at home more especially Jack Power
keeping that barmaid he does of course his wife is always sick or going
to be sick or just getting better of it and hes a goodlooking man still
though hes getting a bit grey over the ears theyre a nice lot all of
them well theyre not going to get my husband again into their
clutches if I can help it making fun of him then behind his back I
know well when he goes on with his idiotics because he has sense
enough not to squander every penny piece he earns[16]

"I see it all now plainly" she claims, and we picture her sitting apart
from and above the novel in which she exists, able to view a moment
many hours old and see into the hearts of men as only some omniscient narrator Joyce would have satirized in "Nausicaa" could. But it is
not that Joyce is positioning Molly as the writer of his epic. That so
much of *Ulysses* shows up in her design is instead evidence that he has
made her responsible for "unwriting" his novel. The artifice of her narrative exposes the apparatus of her own project and finally the conceit
of Joyce's as well. She sees plainly not through a glass (as critics of her
vanity would have it) or an intuitive mind (as admirers of her femininity would) but through hundreds of pieces of the material which allows
her to recreate Paddy's burial and of which she (in her particular contradictoriness) is made, "white ink on black paper" (p. 631). Joyce
described *Ulysses*'s composition as "the progress of a sandblast." "Each
successive episode, dealing with some province of artistic culture
(rhetoric or music or dialectic), leaves behind it a burnt up field."[17]
While he referred to "Penelope" as a "coda," an afterthought to this
catalogue of masculine endeavor and creation, his final episode is not
content to eradicate only woman's artifice, but, in the spirit of Homer's
Penelope, to "unwrite" the product of his eight-years' labor – the
seventeen previous episodes – as well.

Penelope's laborious ploy of weaving in order to unweave is
described three times in *The Odyssey*. First Antinoos, the "most inso-
lent" of her suitors, describes her deception. Later Penelope tells the
story almost word for word to the disguised Odysseus. Finally the soul
of Amphimedon, a suitor Telemachus has killed, tells the story of
coming upon Penelope "undoing the shining fabric" of the robe

which, when finished "resembled the sun or the moon."[18] Each of the three versions differs very little from the others. Penelope, in her desire to outwit the suitors, contrives to weave a large and delicate burial robe for her father-in-law. Each night for three years she undoes what she did during the day and begins again until caught and forced to finish in the fourth year of her deception. This is one of the most famous stories from *The Odyssey*, and yet the weaving of the burial robe is shrouded in mystery. How are we to imagine this activity which takes place always off-stage? For if the great loom is set up "in the halls" in a place where the suitors can "happen upon" it, then there must always be the appearance of a robe worked at for many days. Does Penelope begin each morning with a completely empty loom or does she only remove a certain amount of weft? Does she simply keep going over the same small bit of ground day after day or does she keep in her head an elaborate pattern which she must furiously recreate only to unravel rapidly?

The technique of Joyce's "Penelope" allows for each and all of these possibilities of narrative and craftsmanship to occur simultaneously. The result is like the near cacophony of "Sirens" in which competing musical devices such as "repetition and partial repetition, echo and semi-echo, contrapuntal play of phrase against phrase, percussive explosions, [and] recapitulations in different keys"[19] overlap with and undercut each other. As "Sirens" "represents an elaborate attempt to imitate musical form in words,"[20] "Penelope" represents an elaborate attempt to turn a loom into a blank page, fibers into words, and a weaver into a narrator. While the critical literature on *Ulysses* has no shortage of punning about Molly's weaving her tale, none of this literature has investigated the implications of this wordplay.[21] Leaving out any direct reference to weaving, while the rest of the novel is rife with such allusions, Molly instead plays with a wide range of related words. By omitting apostrophes she puns with several words crucial to her narrative – "cant", "wed", "ill", "wont", and especially "weve". In a passage which clearly illustrates her ability to weave and unweave simultaneously, she shows how women are deserving of contempt and pity: "weve none either he wants what he wont get or its some woman ready to stick her knife in you I hate that in women no wonder they treat us the way they do we are a dreadful lot of bitches I suppose its all the troubles we have makes us so snappy Im not like that" (p. 640). Contradictions are seamlessly woven into Molly's pattern as she moves from "weve none" to "all the troubles we have". Molly's language of romance is also that of the textile worker:

the fun we had running along Williss road to Europa point twisting
in and out all round the other side of Jersey

(p. 627)

I was fit to be tied though I wouldnt give in with that gentleman of
fashion staring down at me

(p. 632)

Knitting, one of the many definitions of weaving that the OED provides, is also critical in her narrative as she twice refers to knitting a
burial sweater for little Rudy, who conveniently shares the name of
Molly's father-in-law. Thus, Joyce establishes a link between Penelope's
pretended devotion to Laertes and Molly's actual devotion to her son.
Through other references to her housewifery, Joyce puns at Molly's
larger task. Her kitchen plates recall the handful of earlier references to
plait and plaited; her frying-pans to the spiders in "Cyclops" and "Oxen
of the Sun." When the Citizen denounces "the adulteress" (Parnell's
wife/Molly) Bloom lets "on to be awfully deeply interested in nothing, a
spider's web in the corner behind the barrel" (p. 266). We too should
see in Molly's eight-part narrative a continuous spider's web. The
purpose of this web is not only to elude her suitors, but to trap her prey.
When Molly considers the modern housewife's alternative to the deadly
spider – "Mrs Maybrick that poisoned her husband" with "white
Arsenic she put in his tea off flypaper" (p. 613) – she is illustrating her
own method for trapping flies, neither husbands nor suitors, but
readers. If we look closely at the passage describing Mrs Maybrick's
crime, we see how Molly ensnares us in her own sticky fibers:

Id rather die 20 times over than marry another of their sex of course
hed never find another woman like me to put up with him the way
I do know me come sleep with me yes and he knows that too at the
bottom of his heart take that Mrs Maybrick that poisoned her
husband for what I wonder in love with some other man yes it was
found out on her wasnt she the downright villain to go and do a
thing like that of course some men can be dreadfully aggravating
drive you mad and always the worst word in the world what do they
ask us to marry them for if were so bad as all that comes to yes
because they cant get on without us white Arsenic she put in his tea
off flypaper wasnt it I wonder why they call it that if I asked him
hed say its from the Greek leave us as wise as we were before she
must have been madly in love with the other fellow to run the
chance of being hanged O she didnt care if that was her nature what

could she do besides theyre not brutes enough to go and hang a woman surely are they

(p. 613)

We are pulled in first one direction, then another. Some readers will stick to Molly's sympathy with the adulteress, others to her sense of moral outrage. Some will at first affix themselves to her apparent loyalty to Bloom above any other of his sex, only to become unglued by her fascination with household poisons. Trying to follow a strand of feminist rhetoric, we will become entangled in her self-portrait as domestic slave.

Yet it is not only the reader but Molly herself who is ensnared in her web. That is, as we come to know Molly through the process of her weaving, how can we hope to tell the weaver from her web? Molly and her text are one: in weaving and unweaving her text, she weaves and unweaves herself.

Weaving involves the process of interlacing rows of fibers from first left to right, then right to left. To textualize this activity is to consider its relationship to two languages crucial to *Ulysses* – English, which is read from left to right, and Hebrew, which is read from right to left. We can also think of this movement as reading forward and backward as Bloom does in "Aeolus" as a typesetter prepares Paddy Dignam's obituary: "Reads it backwards first. Quickly he does it. Must require some practice that. mangiD kcirtaP. Poor papa with his hagadah book, reading backwards with his finger to me. Pessach" (p. 101). And Molly suggests the lure of reading backwards when she remembers passing with Mulvey "the jews burialplace pretending to read out the Hebrew on them" (p. 626). Molly's emphasis on a backward view in her countless references to her bottom and backside has been well-documented. But she always contrasts bottom with top, behind with front:

when he saw me from behind following in the rain I saw him before he saw me

(p. 614)

the bottom out of the pan all for his Kidney this one not so much theres the mark of his teeth still where he tried to bite the nipple

(p. 620)

your blouse is open too low she says to me the pan calling the kettle blackbottom

(p. 631)

We see here how the interdependence of backward and forward movement associated with weaving is inscribed into Molly's sentence structure and diction. She uses a preponderance of palindromes – Madam, HRH, nun, eye, did, pop. HH, XXXXX, and tattarrattat appear nowhere else in the novel. In addition, most of Molly's vocabulary consists of words which form different words in reverse: God/dog, pans/snap, wed/dew, on/no, was/saw, May, deep, nuts, but, mad, ram, pooh, pan, pots, and tons. (Joyce's interest in such a relationship is well-documented throughout the novel as the blind piano tuner who is known by his "tap, tap, tap" is contrasted with the deaf waiter Pat, or Rudolph's dog is given a name antithetical to God – Athos.)

In the forward and backward movement of weaving the vertical (warp) threads remain stationary while the horizontal (weft) threads are in motion. In the plain weave which

> embodies the sum total of weaving and therewith reaches back the furthest ... a weft thread moves alternately over and under each warp thread it meets on its horizontal course from one side of the warp to the other; returning, it reverses the order and crosses over those threads under which it moved before and under those over which it crossed. This is the quintessence of weaving. The result is a very firm structure which, since it is comparatively inelastic, is strong under tension and also easily preserves its rectangular shape. It has an even, uniform surface, with warp and weft appearing in equal measure and producing the same effect on the front and back of the fabric.[22]

Thus, Molly's narrative looks like a piece of woven fabric in that its front and back correspond. As Diane Tolomeo has shown in her work on the structure of "Penelope," its eight sentences form an octagon in which the first and eighth, the second and seventh, the third and sixth, and the fourth and fifth sentences correspond.[23] The episode's apparent formlessness masks the most elaborate structure in the novel. The "woollen thing" that Molly knits for little Rudy in sentence one reappears in sentence eight as "that little woolly jacket I knitted crying". In sentence two, Molly remembers being sent "8 big poppies because mine was the 8th"; in sentence seven, eights again signify an important date – "88 I was married 88"; "that delicate looking student" in sentence three "nearly caught me washing through the window only for I snapped up the towel to my face" while "that fellow opposite used to be there the whole time watching" in sentence six. "That train far away" heard at the end of sentence five makes its first appearance at the beginning of sentence four – "frseeeeeeeeefronnnng". More than the Viconian octagon that Tolomeo has discovered, "Penelope" may also be read as a piece of folded fabric whose top and bottom correspond to Molly's first and eighth sentences.

In the Homeric story Penelope must remain the warp in order that her husband can be the weft. The combination of his motion and her stasis is a bond "strong under tension," a marriage which preserves its shape through years and vicissitudes. The warp and the weft are equally important in the shape, design and texture of the weave. So Odysseus, despite his years of lingering in Calypso's arms or his flirtations with other women, whether making concerted or lackluster attempts at reaching Ithaca, is as crucial to the preservation of his marriage as his wife. For the completion of his journey results in the destruction of the suitors Penelope can merely keep at arm's length. Although Molly, too, remains static, firmly bolted to her bed through her husband's endless journey, she has never been given the same credit for preserving her marriage. Bloom is read as the frightened but faithful one who keeps her memory alive all day and makes his way back to her bed, Molly the adulteress who toys with the ideas of desertion and divorce. But through the weaving of her narrative Molly shows how equally instrumental she is in maintaining the desperate equilibrium of her marriage.

For Molly weaves only so that she may unweave; she does only so that she may undo. She explictly lays out the connection between weaving and unweaving and "doing" Boylan then undoing the act of adultery: "why cant we all remain friends over it instead of quarrelling her husband found it out what they did together well naturally and if he did can he undo it" (p. 639). While the *natural* answer to her question would seem to be no, Molly's narrative does, then undoes her adultery in order to recapture the consummation of her love for Bloom in the memory of her final yes on Ben Howth. We reach the denouement (which derives from *denouer* (F) – to untie, *nodare* (L) – to knot and *nodus* (L) – a knot) only when her narrative is fully unraveled. This unraveling must move backwards in order to go forwards. Virginity can only be attained through sex. Fidelity can only come about through adultery. In order to arrive at the end of the novel at delight in wild mountains, fields of oats and wheat, flowers all sorts of shapes and smells and colours (pp. 642–3), Molly must construct a narrative which follows the logic of the loom, which *goes against nature*.

We have seen that Molly can weave and unweave simultaneously: "not that I care two straws now who he does it with or knew before that way though Id like to find out so long as I dont have the two of them under my nose" (p. 609); "he must have been a bit late because it was 1/4 after 3 when I saw the 2 Dedalus girls coming from school I never know the time even that watch he gave me never seems to go properly" (p. 615).

Or she can wait a dozen lines to contradict herself. She is angry that Bloom is "doing his highness to make himself interesting for that old faggot Mrs Riordan" but "I like that in him polite to old women like that" (p. 608).

She begins her narrative with an image of herself as the recently put upon wife – "Yes because he never did a thing like that before as ask to get his breakfast in bed with a couple of eggs" (p. 608) – but by the end of her unweaving decides that Bloom can make breakfast for both her and Stephen: "if he wants to read in bed in the morning like me as hes making the breakfast for 1 he can make it for 2" (p. 641).

Before beginning the process of weaving with the weft threads, each of the warp threads must be knotted to the loom. Thus, whether we see Molly unraveling a single row of weave, a larger pattern, or an entire piece of fabric, her strategy is to knot in order to unknot and to "not" in order to "un-not." The first word of her soliloquy – "Yes" – may represent the removal of the first of these knots and every one of the many yeses that follows is another "not" undone. That Molly herself is "undone" is the obvious sexual reading of the novel's last lines:

> and the figtrees in the Alameda gardens yes and all the queer little streets and the pink and blue and yellow houses and the rosegardens and the jessamine and geraniums and cactuses and Gibraltar as a girl where I was a Flower of the mountain yes when I put the rose in my hair like the Andalusian girls used or shall I wear a red yes and how he kissed me under the Moorish wall and I thought well as well him as another and then I asked him with my eyes to ask again yes and then he asked me would I yes to say yes my mountain flower and first I put my arms around him yes and drew him down to me so he could feel my breasts all perfume yes and his heart was going like mad and yes I said yes I will Yes.
>
> (pp. 643–4)

In an orgasmic outburst of yeses she rounds off her soliloquy. But the sudden frequency of yeses does not speak simply to sexual climax but to the urgency of Molly's project and to the sudden ease with which the fabric comes apart as less and less weft unravels with greater speed. Like Penelope, Molly is up late at night long after others have gone to bed – for her project must be carried out in private. If

Penelope is represented by the warp threads, Odysseus by the weft, then Odysseus's movement is relatively easy in comparison with the tension of Penelope's stasis. While he encounters fatal obstacles along the way, his larger voyage, like Bloom's, is meandering with time for leisurely meals and contemplation of a life away from Ithaca. Penelope remains in one place but apparently never sleeps. Her hands and mind are constantly occupied with the urgency of her task and this urgency, rather than ecstasy, is what informs the tone and technique of Molly's soliloquy.

Hélène Cixous and other theorists of *écriture feminine* read Molly's unpunctuated sentences as the *jouissance* which carries "*Ulysses* off beyond any book and toward the new writing."[24] But perhaps there are "no stops" in Molly's soliloquy because she has an absolute deadline. Caught up in Molly's web, we must find it an ecstatic experience to be her readers, but Molly's experience of her own text must be both ecstatic and controlled, accelerated and deliberate. Rather than reproducing the uncontrolled, irrational excretions of the female body, her episode must maintain its almost rigid structure. The "flow," which as Derek Attridge has written, is the most frequent way of describing Molly's prose is forever encountering locks and dams.[25] While critics have used "metaphors of rivers, streams, and liquids – and of the barriers they *pour* over ... to characterize the style of the episode,"[26] weaving in the sense of "thread[ing] one's way amid obstructions" (OED) is again a more fruitful metaphor. For while "critics may associate the word 'flow' with femininity, ... *Ulysses* makes no such association. 'Penelope' is one of only five episodes in which the word makes no appearance in any of its forms (nor, for that matter, does it occur in Gerty McDowell's section of 'Nausicaa.')"[27] Rather than wiping out the walls in her path through a flood of words or emotions, Molly must find a way to maneuver her way around them:

> that disheartened me altogether I suppose I oughtnt to have buried him in that little woolly jacket I knitted crying as I was but give it to some poor child but I knew well Id never have another our 1st death too it was we were never the same since O Im not going to think myself into the glooms about that any more I wonder why he wouldnt stay the night
>
> (p. 640)

Again, the urgency of Molly's task to untangle the most persistent weave exposes the leisureliness of Bloom's introspective, often maudlin journey. In "Lestrygonians" Bloom thinks "This is the very worst hour of the day. Vitality. Dull, gloomy: hate this hour. Feel as if I had been eaten and spewed" (p. 135). But this is only the beginning of the movement towards the nadir of Bloom's day. Nine pages later, after the same ecstatic memory of Ben Howth with which Molly ends the novel, Bloom moves from "Kissed, she kissed me" to "Me. And me now. Stuck, the flies buzzed" (p. 144). It is still 1:00 in the afternoon. Bloom has the time to tie himself up in knots. When Molly recounts this moment fourteen hours later, she must vigorously unweave it.

Each day for Penelope is a battle against time. Thus, her experience is more closely related to Joyce's valorization of the quotidian than is her husband's. Odysseus's daily experience is subsumed within the context of nine years of adventure. We remember his exploits in relation to the monsters he eludes, not the hour at which he is cornered. Penelope, however, can sum up her four-years' deception with the same brief words as Antinoos and Amphimedon. Seen as the activity of four years her weaving is uneventful and monotonous. Only on the level of the individual day does her experience vary and acquire meaning. We see in Molly's episode the epic (her largely unchanging narrative) competing with the quotidian (her attempt to introduce new threads). If backing off, changing course, and losing speed and fellow travelers are central to the Odyssean experience, then covering the same ground defines Penelope's. Each novelty in her design is instantly subsumed into her larger story of frustration, aimlessness, and loss. With each row that holds out hope of escape, she is blown back onto shore; with each obstacle passed, another is erected. Introducing a new element into her design, she invites the possibility of hopefulness in the opening words of her soliloquy: "Yes because he never did a thing like that before as ask to get his breakfast in bed with a couple of eggs" (p. 641). Bloom's sudden demands of his slatternly wife suggest that his journey has prepared him for the job of being a more traditional husband. Perhaps something resembling a conventional marriage can take place again. Yet the novelty of this design is immediately unraveled: "since the City Arms hotel when he used to be pretending to be laid up with a sick voice doing his highness to make himself interesting for that old faggot Mrs Riordan" (p. 608). As quickly as it is marveled at, Bloom's behavior is recognized and its significance retracted. While the introductory words offer a promise of breaking away from the loom, the subsequent words pull Molly back into the inevitability of her task, her circumstances, her relationship with her husband.

If Penelope's project is to recreate in its tiniest details the same pattern for four years, then Molly's narrative textualizes the difficulties of this task in the face of attraction to her suitors, despair, boredom, indifference, and particularly the gradual loss of memory of her husband. We may read the simultaneity of her weaving and unweaving as the betrayal and subsequent repression of contradictory impulses. Molly sees a text before her distinct from that which *pours* out of her. Onto the threads of this text she holds and looses. Writing and erasure become competing processes, not in *natural flow* with each other.

Yet flow imagery necessarily persists in discussions of "Penelope," for Molly's episode has come to epitomize the narrative of stream of consciousness. While writers have devoted books to the definition of this term, Gilbert Seldes's use of the term has had particular resonance in readings of Molly: "There is no mistaking the meditations of Stephen for those of Bloom, those of either for the dark flood of Marion's consciousness."[28] Associating this dark flood with her menstrual blood, critics (whether consciously or not) have left us with an image of a consciousness so fluid, so uncontrollable that it is a consciousness unconscious of itself. Molly's stream of consciousness has been read as "the flux of .... thoughts, impressions, emotions, or reminiscences, often without logical sequence or syntax,"[29] but there is a logic to her illogic and the illogic is a necessary component of the logic. Rather than pouring out of her, Molly's narrative reveals an attention to pattern not flux as it consistently falters in its insistence to pin down the correct name, date, or word. On one page, for example, we see Molly repeatedly hesitating in order to think before going any further:

> he saved the one I have but thats no good what did they say they give a delightful figure
> thats all he bought me out of the cheque he got on the first O no there was the face lotion
> for the 4 years more I have of life up to 35 no Im what am I at all Ill be 33 in September will I what O well
> there was some funny story about the jealous old husband what was it at all and an oyster knife

> (p. 618)

Molly's narrative is the result of an overly insistent memory; what it remembers is forgetting. Producing enough verbiage to write a short novel, her narrative always recalls being at a loss for words.

Molly is forever defensive about her limited vocabulary as we see in her feeble attempts to speak Spanish: "she stood there standing when I asked her to hand me and I pointing at them I couldnt think of the word a hairpin to open it with ah horquilla disobliging old thing and it staring her in the face" (p. 624); "I wonder could I get my tongue round any of the Spanish como esta usted muy bien gracias y usted see I havent forgotten it all I thought I had only for the grammar a noun is the name of any person place or thing" (pp. 640–1). Bloom's ability to use fancy words is for Molly evidence of his lack of common sense–"that word met something with hoses in it and he came out with some jawbreakers about the incarnation he never can explain a thing simply the way a body can understand then he goes and burns the bottom out of the pan" (p. 620) – and the gynecologist's "technical" language gives him license to overcharge his patients: "your vagina he called it I suppose thats how he got all the gilt mirrors and carpets getting round those rich ones off Stephens green running up to him for every little fiddlefaddle her vagina and her cochinchina" (p. 633). But there is a suggestion that both metempsychosis and vagina are not unknown, but forgotten words. In a previous incarnation Molly knew horquilla as well as she now knows hairpin. She could once flirt as easily in Spanish as she now can in English. What Molly has lost through years of estrangement from her husband is registered in her narrative through the loss of words. While critics have insisted on studying her emissions, she hints at how both her readers and her gynecologist have gotten her wrong by analyzing what comes out of her rather than noticing what is no longer there: "had I frequent omissions where do those old fellows get all the words they have omissions" (p. 634). The poignancy of this loss should not be overlooked despite the comic stance Molly adopts towards it – "if I only could remember the 1 half of the things and write a book out of it the works of Master Poldy" (p. 621) – for the originary moment toward which Molly is inevitably unweaving is a memory of verbal as well as physical communication, of Bloom's asking "and then he asked me would I" and her replying "and yes I said yes I will Yes." (p. 644)

Molly's desire to write a book out of Bloom's words echoes his own fantasy of "a collaborative venture between Molly and himself"[30]: "Might manage a sketch. By Mr and Mrs L.M. Bloom. Invent a story for some proverb. Which? Time I used to try jotting down on my cuff what she said dressing" (p. 56). Like Molly, Bloom senses the urgency of getting down words before they are forgotten. Without even the time to grab paper, Bloom uses his cuffs. In her every role as wife Molly must undo whatever she has done. Were she the most slatternly of housekeepers, Molly's bon mots are surely long lost in the laundry.

Thus Molly has no text to which to refer. Nor is her project the creation of text, but the preservation of memory through the use of an increasingly faltering one. Her literary inheritance is the journal Blazes Boylan's secretary is reading of Marion (sic) Halcombe and the autobiography Bloom brings her of Molly from Flanders. Like Pamela, she relies on the epistolary mode – we first encounter her in "Calypso" hiding her letter from Boylan, and "Penelope" is replete with memories of letters she once received from former suitors. Yet Molly herself never writes a letter. So desperate is she to receive one in Gibraltar that she mails herself blank pieces of paper (p. 623). Her literary forebears used their writing as proof. Marian is forever consulting the evidence of her diary to assist a supposedly faulty memory, and Mr B. uses Pamela's letters as proof of her virtue and marriageability. Their obsessive narratives produce evidence; Molly's obsessive narrative, as her husband tells her – "you have no proof" (p. 609) – destroys all evidence.

Thus, to get a handle on Molly is virtually impossible. Her overlapping words resist stops, periods, and definitive meanings; she insists on using pronouns so that Bloom, Boylan, and Stephen overlap indistinguishably through the word "he." The quotidian and the epic overlap as do the present, past, and future. Any staged reading of "Penelope" illuminates the limitations of a Molly reading herself as we read her as words on a page. An actress must necessarily read or perform her narrative sequentially. Yet as Diane Tolomeo's structure shows us, her narrative must also be read back and forth like the weave on a loom. Molly's breathlessness is also lost. As an actress stops to catch her breath, sentences (that Joyce never wrote) naturally occur, as meaning (that Molly never intended) is necessarily introduced.

The reader of Molly's narrative must fill in the gaps in her unpunctuated sentences not only to resolve ambiguity, but to find Molly herself. As often as they are accidental, Molly's omissions are deliberate as well. As she cautions us on the first page of her narrative, "the woman hides it" (p. 608). We never know what Molly's face looks like, only that no other rivals hers. One woman is a "dirty barefaced liar" (p. 609), others "brazenfaced things on the bicycles with their skirts blowing up to their navels" (p. 614). A hardened criminal has "a face youd run miles away from" (p. 630) but Bloom can put on a "blackguards face" (p. 619) of his own. Josie's is "beginning to look drawn and run down" (p. 613), Mrs Rubio's is a "mass of wrinkles" (p. 624), and "youd vomit a better face" (p. 629) than Burke's. She complains of prudish Mrs Riordan, "a wonder she didn't want us to cover our faces" (p. 608) but this Penelope (or "countenance of webs," "mask") goes on to hide hers repeatedly – "I wonder did he know me in the box I could see his face he couldnt see mine of course" (p. 610). She cautions "frostyface Goodwin" not to look at her – "Im a fright" (p. 615). Even her lovers don't get a full view – "I was leaning over him with my white ricestraw hat to take the newness out of it the left side of my face the best" (p. 625). Molly repeatedly inverts the reunion of Penelope and her husband. Unlike the long-abandoned wife who, in Joyce's interpretation, "is trying to recollect what Ulysses looks like," she has memorized every face, but her countenance of shifting webs is unrecognizable to others. The medical student "didnt recognise me either when I half frowned at him outside Westland row chapel" (p. 623); she recognizes the fellow in the pit at the Gaiety "on the moment the face and everything but he didn't remember me" (p. 631); and with Stephen "Id have to introduce myself not knowing me from Adam" (p. 641). But perhaps her face is the last thing men take into account. She sums up her encounters with prospective suitors with the same refrain – "I saw his eyes on my feet" (p. 613), "I could feel him coming along skulking after me his eyes on my neck" (p. 614), "I could see him looking very hard at my chest" (p. 619). Her narrative is not about being watched but about watching herself being watched.

Penelope, too, is highly conscious of herself being on display. Her public act, weaving, is pretense or performance motivated by the presence of an audience. In fact, there is no necessity for the weaving – some other ruse would have to be employed – without the audience. By engaging in the daily activity of any other woman, she is acting natural. Like her, Molly need not *be* natural, only *act* natural. Molly's weaving is pretense passing as natural act; her unweaving is the exposure of her natural act as rehearsed, performed, pretended. Thus, unweaving occurs not only on the level of the individual sentence but in the interweaving of evidence which undoes the naturalness of Molly's narrative. Molly weaves into her pattern an understanding of how it can be unwoven. Once it is unwoven, however, we are not left with a clearer understanding of Molly, merely an empty loom. Like Penelope, who uses her weaving to string her suitors along, Molly uses her narrative to string her reader along until her loom is unstrung, until she is able to imagine herself back in her husband's arms, until she is ready to begin her day and her project anew. Her flirtation with the reader – her presentation of a dissected body ostensibly ready to be touched, squeezed, and ogled – is the raison d'être of her narrative. Her pretense of sexual availability allows her to keep her marriage; her pretense of being a natural woman allows her to practice artifice; her pretense of weaving allows her to unweave.

The most persistent evidence of this surreptitious unweaving is, in fact, the verb pretend (or pretended and pretending) which appears only five times in the first seventeen episodes of *Ulysses* but nineteen times in "Penelope." Molly repeatedly chides her husband for his habit of pretending. His laziness is evidenced by his "pretending to be mooching about for advertisements" (p. 619), his ignorance by the fact that he "pretended to understand it all" (p. 637), his desire for female sympathy by his "pretending to be laid up with a sick voice" (p. 608). Although Molly despises his penchant and sees it rubbing off on their daughter–"she pretending to understand sly of course that comes from his side of the house he cant say I pretend things can he Im too honest as a matter of fact" (p. 630) – she thoroughly documents her own talent for pretending during all aspects of lovemaking. With her husband she was always "pretending to like it till he comes" (p. 610), while with Boylan she pulls him off into her handkerchief "pretending not to be excited" (p. 626). Her courtship with Mulvey involved "pretending to read out the Hebrew" (p. 626) while she will "pretend we were in Spain" (p. 641) to initiate her imagined courtship with Stephen. For Molly lovemaking is the equivalent of gameplaying. She weaves and unweaves Bloom's proposal of marriage so rapidly that we cannot be certain of whether she was teasing her husband or only her reader:

> Id just go to her and ask her do you love him and look her square in the eyes she couldnt fool me but he might imagine he was and make a declaration to her with his plabbery kind of a manner like he did to me though I had the devils own job to get it out of him though I liked him for that it showed he could hold in and wasnt to be got for the asking he was on the pop of asking me too the night in the kitchen I was rolling the potato cake theres something I want to say to you only for I put him off letting on I was in a temper
>
> (p. 612)

From "letting on" to being in a temper with Bloom she moves backwards in time to full-fledged lying to Mulvey:

> what did I tell him I was engaged for for fun to the son of a Spanish nobleman named Don Miguel de la Flora and he believed me that I was to be married to him in 3 years time theres many a true word spoken in jest there is a flower that bloometh a few things I told him true about myself just for him to be imagining
>
> (p. 625)

But the lying becomes romantic prophecy as she goes on to marry "Don Poldo de la Flora". For Molly's pretense is linked both to artifice and to nature, both to masturbatory play and to creation.

Her harshest critique of pretense establishes a connection between it and invention:

> I hate that pretending of all things with that old blackguards face on him anybody can see its not true and that Ruby and Fair Tyrants he brought me that twice I remember when I came to page 50 the part about where she hangs him up out of a hook with a cord flagellate sure theres nothing for a woman in that all invention made up
>
> (p. 619)

Invention (or invent) is another of Molly's favorite words. While it here connotes an artist's fancy, it is earlier given a physiological meaning: "nice invention they made for women for him to get all the pleasure but if someone gave them a touch of it themselves theyd know what I went through with Milly" (p. 611). When Molly alternately defines the same word as man-made and natural, the difficulty of pinpointing her debt to artifice or to nature becomes clearer. Consider how she weaves her way in and out of a discussion on art – or is it nature?:

> what are all those veins and things curious the way its made 2 the same in case of twins theyre supposed to represent beauty placed up there like those statues in the museum one of them pretending to hide it with her hand are they so beautiful of course compared with what a man looks like with his two bags full and his other thing hanging down out of him or sticking up at you like a hatrack no wonder they hide it with a cabbageleaf
>
> (p. 620)

Molly simultaneously laughs at the absurdity of God's anatomical design which cries out to be hidden and makes fun of the hypocrisy of covering genitals as if we didn't know what was under hands and cabbage leaves. Neither nature's aberrations nor man's artifice escapes her judgment. By sticking to such a passive construction – "the way its made", "supposed to represent beauty placed up there" – Molly never differentiates specifically between those breasts created naturally and those by the hands of sculptors. Molly's conflation of artifice and nature complicates any reading of her as earth mother or flower of the mountain. Even her final orgasmic outburst may be "unnatural." Is this a memory of "pretending to like it until he comes" or an actual experience of "pretending not to be excited" in order not to awaken her sleeping husband?

Our experience of "Penelope" as an intimate look at a woman's most private moments and thoughts is the ultimate pretension of the narrative. By "Penelope" we have moved far from the public setting of "Circe" or the mediating presence of the catechizer in "Ithaca." We feel we are inside Molly's mind and bed. But this illusion of intimacy between Molly and her reader is destroyed as often as it is created. We are not privileged to be watching her bleed or moan, for her bodily functions and sexuality are always available for public consumption, always part of a staged performance. The least likely place to find Molly making love is in her bed. She kisses Mulvey under the Moorish wall and lies half naked with him in a firtree cove. She lifts her petticoat for Bloom in the rain, consummates her love for him among the rhododendrons, and conceives Rudy while standing in a window watching two dogs go at it in the street. It is difficult to read these as moments of wild, uncontrolled passion when Molly is forever aware of what others will be thinking, hearing, and seeing. When Bartell d'Arcy begins kissing her on the choir stairs, she is thinking about how she can re-enact the moment for her husband: "he said wasnt it terrible to do that there in a place like that I dont see anything so terrible about it Ill tell him about that some day not now and surprise him ay and Ill take him there and show him the very place too we did it" (p. 614). Yet she is worried about making Boylan too jealous if his hotel room and hers with Bloom "were beside each other and any fooling went on in the new bed I couldnt tell him to stop and not bother me with him in the next room" (p. 616). Still her fornicating with Boylan has already been heard "away over the other side of the park" (p. 633) from her old, jingling bed. With her characteristic contradictoriness Molly dresses in front of the window to attract the attention of the medical student on the other side and chides Milly for cocking "her legs up like that on show on the windowsill before all the people passing" (p. 631). She would like to have tattered Bloom's flannel trousers "down off him before all the people and give him what that one calls flagellate till he was black and blue do him all the good in the world" (p. 629) and wouldn't mind taking Stephen in her "mouth if nobody was looking" (p. 638). Molly's pattern of weaving and unweaving never allows us to know with any certainty if public sex is more or less erotic, dangerous, or desirable for her, but it does reveal a woman who lives her most private experiences on stage. Molly's sexual performances are never spontaneous, unselfconscious, "natural." Everything that is seen and heard during them is what she, as Joyce's stage manager, decides will be seen and heard.

Staging her sexuality at one point in her narrative, Molly moves from the role of voice coach – "deep down chin back not too much make it double"–to costume designer – "Ill change that lace on my black dress to show off my bubs" – to sound effects technician – "quietly sweeeee theres that train far away pianissimo eeeee one more tsong" – and finally to lighting designer – "Im sure that fellow opposite used to be there the whole time watching with the lights out in the summer and I in my skin hopping around I used to love myself then stripped at the washstand dabbing and creaming only when it came to the chamber performance I put out the light too" (p. 628). We are privileged to have the lights kept on during tonight's "chamber performance," but does this make it any less of a staged event?

The onset of Molly's period, the moment that Harry Blamires describes as "nature inter[vening] in her monologue,"[31] begins at the end of the sixth "sentence" amid an excessive number of addresses to her Creator. Just before its onset, she cries out to "sweet God sweet God" (p. 632) and as it begins she exclaims "O Jesus wait yes that thing has come on me" (p. 632). She goes on to address "O patience above", and "easy God", and "O Lord" each twice. Yet her period has still not interrupted her obsessive task. Twenty-five lines after discovering that "that thing has come on" Molly is still stuck in the swamp of her bloody sheets, still narrating the tale of an earlier unexpected period, still contemplating how to trick a lover with "red ink" or "blackberry juice" on white linen. She finally calls on Joyce himself to liberate her from the relentless pull of the loom – "O Jamesy let me up out of this pooh" (p. 633). This is the only time in *Ulysses* when a character steps out of the novel long enough to recognize it as fiction and herself as fictional. Acknowledging her creator as she simultaneously calls on the Creator, Molly suggests that her later attack on atheism is actually a defense of artistic license:

> as for them saying theres no God I wouldnt give a snap of my two fingers for all their learning why dont they go and create something I often asked him atheists or whatever they call themselves go and wash the cobbles off themselves first then they go howling for the priest and they dying and why why because theyre afraid of hell on account of their bad conscience ah yes I know them well who was the first person in the universe before there was anybody that made it all who ah that they dont know neither do I so there you are they might as well try to stop the sun from rising tomorrow
>
> (p. 643)

In fact, Joyce has created something which does not allow the sun to rise tomorrow. As Penelope's artifice reproduced in her "shining fabric" the splendor of the sun and the moon, his fiction determines both the rising and setting of the sun and the cycles of the moon. It is his prerogative, not Molly's body that determines the onset of her "flow." And it is not the emission of menstrual blood which intervenes in sentence six, but the spilling of "red ink" (p. 633).

That Joyce tricks his reader with the same fluid with which his character fools her jealous lovers suggests his skill at Molly's "feminine" ruses. And indeed, as he announces his presence hovering over her bed or watching from a corner he destroys the image of a spider happily weaving alone and reveals one caught in a still larger web. Yet, paradoxically, his self-conscious entry into his text at this point indicates his desire not to *pretend* to be the natural voice of a natural woman. When Joyce exposes the moving lips behind the dummy, he breaks the design he has labored so hard to create of a narrative with a "complete lack of authorial omniscience," which comes closest to his ideal of the artist remaining invisible, refined out of existence.[32] He may, at this moment of authorial intervention, have called into question the agency of his tremendously artful female narrator, but he has simultaneously positioned himself before Penelope's loom, weaving a text which must inevitably be unwoven.[33]

Postscript: Further thoughts on the nineteenth century

In 1919 Joyce took exams at the University of Padua in an effort to earn a diploma which would enable him to teach English in the secondary schools of Italy. During this series of exams, he wrote an essay called "The Centenary of Charles Dickens," in which he wrote that:

> we see every character of Dickens in the light of one strongly-marked or even exaggerated moral or physical quality – sleepiness, whimsical self-assertiveness, monstrous obesity, disorderly recklessness, reptile-like servility, intense round-eyed stupidity, tearful and absurd melancholy. And yet there are some simple people who complain that, though they like Dickens very much and have cried over the fate of Little Nell and over the death of poor Joe (sic), the crossing-sweeper, and laughed over the adventurous caprices of Pickwick and his fellow-musketeers and hated (as all good people should) Uriah Heep and Fagin the Jew, yet he is after all a *little* exaggerated. To say this of him is really to give him what I think they call in that land of strange phrases, America, a billet for immortality. It is precisely this little exaggeration which rivets his work firmly to popular taste, which fixes his

characters firmly in popular memory. It is precisely by this little exaggeration that Dickens has influenced the spoken language of the inhabitants of the British Empire as no other writer since Shakespeare's time has influenced it and has won for himself a place deep down in the hearts of his fellow-country-men a honour which has been withheld from his great rival Thackeray.[34]

One of Dickens's most impressively exaggerated characters and one of the most profound influences on the creation of Molly is *Little Dorrit's* Flora Finching. I am certainly not the first person to notice this relationship. Fred Kaplan, for example, has compared two specific monologues by Flora and Molly and showed their striking similarities.[35] But Flora is more than stylistically similar. More than Molly's precursor, she derives from the same literary ancestor, Penelope.

In 1855 Dickens set out to do what Joyce would, to reproduce within a modern city, Odysseus's wanderings in the person of a failed man. The hero of Dickens's novel, Arthur Clennam, has been in exile from his Ithaca – London – for the past twenty years. Chained to a desk at his father's business in China, he has finally been allowed to return to London after his father's death. His story begins in Marseilles where he is quarantined with the world-travelling Meagles family. When Mr Meagles asks him where he will go next, he responds that

'I am such a waif and stray everywhere that I am liable to be drifted where any current may set.'
'It's extraordinary to me – if you'll excuse my freedom in saying so – that you don't go straight to London,' said Mr Meagles.
'I have no will. That is to say – next to none that I can put in action now. Shipped away to the other end of the world before I was of age, and exiled there until my father's death there a year ago, always grinding in a mill I always hated, what is to be expected from me in middle life? Will, purpose, hope? All those lights were extinguished before I could sound the words.'[36]

Like the long-wandering Odysseus, once Arthur arrives in his homeland, he does not immediately make his way back home. Once he finally decides to visit his mother, he, like Odysseus on an earler journey, descends into Hades:

There was the old cellaret with nothing in it, lined with lead, like a sort of coffin in compartments ... On a black bier-like sofa propped

up behind sat his mother in a widow's dress .... There was a smell of
black dye in the airless room, which the fire had been drawing out
of the crape and stuff of the widow's dress for fifteen months, and
out of the bier-like sofa for fifteen years.
'Mother, this is a change from your old active habits.'
'The world has narrowed to these dimensions, Arthur .... '
'Do you never leave your room, mother? ... '
'I never leave my room.'

(pp. 33–4)

While Odysseus is ultimately allowed to end his battles and his wanderings after twenty years' absence, Arthur's battles begin back at home
in his struggle with the modern city, in particular with the
exemplification of bureaucracy – the Circumlocution Office. Like
Odysseus at the gates of Troy, Arthur devotes "himself to the storming
of the Circumlocution Office" (p. 109). There he does battle with many
of Odysseus's enemies. His Cyclops comes in the form of Barnacle, Jr,
who perpetually attempts to stick an eye-glass into one of his eyes in
such an "inflammatory" (p. 104) manner that he is evidently "going
blind on his eye-glass side" (p. 104). He attempts to pin down his
Proteus, Mr Tite Barnacle who "never on any account, whatever, gives
him a straightforward answer" (p. 107). And, while he cannot hope to
be rewarded for his efforts, he is repeatedly urged to make offerings "to
the presiding Idols of the Circumlocution Office" (p. 111).

The novel is rife with allusions to shipwreck and unheroic modern
stock. Bakhtin has noticed that the introduction of the corrupt capitalist,
Merdle, is Homeric.[37] More than any other Dickens's novel, *Little Dorrit* is
concerned with the world and nearly every one of its characters – with
the notable exception of Flora Finching, Arthur's Penelope – has been or
becomes an extensive traveler.

If Joyce's novel considers the dangers of a faithless Penelope, then
Dickens's considers an arguably scarier possibility. What happens when
your Penelope has grown fat and middle-aged and is still waiting for
you? Flora has always been read as Dickens's portrait of Maria Beadnell.
(She and Molly share the same initials.) Maria was the love of his youth
who rejected him and two decades later, shortly before he began
writing *Little Dorrit*, chose to be in touch with him again. Dickens was
horrified by the changes in her. In a letter to him before their meeting
she had described herself as "toothless, fat, old and ugly."[38] While this
was a purposeful exaggeration, Dickens found her to be more like the
Catherine Dickens of the present, the woman he would leave within a

year of completing *Little Dorrit*, than the Maria Beadnell of the past. But there is a clear distinction between Flora and Maria. Maria left Dickens and suddenly reappeared in his life. Flora is taken away from Arthur and, though she has briefly married, has clearly never stopped waiting for his return. She, like Penelope, has never left him.

Like Penelope before her, like Molly after her, Flora endeavors to erase time. But Dickens punishes her for her futile attempts to stop the clock in the person of her father, Christopher Casby, who is "recognisable [to Arthur] at a glance – as unchanged in twenty years and upwards as his own solid furniture – as little touched by the influences of the varying seasons, as the old rose-leaves and old lavender in his porcelain jars" (p. 138). "Look at Papa," Flora screams, "is not Papa precisely what he was when you went away, isn't it cruel and unnatural of Papa to be such a reproach to his own child, if we go on in this way much longer people who don't know us will begin to suppose that I am Papa's Mama" (p. 143).

Clennam's first impression of Flora is that he had left her a lily and returned to find her a peony. Joyce's "flower of the mountain" is clearly alluding to her literary progenitor when she tells Mulvey that she's engaged to Don Miguel de la Flora or when she goes on to marry Don Poldo de la Flora, for Molly owes something of her rapid, unpunctuated speech to Flora. Dickens writes that "whatever she said, [she] never once came to a full stop" (p. 143) and that she pointed "her conversation with nothing but commas, and very few of them" (p. 144).

Flora is only able to tell one story (what Peter Brooks might term a classic example of waiting, suffering, and enduring) and she tells it repeatedly. After years of pining away for Arthur, Flora Casby finally decides to accept the seventh proposal of Mr Finching. Returning from their honeymoon, he dies of the gout, and Flora Finching returns to her father's house to await Arthur's return. But like Molly, Flora is not simply babbling. Like Molly's, there is a pattern to Flora's speech. For, like Penelope, she is forced to cover the same ground over and over again in order to sustain the limited memory she has of her former love, in order to stop time, in order to refuse to move forward and abandon her past. Like Molly, she daringly attempts to introduce new threads and then quickly retracts them. Her particular verbal tic wherein she simultaneously remembers and forgets is when she refers to her former lover as Arthur only to remember that it is far more proper to call him Mr. Clennam. As Flora's appearances in the novel persist, her speech becomes more frenetic, less punctuated. Each time she enters she must begin from the beginning again and furiously catch herself up to this particular moment in the narrative.

So when Arthur first meets Flora after his twenty-year absence, she says:

'[O]nly to think of the changes at home Arthur – cannot overcome it, seems so natural, Mr. Clennam far more proper ... – as no one could have believed, who could have ever imagined Mrs. Finching when I can't imagine it myself .... Finching oh yes isn't it a dreadful name, but as Mr. F said when he proposed to me which he did seven times and handsomely consented I must say to be what he used to call on liking twelve months after all, he wasn't answerable for it and couldn't help it could he, Excellent man, not at all like you but excellent man!'

(p. 145)

When she meets Little Dorrit two hundred pages later, she must begin where she began with Arthur:

'Romance ... as I openly said to Mr. F when he proposed to me and you will be surprised to hear that he proposed seven times once in a hackney coach once in a boat once in a pew once on a donkey at Tunbridge Wells and the rest on his knees, Romance was fled with the early days of Arthur Clennam, our parents tore us asunder we became marble and stern reality usurped the throne, Mr F said very much to his credit that he was perfectly aware of it and even pre-ferred that state of things accordingly the word was spoken the fiat went forth and such is life you see my dear and yet we do not break but bend, pray make a good breakfast while I go in with the tray.'

(pp. 275–6)

When she is reacquainted with Mrs Clennam after twenty years and another 400 pages, she must again begin at the beginning.

'Ah dear me the poor old room, looks just as ever Mrs Clennam I am touched to see except for being smokier which was to be expected with time and which we must all expect and reconcile ourselves to being whether we like it or not as I am sure I have had to do myself if not exactly smokier dreadfully stouter which is the same or worse, to think of the days when papa used to bring me here the least of girls a perfect mass of chilblains to be stuck upon a chair with my feet on the rails and stare at Arthur – pray excuse me – Mr Clennam – the least of boys in the fright-fullest of frills and jackets ere yet Mr. F appeared a misty shadow on the horizon paying attentions like the well-known spectre of some place in Germany beginning with a B is a moral lesson inculcating that all the paths in life are similar to the paths down in the North of England where they get the coals and make the iron and things gravelled with ashes!'

(p. 665)

Joyce found then in Flora a model for his own Penelope. He read her rapid, unpunctuated sentences as neither empty drivel nor ecstatic feminine speech, but as the desperate urgency to outrun the sun, to complete her daily task before the next day dawns. He saw the mind required of a Flora, a mind which could remember and furiously recreate an elaborate pattern. Above all, he found in Flora's language the pattern of weaving in order to unweave which is the basis of Molly's soliloquy. For Flora repeatedly recreates the story of her first courtship, her eventual marriage, her widowhood and her renewed hope for Arthur only to unravel it again. When Flora admits that "I know I am not what you expected, I know that very well," (p. 146) Dickens notes that

> In the midst of her rapidity, she had found that out with the quick perception of a cleverer woman. The inconsistent and profoundly unreasonable way in which she instantly went on, nevertheless, to *interweave* their long-abandoned boy and girl relations with their present interview, made Clennam feel as if he were lightheaded.
>
> (p. 146, emphasis added)

This interweaving of sweet nothings which Flora whispers in Arthur's ear:

> there *was* a time and ... the past was a yawning gulf however a golden chain no longer bound him and ... she revered the memory of the late Mr. F and ... she should be at home tomorrow at half-past one and ... the decrees of Fate were beyond recall and ... she considered nothing so improbable as that he ever walked on the northwest side of Gray's Inn Gardens at exactly four o'clock in the afternoon

is the same interweaving of hope and despair found in Molly's soliloquy. Because of Flora's capacity to leave half of her eighteen-year-old self in the past and to graft the other half onto the widow of the late Mr Finching, Dickens refers to her repeatedly as a mermaid. Clearly neither he nor Arthur responds to this siren's song. His hero goes on to marry a woman with no desires to speak, write or narrate – the quiet, thin, young Little Dorrit. But as Molly Bloom would have said, "God help the world if all the women were her sort" (p. 608).

Conclusion: Refusing to Tell

I began this book by suggesting that women narrators have made themselves unknowable to their readers and yet, paradoxically, have encouraged a degree of intimacy which has invited an overwhelming amount of (often misguided) criticism. I end by looking at a twentieth-century fantasy, "a romance," A.S. Byatt's *Possession*. *Possession* is about a disparate group of contemporary literary critics – Roland Michell, Maud Bailey, Leonora Stern, Beatrice Nest, Mortimer Cropper, and James Blackadder – who, through reading letters, journals, and poems, are investigating the newly-discovered relationship between two fictional Victorian poets – Randolph Henry Ash and Christabel LaMotte. Previous research on Randolph's marriage to his wife, Ellen, and Christabel's lesbian relationship with Blanche Glover is suddenly thrown into question. While Byatt clearly supports efforts to unearth women's poetry and to write women's biographies, she is concerned that feminist critics not inflict a new kind of damage in the process. The novel's lesbian critic, Leonora Stern, is as much a subject of ridicule as old-fashioned critics like Cropper and Blackadder, who see no value in reading Ellen Ash's journals or Christabel LaMotte's poetry.

I hope to show here how Byatt's novel has inspired this project, how her understanding of the tension between the female narrator's desire to conceal and the feminist literary critic's urge to uncover informs my readings of these novels. I want to show as well, however, that the narrative strategies which I have celebrated throughout this study are both respected and maligned by Byatt. Jane's, Esther's, and Molly's lives with men are made possible through their narrative trickery. Ellen Ash and Christabel LaMotte are exaggerated versions of Marian Halcombe – women whose desire for privacy and unknowability becomes pathological. So that while Ellen and Christabel successfully defend themselves against the outrages of feminist literary critics, both inside and outside the novel, they destroy their own lives in the process. Unlike Nelly or Molly, they leave behind texts, but they refuse to live or write their own stories.

The central difference between Byatt's fantasy and the novels which precede hers is that she allows for no gendered struggle for narrative authority – except that invented by literary critics. Byatt's hero, Randolph Henry Ash, poses no threat sexually or editorially to any woman. The attempts by feminist critics within the novel to prove that "Randolph Ash suppressed Ellen's writing and fed off her imagination"[1] fail along with their efforts to discover evidence of Victorian sisterhood. Byatt most forcefully undermines their agenda by rewriting an icon of Victorian feminism, Christina Rossetti's "Goblin Market."[2] Christabel LaMotte's life and poetry are modeled after both Emily Dickinson's and Rossetti's, and Byatt's novel revises and inverts the moral of the latter's most famous work.

When Ash enters Christabel's life, her lover Blanche writes in her journal:

> Something is ranging and snuffing round our small retreat, trying the shutters and huffing and puffing inside the door. In old days they put mountain ash berries and a cast horseshoe over the lintel to frighten away the Fairy Folk .... This Peeping Tom has put his eye to the nick or cranny in our walls and peers shamelessly in. She laughs and says he means no harm ... it amuses her to hear him lolloping and panting round our solid walls, she thinks he will always be Tame ....
>
> (pp. 52–3)

Blanche must warn her more daring companion of the approaching danger as Lizzie did Laura in Rossetti's poem:

> 'Come buy,' call the goblins
> Hobbling down the glen.
> 'Oh', cried Lizzie, 'Laura, Laura,
> You should not peep at goblin men.'
> Lizzie covered up her eyes,
> Covered close lest they should look;
> Laura reared her glossy head,
> And whispered like the restless brook:[3]

Like the "listless" Laura who "no more swept the house,/ Tended the fowls or cows,/ Fetched honey [or] kneaded cakes of wheat" (p. 30) after her encounter with the goblin men, Christabel does not help Blanche with the annual jelly making and writes fewer and fewer poems. To rescue her lost lover Blanche first tries to gain Ellen Ash's sympathy and finally, like Lizzie, sacrifices herself to ensure Christabel's happiness. Although Lizzie and Laura are wives by the end of "Goblin Market," no husbands appear in the poem, and their children, who seem to have arrived through some parthenogenetic reaction, learn the story's moral: "there is no friend like a sister" (p. 53). But Christabel and Blanche's dream of "living useful and fully human lives, in each other's company, and without recourse to help from the outside world, or men" (p. 333) fails. As lovers and surrogate sisters they betray each other. Christabel must turn to her real sister, Sophy, to shelter her and her daugher. Sophy's exchange rate, however, is worse than any goblin man's; she gives Christabel a home and takes her child as her own. The two do not pass their lives in communion with each other. Sophy is a happy wife and mother, Christabel "an old witch in a turret, writing my verses by licence of my boorish brother-in-law, a hanger-on as I had never meant to be, of my sister's good fortune ... " (p. 543). Relations between all sisters and would-be sisters in the novel are strained. Christabel forbids any closeness between herself and her cousin Sabine. Ellen lies to her sisters, Patience and Faith, about her marriage. And the hope for sisterhood among the novel's feminist critics proves farcical. Poor Ariane Le Minier, the French researcher working on Sabine de Kercoz, photocopies Sabine's journal for Maud, believing that "we should share our information, should we not – it is a feminist principle, co-operation" (p. 363). Maud, of course, has obtained the journal by stealing Leonora's lead; Leonora has teased her with the lead as a prelude to full-blown sexual harrassment.

In their quest to "know" Randolph Henry Ash the literary critics in *Possession* steal a letter from the British Library, rip up an antique doll's bed, bribe Christabel's hapless relatives, trespass on gun-patrolled property, and desecrate a century-old grave. Their criticism is, in short, dependent upon violation. In contrast, the subject of their inquiry is extraordinarily respectful of other's privacy and autonomy. The nineteenth-century portions of *Possession* read as a series of acts of violation which never take place. Randolph does not rape Ellen, betray her secret to Christabel, question Christabel about her sexual past, claim his infant daughter, or "hurt" her as a young girl by revealing his identity. In an unmailed letter to Christabel he reminds her of his confirmed gentleness:

> I feel I stand accused, also, by your actions, of having loved you at all, as though my love was an act of brutal forcing, as though I were a heartless ravisher out of some trumpery Romance, from whom you had to flee, despoiled and ruined. Yet if you examine your memories truthfully – if you can be truthful – you must know that it was not so – think over what we did together and ask, where was the cruelty, where the coercion, where, Christabel, the lack of love and respect for you, alike as woman and as intellectual being?
>
> (p. 495)

In *Possession*'s final sentences Ash must choose between the two impulses which motivate him throughout the novel: whether to communicate with or to respect the privacy of Christabel. This scene, in which he meets his daughter for the first and only time, is clearly taken from "Goblin Market." When the merchant men tempt Laura with their fruit, and she has no coin with which to buy, they take her hair instead:

> 'You have much gold upon your head ...
> Buy from us with a golden curl.'
> She clipped a precious golden lock.
>
> (p. 17)

When Ash makes his final appearance in the novel as the man Christabel feared would steal her child, he offers to make his daughter a crown:

> 'But you must give me something in exchange.'
> 'I haven't got anything to give.'
> 'Oh, just a lock of hair – a very fine one – to remember you by .... '
> He took out a little pair of pocket scissors, and cut, very gently, a long lock from the buttercup-gold floss ....
>
> (p. 554)

As always, Ash is an inadequate trespasser; his tentative message to his daughter – "Tell your aunt ... that you met a poet ... who sends her his compliments, and will not disturb her ... " (p. 555) – is never delivered. May, whether out of thoughtlessness or willfulness is, like her mother and father, disinclined to cause a disturbance or generate a plot. Thus Randolph, despite Blanche's, Beatrice's, Leonora's, or Maud's best efforts to portray him as one, is no goblin man, and Blanche and Christabel are no Lizzie and Laura.

*

What we will see then in Byatt's novel is every convention of the Victorian age: the fallen woman, the bastard, the Thames suicide, the self-sacrificing housewife. But we will see each as if through the crystal ball used by Sybilla Silt, the phony medium of Randolph Henry Ash's poem "Mummy Possest."[4] If anyone among the gallery of poets, scholars, and hangers-on who people the novel stands in for Byatt herself, it must be Sybilla, who instructs her young protégée to

> Take up the crystal ball, sweet Geraldine.
> Gaze on the sphere. Observe how left and right,
> Above, below, reverse themselves in this
> And in its depth a glittering chamber lies
> Like a drowned world
> With downward-pointing flames,
> This room in miniature, all widdershins.

(p. 439)

Byatt's novel could aptly be titled "The Crystal Ball" (a near homophone for Christabel) for she asks her reader to look past the facade of late twentieth-century academia into a Victorian England turned "all widdershins." In the fantastical world reflected back at us, some writers strive for dullness, others obscurity; sexuality is enviable and virtue shameful. While *Possession* develops naturally out of the tradition of the female narrative and the narrative of the fallen woman – *Adam Bede, Ruth, Tess of the d'Urbervilles* – Byatt disallows traditional feminist approaches to her novel. *Possession* manages to conflate these two novelistic traditions while eschewing critical readings about oppression, violation, forcible silencing, and sexual taint.

Byatt's inverted Victorianism is most striking for its surface normality, its seeming decorousness and dullness. After Sybilla tantalizes Geraldine with the life of the occultist:

> Come into this reversed world, Geraldine,
> Where power flows upward, as in the glass ball,
> Where left is right, and clocks go widdershins,
> And women sit enthroned and wear the robes,

> The wreaths of scented roses and the crowns,
> The jewels in our hair, the sardonyx,
> The moonstones and the rubies and the pearls,
> The royal stones, where we are priestesses
> And powerful Queens, and all swims with our Will.

she assigns her her nightly duty, posing as a submissive Victorian servant:

> But now you must be decorous and show
> Deference to the ladies, gentle tact
> To the rough male-folk, bring them cups of tea
> And smile, and listen, for we need to know
> All that their innocent gossiping reveals.

(p. 444)

It is crucial that Geraldine not view this period of servitude and submissiveness as a form of punishment. According to Sybilla a woman's ability to bow and scrape allows her admission to this promised reversed world; it is in fact the source from which her power derives. When a medium tells Randolph Henry Ash the source of her powers, he believes he has discovered an analogy for his own: "You should not mock. I have no power to summon spirits. I am their instrument; they speak through me, or not, as they please, not as I please." He said, "They speak to me too, through the medium of language" (p. 427).[5] Ash, a monologist modeled on Browning, sees a connection between the medium's calling and his own as "The Great Ventriloquist."

Ventriloquism was once viewed as a form of witchcraft whose practitioners were able to "form words and voices in their stomach, which shall seem to come from others rather than the person that speaks them." By the nineteenth century, however, ventriloquism was a respectable form of entertainment and the ventriloquist almost an interchangeable term for the poet. (Coleridge noted how Jonson practices ventriloquism in his play *Sejanus His Fall* because "Sejanus is a puppet out of which the poet makes his own voice appear to come;" Tennyson's "Maud" was reviewed as "as striking an instance as could be named of what we call poetical ventriloquism"(OED).) Unlike the medium, Ash lays claim to his gift for voices. His ventriloquism is that of the master showman and show-off, while the medium's is what so terrified the early observers of ventriloquy, unattributable agency. In Byatt's romance men exercise their powers visibly and audibly, but they are no more and no less powerful than women whose agency is silent and invisible. The essential difference between men and women is in their self-presentation. Men do not choose among the five or six faces they may present to the world; they simply present themselves. But there are two Vals. One belongs in a Putney basement with her penniless boyfriend, Roland; the other is primed to marry a wealthy solicitor. Should she choose to be the one with the "lustreless brown hair, very straight, hanging about a pale, underground face" or the one who "was carefully made up with ink and brown eyeshadow brushed blusher along the cheekbone and plummy lips?" (p. 18). Maud Bailey does daily battle with her naturally blonde hair. Should she crop it, tie it up, let it hang loose? Will her style label her a radical lesbian feminist, a prude, or a bimbo? Should she hide behind it, apologize for it or flaunt it? Beatrice Nest perceives herself in terms of the "unacceptable bulk of her breasts" (p. 130). Should she corset them, let them hang or mold them into a devastating cleavage? Will they alert younger scholars to her motherliness, her repression, or her unregenerate lesbianism? For Victorian women questions of self-presentation are more easily answered. Their advantage lies only in their unobtrusiveness, but this too is a pose. Randolph

> saw or thought he saw, how those qualities had been disguised or overlaid by more conventional casts of expression – an assumed modesty, an expedient patience, a disdain masking itself as calm. At her worst – oh, he saw her clearly despite her possession of him – at her worst she would look down and sideways and smile demurely, and this smile would come near a mechanical simper, for it was an untruth, it was a convention, it was her brief constricted acknowledgement of the world's expectations.

> (p. 302)

In hidden letters and deliberately unreadable confessionals, from under masks of self-deprecation, while performing life-long charades of subservience and submission Christabel and her contemporaries exercise their influence over language and events. Like Ash they have great facility with language; like the medium, they present themselves as powerless, mute instruments. Thus, in Byatt's scheme the nineteenth-century woman can be a demonic ventriloquist only by posing as her own wooden dummy.

Byatt seizes on the paradoxical possibilities of ventriloquism early in *Possession*. Val's thesis, "Male Ventriloquism: the Women of Randolph Henry Ash," is discounted by her examiners as largely written by her boyfriend, Roland, who has in fact disagreed with its premise and refused to read it. But ventriloquism is about such invited misreadings and false constructs of domination and oppression. The block of wood must always seem smarter than the puppeteer. The one manipulating the dummy must seem appalled by the words coming out of it. Byatt is less interested in the unanswerable questions ventriloquy poses – who is manipulating whom? who is speaking for whom? – than in the need to turn the most solipsistic of activities – a performer in conversation with him/herself – into a model of power relations. Christabel LaMotte and Ellen Ash never aspire to Ash's fame, because their writing is designed not to communicate with others but to discover voices to talk to themselves. They are not forcibly silenced by patriarchal puppeteers; they impose silence upon themselves. Thus, though their writing evokes such female narrators as Pamela, Jane, and Esther, they are not in fact narrators. They use their invisible agency not to further but to prevent plot.

> 'I feel as [Christabel] did,' says Maud. 'I keep my defences up because I must go on doing my work. I know how she felt about her unbroken egg. Her self-possession, her autonomy. I don't want to think of that going .... I write about liminality. Thresholds. Bastions. Fortresses.'
>
> (p. 549–50)

"Invasion. Irruption," Roland replies. And yet the two critics hold so little stock in autonomy that they commit various acts of violation and invasion in the belief that privacy can be destroyed, that ultimate knowability can be achieved. Ironically, the three most informative sections of *Possession* – the details of Randolph and Christabel's love affair, the secrets of Randolph's honeymoon, and the truth about Ellen's journal, together with the encounter between Randolph and his daughter – are unavailable to Roland, Maud and their colleagues. Yet the extraordinary revelations of Christabel's letters and Sabine's journal do nothing to alter their impression that they "know" these figures. When Roland finds the first letter linking Randolph to Christabel, he is shocked for "he thought he knew Ash fairly well ... " (p. 10). His research allows him the mistaken impression that he knows the poet far better. Even as lightning strikes and buried treasure is unearthed, Maud clings to the idea that timidly poring over pages of books allows us access to a person. "Beatrice, you know Ellen. Why do you think she put [Christabel's letter] in the box with her own love letters?" (p. 547). Beatrice, who will never discover the misdirection of her life's work, is overcome with emotion at finding Christabel's unopened letter. She sees the tragedy of Christabel's "[writing] all that for no one," not the irony of Ellen writing her private journal for Beatrice.

In her Victorian fantasy, in which no boundaries are crossed, no confidences betrayed, Byatt complicates the formation of power relations. The feminists' failed attempt to paint Randolph Ash as a patriarchal oppressor of his wife is sneeringly summed up by Blackadder:

> 'They haven't any time for Ash. All they want is to read Ellen's endless journal. They *know* what there is to find before they've seen it. All they've got to go on is that she spent a lot of time lying on the sofa, and that's hardly unusual for a lady in her time and circumstances. Their real problem – and Beatrice's – is that Ellen Ash is *dull*. No Jane Carlyle, more's the pity. Poor old Beatrice began by wanting to show how self-denying and supportive Ellen Ash was and she messed around looking up every recipe for gooseberry jam and every jaunt to Broadstairs for *twenty-five years*, can you believe it, and woke up to find that no one wanted self-denial and dedication anymore, they wanted proof that Ellen was raging with rebellion and pain and untapped talent.'
>
> (p. 36)

The joke on the critics, of course, is that Ellen's talent has not remained untapped. For decades she has manufactured a fictional life for herself and her husband in the pages of her journal. That critics of *Possession* have agreed with Blackadder and considered Ash's wife dull implies not so much a misreading of the novel as a testament to Ellen's power of self-caricaturization. We do not learn from Ellen's own muted voice what Byatt shares with her reader but withholds from her literary critics:

> The eagerness, the terrible love, with which she had made it up to him, his abstinence, making him a thousand small comforts, cakes and tidbits. She became his slave. Quivering at every word. He had accepted her love. She had loved him for it. He had loved her .... She howled. 'What shall I be without you?'
>
> (p. 499)

Even in this passage Ash does not make a compelling oppressor. He does not appear to have enslaved his wife, but to have allowed her to insinuate herself into his life. She is depicted here as less a slave than a hanger-on, a groupie. If Ellen has given up something of her life by devoting herself to him, then Randolph is enslaved by her to his semblance of a marriage. When Christabel writes to Ellen, "I am in your hands," she is unwittingly acknowledging Ellen's profound manipulation of events. She, not her husband, turns out to be the master puppeteer. But her manipulation throughout is a manipulation by omission. With Christabel's unopened letter in her fingers she handles the situation so as to deny everyone something: her husband final contact with his lover, Christabel a chance to repent, and herself a chance to know. Had she spoken about their unnatural living arrangement, had she broken the silence between them years before, they might have parted. Had she confronted her husband with Blanche's stolen letter, she might have initiated the argument that would have sent him off with his lover for good. Instead, through her silences and her omissions she hangs onto him. "Had she done well, or ill? She had done what was in her nature, which was profoundly implicated in not knowing, in silence, in avoidance, she said to herself, in harsher moments" (p. 494). Ellen's greatest strength is her passivity. By manipulating lives as an invisible agent, she makes way for the misreading of her own life as a victimized jam-maker.

The female narrative has been characterized since its beginnings by a desire to communicate and maintain privacy simultaneously. Even while madly scratching out a letter on her knees, Pamela is devising ways to hide it under a rock or sew it into her undergarments. Esther's relentless self-effacement – "I don't know how it is, I seem to be always writing about myself" – goes far in deceiving her reader as to whose story she is writing. Just as she allows herself no confidants – she bars Ada from her sickroom; she is grateful that her deformed face will not betray her mother's identity – her confessions to her reader are made always tentatively and only after their impact has been defused. Even then, they are highly suspect, for why admit that she will never confess her love to Dr. Woodcourt when she is writing her memoirs as Mrs. Woodcourt?

Ellen Ash's journal is an impossible conflation of Pamela's extempore prose and Esther's self-imposed innocuousness. She writes her experience as it actually or ostensibly happens with the advantage of *Possession*'s twentieth-century perspective. Her writing is labored and calculated yet fosters the impression of Richardsonian spontaneity. Thus, Byatt allows Ellen what Dickens could only provide in a retrospective narrative – the opportunity to construct privacy and narrative authority. Ellen's journal forearms itself against any possibility of accurate postmodern criticism. "My life ... has been built round a lie," (p. 496) Byatt writes of her, but it is a beautifully constructed lie.

Byatt's novel underscores the difficulty of fashioning power relations in an environment where people do not believe they can or do not attempt to know each other. Ellen does not empower herself (as Geraldine does) by eavesdropping or by extracting confessions from others, but by denying herself confidants, by remaining outside potential conflicts of power. She views her journal as her ultimate challenge, the unsympathetic obstacle to whom she must reveal nothing. She labors over her journal – "both a defence against, and a bait for, the gathering of ghouls and vultures" (p. 501) – to find a voice in which she can most adequately misrepresent herself. Ellen's journal fascinates because of its "systematic omission" (p. 241). She literally writes the plot out of her fictional narrative. There are large gaps in Sabine's journal because she attempts to do the same. In February she writes: "I have noticed that I have lost pleasure in this journal. For some time now it has been neither writer's exercise nor record of my world, only a narrative of jealousy and bafflement and resentment .... I shall give it up for the time being." In April she resumes: "I am witnessing something so strange, so strange I must write about it, though I said I would not, in order to help myself to understand" (p. 402). Both in her compulsion to write and in the unintentionality of her narrative Sabine is reminiscent of Pamela. Sabine's journal, intended neither to communicate nor miscommunicate with anyone, is a more overtly solipsistic exercise than Ellen's. In her first diary entry she questions her motivations for writing:

> Am I writing this for Christabel to see, as a kind of devoir – a writer's exercise – or even as a kind of intimate letter, for her to read alone, in moments of contemplation and withdrawal? Or am I writing it privately to myself, in an attempt to be wholly truthful with myself, for the sake of truth alone? I know *she* would prefer the latter. So I shall lock away this volume – anyway during its earliest life – and write in it only what is meant for my eyes alone ....
>
> (p. 365)

Sabine's journal writing is more conspicuously self-conscious than Ellen's. It is clearly not the highly polished retrospective writing that Ellen produces, but extempore prose peppered with self-criticism – "I have much to learn about the organisation of my discourse" (p. 368); "I see one of my faults as a writer will be a tendency to rush off in all directions at once" (p. 370). Sabine pours her heart out to these pages; Ellen stands back from and protects herself against them. Yet the two journals should be read as companion pieces, as the uncannily similar writings of women occupying parallel universes.

The novel is, of course, constructed around parallel worlds. As Val tells her boyfriend so eloquently, "you have this thing about this dead man. Who had a thing about dead people" (p. 23). While Maud and Roland retrace Christabel and Randolph's journeys and relive their experiences, Ash, like Robert Browning, inhabits the heads of long-dead geniuses. In his poem "Swammerdam" he imagines the thoughts of the inventor of the microscope. How, Ash wonders, did he come to realize the existence of teeming worlds invisible to the human eye? And when, Swammerdam asks, may we come to realize that we too are the bacteria that inhabit some other universe? In many ways Byatt figures her contemporary critics as those lower life-forms feeding off the dead bodies of previous generations. While the vast majority of these parasites denigrate Ellen, she, more than any other character in the novel, anticipates their arrival. Her journal awaits the parallel world to come, the business of literary studies.

When Ellen's journal is read alongside Sabine's, Byatt's project of writing her nineteenth-century women as constructs of a twentieth-century imagination is made clear. Ellen systematically uses her neuresthenia and the boring details of housework as foils for her fears of sex, childbirth, and abandonment (is she named for the great celibate homebody of Victorian fiction – Ellen Dean?). Sabine uses similar metaphors. Ellen's journal of June 4 1859 begins:

> The house is echoing and silent without my dear Randolph. I am full of projects for improvements in his comfort to be effected whilst he is away. The study curtains and those in his dressing- room must come down and be beaten out thoroughly on the line. I am in doubts as to the wisdom of attempting to *wash* the upper ones. The drawing-room pair I attempted have never been the same, either as to lustre or as to the "hang" of their folds. I shall set Bertha to a diligent beating and brushing and see what can be done. Bertha has been somewhat sluggish of late; she comes slowly when called and leaves tasks not rounded-off ... I wonder if something is amiss with Bertha .... I shall shut this book and betake myself to my pillow to fortify myself for the curtain-battle and the questioning of Bertha.
>
> (pp. 242–3)

What is "amiss" with Bertha is immediately evident to the reader. Ellen's unsubtle suggestions indicate that she is either relating the discovery of Bertha's pregnancy in retrospect, or manufacturing a fictitious character who conveniently appears in the journal as she learns of Randolph's affair, and disappears as she awaits his return. There are even suggestions that Bertha, whether real or invented, has been impregnated by Ash. "I do not believe my dearest Randolph would ever consider applying his hand – or anything else – to any young person in our employment" (p. 246). "Perhaps Bertha is gone to the man who [passage crossed out illegibly]" (p. 251). As Ellen arranges for where Bertha should "be brought to bed" (p. 247), she retires repeatedly to her own: "I have had a sore throat and violent attacks of sneezing – maybe from all the dust aroused by the cleaning efforts – and retired to my couch for the afternoon, behind closed curtains" (p. 244); "I have resolved to consult Herbert Baulk about Bertha. I felt a headache coming on, and a sense of being flustered by the sudden silence and emptiness of my house again. I retired to my room and slept for two hours ... " (p. 247); "Another bad day. I lay all day in bed with the curtains open, for I became superstitiously afraid of spending so long in a house with drawn curtains" (p. 252); Thus, Ellen's neuresthenia with its repeated associations with Bertha, the curtains and the housecleaning is linked both to her fear of sex and to the threat posed by Christabel. Her desire to treat Bertha with Christian compassion – "Patience has a strong sense that it is contaminating to continue in the presence of sin. I said I felt we were enjoined to love the sinner ... " – is counteracted by her terror of childbirth – "We talked ... of the trials dear Mamma must have borne, giving birth to fifteen infants, of whom we four girl children only survived" (p. 245). She is so incapacitated by her servant's overt display of sexuality that she cannot bring herself to pursue and help the wayward woman, but instead takes to her bed vowing that "when he returns, I must be quick and lively. It must be so" (p. 252). Yet could we read these pages as having been written months after Randolph's return? For Ellen's inability to cope with or contemplate the fate of the vanished servant either anticipates or echoes her response to Randolph's confession about Christabel:

> 'I do not know what to say, Ellen. I do not expect to see her – Miss LaMotte again. We were agreed that – that this one summer must see the end – of – the end. And even if that were not so – she has vanished, she has gone away' – 'She had heard the pain in that, had

noted, it, had said nothing. 'I cannot explain, Ellen, but I can tell you – ' 'No more. No more. We will not speak of it again.'

(p. 493)

Maud Bailey reads Ellen's reaction to Bertha as naive, – "It must have been terrible for Bertha. She – Ellen – doesn't seem to see" (p. 252). Like critics of *Jane Eyre* who overlook or deny Jane's retrospective power to make sense of Bertha, Maud cannot see that we get only as much of a portrait of Ellen's real or fictional Bertha as the diarist wants us to have.

A woman of a different generation, country, and background, Sabine de Kercoz uses similar metaphors not to write about Christabel's bogey, but her flesh-and-blood cousin:

> My mother's bed had heavy velvet hangings with braid and embroidery. My father asked me to clean these two months ago; he did not say why; I formed the mad idea that he had some project of marrying me, and was preparing my mother's room as a bridal chamber. When we took down the hangings they were heavy with dust, and Gode made herself very ill with beating them out in the courtyard, her lungs were stuffed with a lifetime's (*my* lifetime's) spiderwebs and filth. And then, when they were beaten, they were nothing, all their substance was gone with their encrustation, so that huge rents and ragged tatters appeared everywhere. Then my father said, 'Your cousin from England is coming, and new bed furniture must be had somewhere.'

(p. 367)

While Ellen's servants obsessively dust and scrub in preparation for Randolph's return, Ellen herself takes to her bed as if protecting it against a possible usurper. Sabine makes up the usurper's bed herself. Her ambiguously-worded confession – "I formed the mad idea that he had some project of marrying me, and was preparing my mother's room as a bridal chamber" – does not suggest that her father intends to marry her off, but that she will officially take her mother's place. The longer Christabel stays, the more jealous Sabine, who has never had a lover, admits to being of her: "I have never shared my father or my home with another woman, and was afraid I should not like this, afraid of nameless interferences or criticism or at the least embarrassment. Perhaps I still feel all these things" (p. 371). Or:

> I wanted her to stay, to be a friend, to be a companion. Not to replace me. Not to replace my mother. Those are distinct things. I have not aspired to my mother's place, but my place is what it is

because she is not there. And I do not want another to have the care of my father, or the first right to hear his thoughts or his discoveries. Or steal his kiss, write it, that is what I felt, or steal his kiss.

(p. 393)

Before she has guessed Christabel's condition, she is preparing her mother's childbed for her childbed. Before she can judge her immoral, she already hates her for being "the thief in the night" (p. 393).

From *Pamela; or Virtue Rewarded* through *Jane Eyre, Wuthering Heights,* and *Bleak House*, the female narrator is always a virtuous character confronted with another woman's sexual taint. After writing for hundreds of pages about the necessity of protecting her virtue (read marriageability), Pamela learns about Sally Godfrey, the abandoned mother of Mr B.'s illegitimate daughter. Pamela hears about Sally with neither resentment nor horror. Her own chastity has earned her a position where she can afford to be charitable to a woman lacking her strength of character. Jane Eyre leaves Rochester as he begs her to become his fourth mistress and returns only after she can become his legal wife. The young, impulsive Nelly Dean can justify her destructive behavior because it punishes Catherine for loving one man while the wife of another. Esther Summerson lovingly embraces her estranged sinner of a mother. Yet she is grateful that her pock-marked face will never betray her sordid heritage. Thus, the female narrative in the Victorian period is a record of a woman's fortitude in the face of sexual temptation or corruption. Fallen women – Lady Dedlock, Hetty Sorrel, Gaskell's Ruth, Tess of the d'Urbervilles- never write their own narratives. When they are given tongues, as Hetty is after killing her baby or Lady Dedlock after meeting Esther, they voice their despair, their friendlessness, their remorse, their self-disgust. *Possession* conflates and inverts these two traditions. Christabel and Randolph's correspondence is not that between a threatened virgin and her protective parents nor that between a victim and her would-be rapist, but the letters of a man and a woman together negotiating a way into bed with each other. Ellen and Sabine do not sit in judgment of Christabel. In her blatant sexuality they see reflected back at them their own prolonged virginity. Ellen's shame and self-loathing rival Lady Dedlock's.

Ellen remembers herself on her honeymoon as a space to be penetrated: "The approach, the locked gateway, the panic, the whimpering flight," (p. 498) and indeed in his courtship of Christabel, Randolph figures her in similar terms:

> I was invited to take exercise with friends in the Park, and felt a vague
> unease as though its woody plantations and green spaces were girdled
> with an unspoken spell of prohibition – as your Cottage is – as Shalott
> was to the knights – as the woods of sleep are in the tale, with their
> sharp briar hedges …. It may be even that I might not have come to
> ride in the park if it had not had the definite glitter and glamour of the
> enclosed and barred … I will not exchange my imagined rose-bower
> for reality until I am invited to step inside it – which may be never.
>
> (pp. 198–9)

Christabel hesitates to invite him inside, not because of propriety or
morality, but because of her fear of the act of invasion itself.

> You see, Sir, I say nothing of Honour, nor of Morality – though they
> are weighty matters – I go to the Core, which renders much disquisi-
> tion on these matters superfluous. The core is my solitude, my soli-
> tude that is threatened, that you threaten, without which I am
> nothing – so how may honour, how may morality speak to me?
>
> (p. 213)

Ellen and Christabel are women protective of their space, not their
honor, and they are punished finally not for their sexual predilections,
but for a self-protectiveness which resists narrative.

Christabel has a voice in a way that Hetty, Lady Dedlock, Ruth and
Tess do not, and yet she chooses not to use it to further a narrative.
Her letters stop as her sexual liaison ends, and she waits thirty years to
write another. During her pregnancy, she remains pathologically mute.
Her pregnant body itself obstructs narrative. In *Bleak House*, for
example, sexual contamination literally propels the narrative forward.
Sally Shuttleworth has argued that much sensation fiction is motivated
by the "anarchic disruptions" of the maternal body.[6] But Christabel's
pregnant body is figured not as a site of terrible passions, but of
remarkable passivity. She is not the locus of contamination, but a text
to be read or misread. Sabine writes of her:

> My cousin is now so big, so ripe, so heavy, it must be soon, and yet
> she has allowed no word of discussion of her condition or her
> expectations. And she has us all under some spell, for no one of us
> dare take her to task, or bring into the open, to be spoken of, what
> is already in full view and yet hidden.
>
> (p. 402)

The Victorian woman's pregnancy, obvious and yet obscured under her voluminous skirts becomes in Byatt's hands a metaphor for the obliqueness of female narrative. Christabel never speaks or writes about her relationship with Randolph but hints at it in her Lincolnshire descriptions in "The Fairy Melusina" and in her cryptic clues to his letters' hiding place in "Dolly Has a Secret." Ellen refuses to speak of Christabel and yet writes down her reactions to "The Fairy Melusina"; she buries Christabel's letter and then tells her journal where it is. Christabel and Ellen place their concerns directly before the reader and then cover them in layers of skirt.

Christabel is punished, as she confesses in her last letter to Randolph, not for having a sexual past, but for having no past at all. In order to keep her daughter in the dark she has denied herself a personal history. Her asexuality terrifies: "I fill her with a sort of fear, a sort of revulsion – she feels, rightly, a *too-much* in my concern for her – but misreads that, which is most natural, as something *unnatural*" (p. 544). In order to keep Randolph in the dark she has prevented any further narrative possibilities:

> You will think – if the *shock* of what I have had to tell you has left you any power to care or to think about my narrow world – that a *romancer* such as I (or a true dramatist, such as you) would not be able to keep such a secret for nigh on thirty years (think, Randolph, thirty years), without bringing about some *peripeteia*, some *denoue-ment*, some secret hinting or open scene of revelation. Ah, but if you were here, you would see how I dare not. For her sake, for she is so happy. For mine, in that I fear – I fear the possible horror in her fair eyes. If I told her – *that* – and she *stepped back*? ... I am the spinster aunt who is not loved. So I am punished, in some sort, for keeping her from you.
>
> (pp. 544–5)

It is crucial that Christabel neither writes nor enacts a romance on the order of the one she hears early in her pregnancy. This, the tale of the miller's daughter who murders her baby, is told by Sabine's servant Gode. Gode's is the only spontaneous, unguarded female narrative in the novel. It tells the tale of a woman, abandoned by her lover, who kills her baby and goes mad with grief. She hears her child dancing in the streets and follows it over a cliff and to her death. Her skeptical lover, confronted by her dead body, finally hears the child as well and goes mad with the sound of its dancing feet. Gode's tale has a strong but false resonance which misdirects both Byatt's readers and her literary critics for nearly two hundred pages: "'[Christabel] wrote a lot about Goethe's *Faust* round about then. It's a regular motif, the innocent infanticide, in European literature at that time. Gretchen, Hetty Sorrel, Wordsworth's Martha in "The Thorn." Despairing women with dead babies'"(p. 457). Part of the tragedy in the traditional narrative of the fallen woman is the fate of her bastard child. Hetty's baby is killed, Martha's and Tess's babies die, Esther Summerson is deformed, Sally Godfrey's baby is abandoned by her mother, and the son of Gaskell's Ruth is ostracized. But the tragedy of Christabel's story is that her child suffers not at all. Her story has no resonance in her child's life. May is born, grows up "extraordinarily happily" (p. 554), marries and has ten children. She meets her father on one occasion and immediately forgets him. Randolph returns to his wife and Christabel retires to her room. Addicted to silence, frightened of communication, Christabel plays out what Sabine defines as "the essence of tragic drama, in the case of most women"–"inaction" (p. 369). Christabel is explicit in her confession to Randolph; she has been punished not for a sexual sin, but for a sin of omission. In the end she and Ellen suffer the same despair, for Ellen is punished not for the "unnaturalness" of her sexuality but for keeping Randolph and his family apart.

We see here that Byatt is not unequivocal in her defense of her characters' narrative strategies. While these women derive their greatest strength from their ability to construct privacy, they cause the greatest harm to themselves and others through their self-protectiveness. Yet this tension between the desire to withhold and the desire to betray information informs Byatt's own narrative technique as well. She takes the most intimate information and that which propels the narrative forward out of the hands of specifically named narrators, so that the details of Christabel and Randolph's marriage, and the meeting between Randolph and his daughter may be said to be part of her own narrative. Unlike her fictional creations, Byatt is not afraid to tell a story, and yet these most revelatory sections of the novel are the only ones withheld from her literary detectives. Like Sabine, who writes for herself alone, or Christabel, who writes for her lover alone, or Ellen, who writes exclusively for those who will never know her, Byatt composes these scenes with a specific audience in mind. Her tendency in these sections is always to reveal slowly and gradually, to disorient us by identifying neither a narrative voice, nor the subjects of her narrative, to give us the impression of being intruders on a private moment to which we are given limited access. Thus, a nearly erotic scene between Roland and Maud moves imperceptibly into a chapter about Randolph and Christabel: "The man and the woman sat opposite each other in the railway carriage" (p. 297). Several paragraphs later we can firmly situate ourselves in the nineteenth century. Within several more we can identify Randolph and Christabel as the train passengers. Byatt further toys with her reader in the next "concealed" section of her novel. We know it is November 27th 1889, but whom are we observing?

> The old woman trod softly along the dark corridors, and climbed the stairs, standing in uncertainty on various landings. From the back – we are going to see her clearly now – from the back and in the shadow, she might still have been any age.
>
> (p. 485)

Byatt stages this scene so as to have Ellen move slowly into the light, but even as we see her – "She wore a velvet dressing gown, and soft embroidered slippers .... " – we cannot identify her. In fact, throughout this section, she is named only by those with whom she is in conversation. Ellen is the novel's most secretive character, the one least known to us as we reach this point in the novel, and Byatt remains respectful of her privacy (or reminds us of our own intrusiveness) by never naming her while revealing the most intimate details of her life. Finally in her postscript, Byatt introduces Randolph and May as "two people [who] met on a hot May day, and never later mentioned their meeting" (p. 552). As Ash never identifies himself to his daughter, Byatt never names him to the reader.

Yet, as I suggested earlier, Byatt makes her most formidable appearance as Sybilla Silt in "Mummy Possest." The poem is a reworking of Browning's "Mr. Sludge 'the Medium'," in which a crank medium explains and apologizes for his methods to a disgruntled client.[7] The lengthy apology, however, is revealed in the poem's last lines as yet another lie. "Mummy Possest" is an apology for Byatt's own lies – for creating a phantom world so convincingly real – but her apology is contained within a still larger lie. The premise of the poem seems to be Ash's desire to punish Christabel for her crime against his child. In its last lines he tortures her with his own uncertainty:

> Here is a lock of hair – the housemaid's hair –
> As golden as her son's, and just as fine –
> Which at some aptest moment you let fall
> You understand me – in her lap – or on

> Her clutching fingers – that will do such good –
> Will give such Happiness that you and I
> May grow and prosper in its lovely warmth.
> We shall have gifts and she her moment's hope,
> Nay more, her certainty …
>
> (p. 445)

And yet within the body of the poem lies proof of Ash's certainty:

> Her only son, a year since, when he was
> Scarce more than lisping Babe of two years' growth
> Snatched by a fever in a summer Tour.
> His small voice has been heard in broken sounds –
> He makes, he says, perpetual daisy-chains
> In wondrous meadows – but she weeps and weeps,
> And will not be consoled, and takes with her
> Where'er she goes, a lock of his bright hair …

He has not written this poem in the first days of grief after the seance, but years later after making daisy chains with and taking a lock of hair from his daughter. But is this hint too obscure for Christabel to read any meaning into it? She is supposed to pick up on the obvious references to herself – to Coleridge's Geraldine, to the dead child. But is she supposed to see Ash's hope and despair or his certainty? It is crucial that Ash puts this monologue into the mouth of a woman, for it is meant not to communicate, but to baffle.

Like Ellen's journal, which both attracts and defends itself against "ghouls and vultures," "Mummy Possest" both entices and permanently misdirects those literary scholars who equate knowledge with possession. (Cropper becomes an expert on his subject by buying up Ash memorabilia, Beatrice by hoarding Ellen's diaries for twenty-five years, Blackadder by enslaving poor graduate students in his "Ash Factory," Leonora by seducing hapless colleagues.) In *Possession*'s last pages Byatt conjures up this poem again to remind us that this novel is not about acquisition, but loss. We remember that even as Ash is "knowing" Christabel he feels as though "it was like holding Proteus … as though she was liquid moving through his grasping fingers" (p. 308). In order for Ash to have held onto Christabel, he would have to have done violence to her. But Byatt allows for no such reading of her poet-lovers. "Mummy Possest" is itself a protean mass. It refuses to be pinned down; it refuses to be held. Byatt leaves her feminist critics both inside and outside her novel with this terrible prospect: get your hands on and impose your anti-patriarchal concerns on these texts, but only at the risk of perpetrating your own form of violence.

*

The Last Chapter

The cover of this book – Robert Braithwaite Martineau's *The Last Chapter* – does not show a woman writing or speaking, but rather reading. I have explained in my introduction the dangers of visually representing what happens within the body of each of these novels, but *The Last Chapter* could not illustrate any moment in the finished *products* I have discussed. Rarely do any of these novels depict a woman taking pleasure in her own words. Marian writes with too much urgency, Esther, Christabel, and Sabine with too much self-criticism. Revealing their experience of pleasure would expose the agendas of Ellen Ash or Jane Eyre. But this painting might capture a necessary moment from the *process* of narration. I can picture Marian Halcombe in such a pose selecting portions of her diary to read aloud to Walter, or Jane Eyre receiving her copy of her autobiography from Smith, Elder and Co., and sneaking a peek at it after putting her husband to bed. I can imagine that even a housewife as attentive to her draperies as Ellen Ash could become so engrossed in the reading of her own diary that she might forget to draw the curtains and light a lamp.[8] This is a rare image of a Victorian woman alone clearly enjoying her solitude. The most famous images from the period are of women from the pages of literature dying (John Everett Millais's *Ophelia*, John William Waterhouse's *The Lady of Shalott*, Dante Gabriel Rossetti's, *Beata Beatrix*), of fallen women repenting (William Holman Hunt's *The Awakening Conscience*, Augustus Egg's *Past and Present*), of sleepless seamstresses starving (Richard Redgrave's *The Sempstress*), of patient lovers waiting, suffering, and enduring (Arthur Hughes's *The Long Engagement*, Frederick Sandys's *If*), and of stoic wives valiantly moving on (Ford Madox Brown's *The Last of England*). The most famous models of the period – Jane Morris, Fanny Cornforth, and Elizabeth Siddal – are remembered for their wild hair, their ethereal or enormous features, certainly not for their smiles. I love *The Last Chapter* because it is an unusual example from Victorian art of a woman alone, not waiting, suffering, and enduring, but experiencing undisguised pleasure at the very fact of her solitude. It is, of course, a rare image, for as Florence

Nightingale reminds us in "Cassandra," the opportunity to enjoy the pleasures of a book in private were so often denied middle-class Victorian women.

Should feminist criticism be suspicious of pleasure? Laura Mulvey (who has since reversed herself) famously insisted that it should in "Visual Pleasure and Narrative Cinema" because narrative cinema produces pleasure through the objectification of women.[9] Since Mulvey, many other feminist critics have attempted to destroy the pleasures of visual, cinematic, and literary texts. But not even as prescient a critic as Byatt could have foreseen how far they would go in their efforts. When she published *Possession* in 1990, Byatt was prepared to protect her male characters against charges of silencing women – could she have foreseen a time when feminist critics would deem politically incorrect the exercise of female speech, the promulgation of women's writing? But that is, of course, what has happened to recent feminist criticism. In Nancy Armstrong's latest reading of *Jane Eyre* – "Captivity and Cultural Capital in the English Novel" (1998) – female literacy comes under sharp attack. Armstrong claims that "the only people to survive Jane's narrative are those who resemble Jane and fit into her social circle. By the time Jane Eyre tells her story, however, the individual cannot exist as such and claim full human status unless or until she has the kind of literacy that presupposes such internal wellsprings of humanity.... What makes one human in Brontë's novel," Armstrong asserts, are "education" and "possession of the prestige dialect, or writing."

> [Brontë] differentiates her heroine ... from women who lack her verbal ability and thus the basis for accumulating cultural capital. Brontë does this by describing her heroine's subcultural counterparts in the xenophobic terms of the period, as racially incompatible. This holds true not only for her memorable representations of Bertha Mason, who lacks all capacity for literacy, but also for Jane's young charges in the rural school, among whom she confesses to feeling 'degraded ... dismayed at the ignorance, the poverty, the coarseness of all I heard and saw round me.' As Cora Kaplan explains, 'these little peasant girls, though they may be "of flesh and blood as good as the scions of gentlest genealogy," are nevertheless part of the Africanist discourse of the novel.'[10]

Of course, Armstrong's own possession of "cultural capital" makes her the envy of most academics in her field, her own mastery of the "prestige dialect" gives her license to do such violence to this unsuspecting novel. What evidence does the text provide of Bertha's illiteracy?[11] Where does it conflate rural Yorkshire and Africa? How can girls of Jane's own race be "racially incompatible" with their teacher? Armstrong has it both ways in her analysis. Language is powerful enough to make "the telling difference between the subject and ... object in this narrative," yet Brontë makes "something out of nothing at all – a self [Jane Eyre] out of little else but language."[12] Does Armstrong despise Jane because she has nothing but her language or because she proves that language is everything? Clearly Armstrong and some of the critics whose readings she uses to build her own (particularly Gayatri Spivak and Cora Kaplan) teach us how to despise both *Jane Eyre* and Jane Eyre. My book has not disguised my admiration for Charlotte Brontë or *Jane Eyre*. I hope that my reading has given readers a new way to respect and marvel at a book they may have once uncritically but viscerally adored. And I hope it will have done so not because Jane Eyre has "cultural capital," but because the joys of constructing and reading an elegant sentence cannot be reproduced by any experience on the stock exchange or at the mall, because it is still valuable to analyze literature without employing the vocabulary used to critique capitalism.

I began this study by departing from Susan Lanser's work. Let me revisit her reading of *Jane Eyre*:

> If the powerful voice achieved by Jane Eyre helped to foster a tradition of outspoken white female narrators in novels since the mid-nineteenth century, the very hegemony of that tradition, brought into being by the dramatized silencing of Bertha Mason, must also have helped to foreclose narrative possibilities for women novelists of color writing in the West.
>
> (p. 192)

My study, with its emphasis on artfully covert tactics, has found no evidence of a tradition of "outspoken white female narrators." The diversity of these narrators' hidden agendas negates any simple reading of a hegemonic tradition. But it is as a teacher, rather than as a critic, that I must finally take exception to Lanser's argument. How willingly will our students seek to discover the *actual* causes and effects of racism when they have been taught to blame English literature? Isn't it easier to ask them to accuse timid, isolated Charlotte Brontë for creating the current state of affairs than to have them study history and politics? Isn't scapegoating a long dead white woman more convenient than asking them to examine the source of their parents' income or the investment history of their academic institution? Instead of demanding that our students learn about racism in Brixton, Oldham, Crown Heights or Los Angeles, we show them how to *invent* racism. "Rochester's white Creole wife," is in Cora Kaplan's analysis somehow magically "metamorphosed by marriage, madness, and incarceration into a fully racialized figure."[13]

Feminist criticism has reached an impasse by insisting that the pleasure to be found in canonical texts is ideologically untenable. If the reader of this book remains convinced that we should loathe or feel superior to the novels I have discussed, then I have failed. But I am not alone in my attempt to celebrate the pleasures of the text. Other feminist critics – including Linda Nochlin, Maria DiBattista, and Nina Baym – are offering us escape routes. These women, whose writing I greatly admire, work in different disciplines and fields and use different methodologies, but they all approach a piece of art without a preconceived and inflexible notion of its ideology. While many other critics have stopped discussing questions of value and aesthetics, these women continue to prove that explaining why something is "good" is invariably more difficult and rewarding than denigrating it. Possibly the most influential of all feminist art historians, Linda Nochlin, questions in her most recent book

the possibility of a single methodology – empirical, theoretical, or both, or neither – which is guaranteed to work in every case .... [W]hat underlies and binds each instance of my work is a sense of moral and ethical commitment, combined, perhaps surprisingly, with a highly developed sense of play and a deep, and often contradictory, love of the sheer visual seductiveness of some kinds of art and the adventurous refusal of conventional formal value of others: the undeniable pleasures of the visual text. What single methodology could ever cope with such disparate elements? I like Claude Levi-Strauss's concept of 'bricolage' – constructing your method as you go along to suit the needs of the material and the evolving argument and, in turn, examining the material in the light of the argument so constructed .... [14]

In her spectacular defense of the screwball comedy, *Fast Talking Dames*, Maria DiBattista reclaims for women the "visual pleasure" denied them by Laura Mulvey, Mary Ann Doane, Kaja Silverman, and others. Blithely dismissing "the feminist critique of film as a tool of ideological oppression and the camera as an instrument of the 'male gaze' catering to voyeurs and fetishists," DiBattista celebrates the fact that the "fast talking dame doesn't stand or sit or lie still long enough to satisfy such customers."[15] Her book reminds us that a woman's body can be more than sexualized, that physicality can be audaciously liberating for both the actor and the audience as she marvels at Carole Lombard boxing with Frederic March, Barbara Stanwyck gracefully tripping Henry Fonda or Katharine Hepburn going leopard hunting with Cary Grant. But this physical prowess is more than matched by an agile and ferociously witty tongue:

> We live in a culture in which the question of our speech is very much alive, but primarily as a negative demonstration of the power of words to inflict harm or take unfair advantage of those less articulate or well spoken than ourselves. Hate speech is a national shibboleth that has driven out of public consciousness the simple fact that words can do more than give offense. Perhaps the time has come to rephrase the question of our speech and address ourselves to how the American language might work the same positive magic on the national character as it did when the movies first learned to talk. If we take the time to revisit that cultural moment when the fast-talking dame was in her heyday, we will find women to instruct us in the happy boldness of their speech. At the very least we might be thrilled, even heartened, by those animated visions of irrepressible life racing past us in a torrent of words.[16]

For twenty years Nina Baym has been critiquing feminism's use of theory:

> [F]eminist theory addresses an audience of prestigious male academics and attempts to win its respect. It succeeds, so far as I can see, only when it ignores or dismisses the earlier paths of feminist literary study as 'naive' and grounds its own theories in those currently in vogue with the men who make theory: deconstruction, for example, or Marxism. These grounding theories manifest more than mere indifference to women's writing; they are irretrievably misogynist. As a result of building on misogynist foundations, feminist theorists mainly excoriate their deviating sisters. Feminism has always been bifurcated by contention between pluralists and legalists. Pluralists anticipate the unexpected, encourage diversity; legalists locate the correct position and marshal women within the ranks. As for recent literary theory, it is deeply legalistic and judgmental.

Infractions – the wrong theory, theoretical errors or insouciant dis-
regard for theoretical implications – are crimes .... Such totalizing by
feminist theorists reproduces *to the letter* the appropriation of
women's experience by men, substituting only the appropriation
and naming of that experience by a subset of women; themselves.[17]

As a pluralist Baym has written particularly persuasively about the need
in the classroom for feminists to acknowledge the pleasures of reading.
If the feminist teacher aims "to rupture the blissful uncritical connection between reader and text and to erase the memory of that connection by enforcing a new, unpleasurable, feminist interpretation," then
she will inevitably be silencing those women students afraid to own
and to own up to their own experience of pleasure.[18] Baym advocates
teaching "a wide range of works in a variety of ways, to rethink the
dominance of interpretive activity in the classroom, to remember that
all interpretations (even our own) are contingent and none absolutely
correct. If we don't try to do these things, the only voice in the class-
room will be the teacher's, and then it makes no difference if her voice
is feminist or not."[19]

What case then have I made for pleasure? Some feminist readers will
find pleasure in *Jane Eyre*'s conclusion when the poor, plain girl finds
money and marital happiness; others will find such a neat ending too
comfortable, too conservative.[20] But what if both sets of readers have
mistaken ongoing conflict for resolution? Are there new pleasures to be
discovered once we read the novel not as product, but as process?

When we read *Jane Eyre* as a product, we see marriage as the goal of a
teleological narrative. When we read it as a process, we see marriage as
the starting point from which a different story can be told. As a
product *Wuthering Heights* is the account of twenty-year old events; as a
process it is a story being reinvented minute by minute. As a product it
is the story of a doomed passion; as a process it is the attempt to forge
a different kind of love. As a product *Bleak House* is allowed to end with
Esther tying up the loose strands of a massive story; as a process it
cannot end, for the struggle for self-definition goes on after the story is
told and outside the confines of the plot. As a product *The Woman in
White* affirms the truths that Walter Hartright sets forth to prove; as a
process it denies the possibility of proving anything true. As a product
"Penelope" is the portrait of Molly we have expected from *Ulysses*'s
previous chapters; as a process it is the undoing of all our previous
conceptions.

I have tried, when writing about these books, not to stand apart from and look down on them as completed products, but to try to experience them as their narrators themselves (were they real women) would, as works in progress. I have tried to imagine what Marian would do with three nights alone with Walter, why Molly never says anything without eventually negating it, how Jane would remember ten-year-old events, why Nelly has abandoned housekeeping for storytelling, what and for whom Esther thinks she is writing. I have tried to imagine how difficult is the experience of narrating for Nelly or Molly or Marian under the pressure of a deadline. I have tried to understand why with all their other responsibilities Esther or Jane would undertake such a time-consuming task.

I believe that Dickens, Collins, and Joyce want us to ask such kinds of questions because their novels are so self-consciously written. Each breaks the illusion that Henry James deemed necessary in the writing of fiction. Dickens destroys the conceit of superhuman omniscience by suddenly revealing his unnamed narrator's humanity and mortality. Collins uses his most colorful character (Fosco) to comment on the fictional text in which he exists, to talk back to his own creator. And Joyce gets so caught up in the frustration of Molly's task that he allows her to call on him to pull her out of it. Through these overt intrusions these authors are drawing attention to their own ventriloquy. They are not claiming Esther's, Marian's, or Molly's as the voices of real women but highlighting the *process* by which they have created and given voice to fictional narrators.

So by advocating process over product I am suggesting a reading practice that takes into account the experience of the novelist writing, the imagined experience of the narrator narrating, and especially the unrepresented but imaginable experience of the narrator as she prepares to narrate or looks back on narrating. By advocating process I am showing how great works of literature do not end, but by their very construction demand rereading. The ambiguity of each of these novels' endings – Why does *Jane Eyre* end with St. John and Revelation? Why does *Wuthering Heights* end without the marriage of Lockwood and Cathy? Why does *Bleak House* end in mid-sentence? Why does *The Woman in White* end with Walter focusing on Aunt Marian? Why does *Ulysses* end with a yes? – suggests that these are not stable products with clearly defined meanings and agendas. And no pleasure-denying ideological critique can force them into teleological straitjackets or dissipate their incalculable energies.

More overtly than these other novels, *Possession* shows the impossibility of narrative closure. When Random House recorded the romance on audiotape, it chose to end with the last chapter and Roland and Maud finally getting into bed, not with the postscript in which Randolph meets and does not claim his daughter. In the audio version (perhaps more palatable to a contemporary audience) the novel is about consummation and acquisition, not repression and loss. And yet, of course, Byatt has made it clear that consummation – both the fulfillment of the characters' sexual desires and the realization of our readerly expectations – is neither the only, nor the most preferable kind of pleasure her text offers. (To my mind the most beautiful scene in the novel – Randolph on his deathbed – remains a tantalizing mystery unless *Possession* is reread.)[21] The sexual relationship Roland and Maud have longed for is far less poignant than the verbal connection Christabel and Randolph have lost. In Christabel's final letter to Randolph she declares it "so dangerously sweet to speak out, after all these years .... " She misses "our old letters, of poetry and other things, our trusting minds which recognised each other," not "those few sharp sweet days of passion – which might have been almost anyone's passion, it seems, *for all passions run the same course to the same end* " (p. 544, emphasis added). If we look past *Jane Eyre*'s, *Wuthering Heights*'s, or *The Woman in White*'s illusions of closure we will find each of their authors offering us alternatives to "the same end." The pleasures we may have derived from reading these as perfectly resolved, morally certain products may be replaced by the new pleasures of being surprised, outwitted, and ensnared in an ethical or aesthetic maze.

Because histories of the novel have studied all of these works as products, marriage, children, narrative closure and fulfillment have been seen as the defining characteristics of the Victorian novel's ending. Because *Ulysses* has been read as a radical break from this tradition, its ultimate goal has not been read as the affirmation of the marital state. In Byatt's double ending she cautions her scholar-lovers against what has driven them all along, the overwhelming need for narrative closure. Maud and Roland have learned that the histories of Victorian poetry and of the Victorians themselves have lacked crucial information. *We* know that the histories Maud and Roland will come to write will be similarly lacking. I have tried to show how histories of the novel may need to be reconsidered. But I hope that I have also shown that these artful narratives will not allow any history to arrive at some comfortable narrative resolution.

Notes

Introduction: Designing a narrative

1 Susan Sniader Lanser, *Fictions of Authority: Women Writers and Narrative Voice* (Ithaca: Cornell University Press, 1992), p. 8. In particular I will avoid conventional narratology's specialized vocabulary, preferring retrospection to analepsis, first-person narration to homo- or autodiegetic narratives.

2 Lanser, pp. 4–5.

3 Lanser, p. 192.

4 Richard Rorty, "The Pragmatist's Progress" in Umberto Eco, *Interpretation and Overinterpretation* (Cambridge: Cambridge University Press, 1992), p. 106.

5 Peter Brooks, *Reading for the Plot* (New York: Random House, 1984), p. 330.

6 Wayne Booth, *The Rhetoric of Fiction* (Chicago: University of Chicago Press, 1961), p. 159.

7 Booth, pp. 158–9. Great works of irony such as Browning's dramatic monologues, Ford's *The Good Soldier*, or Nabokov's *Lolita* are notable for their game-playing and narrative trickery. Yet to my mind they are ultimately about self-deception and self-exposure. The narrators of these texts cannot gain our sympathies to the degree that the narrators in this study can, for the former insistently reproduce evidence against themselves, evidence that has already been destroyed.

8 Shlomith Rimmon-Kenan, *Narrative Fiction: Contemporary Poetics* (London: Routledge, 1999), p. 100.

9 Booth, p. 307.

10 John Kucich, *The Power of Lies: Transgression in Victorian Fiction* (Ithaca: Cornell University Press, 1994), pp. 27–8.

11 Nina Baym, "The Madwoman and Her Languages: Why I Don't Do Feminist Literary Theory," *Feminisms*, ed. Robyn R. Warhol and Diane Price Herndl (New Brunswick, NJ: Rutgers University Press, 1991), pp. 160–2.

12 Although Mulvey has distanced herself from many of her own contentions in "Visual Pleasure and Narrative Cinema," her essay continues to exert enormous influence. See *Feminisms*, ed. Robyn R. Warhol and Diane Price Herndl (New Brunswick, NJ: Rutgers University Press, 1991), pp. 432–42.

13 See Domna C. Stanton, "Language and Revolution: the Franco-American Disconnection," *The Future of Difference* (Boston: Hall, 1980), p. 86.

14 In light of Bill Clinton's legacy might it be time to note that the phallic need not be associated with the rational, logical, deliberate, or cautious?

15 Mary Poovey, *Uneven Developments: The Ideological Work of Gender in Mid-Victorian England* (Chicago: University of Chicago Press, 1988), pp. 37, 46. Kucich, whom I quote, supports Poovey's claim, p. 11.

16 Ian Watt, *The Rise of the Novel* (Berkeley: University of California Press, 1957), p. 26.

17 George Levine has done an admirable job of showing how Victorian realism is far more self-aware than is usually thought. "The great novelists of the

nineteenth century were never so naive about narrative conventions or the problems of representation as later realists or modern critics have suggested." See *The Realistic Imagination: English Fiction from Frankenstein to Lady Chatterley* (Chicago: University of Chicago Press, 1981), especially pp. 3–22. Caroline Levine (no relation) in her unpublished manuscript *The Realist Experiment* also passionately defends the sophistication of Victorian realism.

18 See for example, Watt's discussion of Richardson's contribution to the novel: he "achieved for the novel what D.W. Griffith's technique of the 'close-up' did for the film: added a new dimension to the representation of reality," p. 27, or Gérard Genette's discussion of retrospection in *Remembrance of Things Past* which involves the " 'replay' of the main episodes of [Marcel's] existence," *Narrative Discourse*, trans. Jane E. Lewin (Oxford: Basil Blackwell, 1980), p. 56.

19 Nancy Armstrong, *Desire and Domestic Fiction* (New York: Oxford University Press, 1987), p. 30.

20 Armstrong, p. 43.

21 Armstrong, p. 42. Armstrong has continued to misread this crucial scene. In her recent article, "Captivity and Cultural Capital in the English Novel," *Novel: a Forum on Fiction* (Summer 1998) 388 she writes that "What propels [Jane to her own home] is neither family, nor fortune, nor beauty, nor wit, nor even exactly Jane herself, but something that she has and others lack, call it a capacity for self-production. 'Ere I had finished this reply,' she claims in recalling one of several such self transcendent moments, 'my soul began to expand, to exult, with the strangest sense of freedom, of triumph, I ever felt.'" Armstrong makes speaking look a good deal easier for Jane than it actually is. Within half an hour Jane sees "the madness of [her] conduct, and the dreariness of [her] hatred and hating position." "Something of vengeance I had tasted for the first time; as aromatic wine it seemed, on swallowing, warm and racy: its after-flavour, metallic and corroding, gave me a sensation as if I had been poisoned." See Charlotte Brontë, *Jane Eyre*, ed. Jane Jack and Margaret Smith (Oxford: Clarendon Press, 1969), p. 38.

22 Armstrong, *Desire and Domestic Fiction*, p. 49.

23 Daniel Defoe, *Moll Flanders* (London: Penguin, 1989), p. 37.

24 Virginia Woolf, *A Room of One's Own* (London: The Hogarth Press, 1959), pp. 102–3.

25 Woolf, p. 104.

26 Charlotte Brontë, *Jane Eyre*, ed. Jane Jack and Margaret Smith (Oxford: Clarendon Press, 1969), pp. 110–11.

27 Harriet Martineau, *Harriet Martineau's Autobiography* Vol. I (London: Virago, 1983), pp. 100–1.

28 Florence Nightingale, *Cassandra and other Selections from Suggestions for Thought*, ed. Mary Poovey (London: Pickering & Chatto, 1991), p. 213.

29 Margaret Oliphant, The Autobiography of Margaret Oliphant, ed. Elizabeth Jay (Oxford: Oxford University Press, 1990), p. 15.

1   Jane Eyre: Hazarding confidences

1 More than a month later Nussey wrote the following comment which she left among her notes: "The naiveté respecting the last new novel was on

Charlotte's side in supposing that I, though silent, was uninformed. *Specially* informed I was not; but I had seen proof-sheets corrected (at Brookroyd) and passed them to the house letter-bag without glancing at the address. Perceiving that confidence was not volunteered, it was not sought. Charlotte confessed afterwards what a struggle it cost her to retain silence; but the sisters had pledged themselves to keep their attempts at Authorship unknown to any but themselves." See *The Brontës: Their Lives, Friendships and Correspondence*, ed. Thomas James Wise and John Alexander Symington (Philadelphia: Porcupine Press, 1980), II, pp. 211–28.

2 Brontë's letters to Nussey in the year after the publication of *Jane Eyre* are nearly always about the progress of Ellen's spring cleaning or the health of Ellen's acquaintances. Meanwhile, Brontë (under a pseudonym) was carrying on a rigorous correspondence with her publisher, W.S. Williams, in which she was more prone to discuss such issues as the status of women in society than the domestic concerns she shared with Nussey.

3 Charlotte Brontë, *Jane Eyre*, ed. Jane Jack and Margaret Smith (Oxford: Clarendon Press, 1969), p. 326. Further references to this work appear in the text. In Jane's one address to the "gentle reader" she is clearly imagining a sister in misery: "Gentle reader, may you never feel what I then felt! May your eyes never shed such stormy, scalding, heart-wrung tears as poured from mine. May you never appeal to Heaven in prayers so hopeless and so agonised as in that hour left my lips: for never may you, like me, dread to be the instrument of evil to what you wholly love." She is certainly addressing a woman when she pleads, "oh, romantic reader, forgive me for telling the plain truth" (p. 111). And she is searching for female sympathy when she rejects St. John's marriage proposal: "Reader, do you know, as I do, what terror those cold people can put into the ice of their questions?" (p. 417). Unlike Sylvère Monod, then, who finds thirty male readers, I find thirty-five female readers. Brontë's seduction of the reader is not a sexual but an intellectual, and far more lasting and potentially damaging, one. See Sylvère Monod, "Charlotte Brontë and the Thirty 'Readers' of *Jane Eyre*," Charlotte Brontë, *Jane Eyre*, ed. Richard J. Dunn, (New York: W.W. Norton & Co., 1971), pp. 496-507. The thirty-five references to the reader can be found on the following pages of the Clarendon edition of *Jane Eyre*: 53, 91, 103,112, 133, 153, 181, 216, 218, 231, 232, 325, 348, 362, 381, 406, 411, 419 (2 references), 420, 440, 468, 487, 490, 501, 509, 519, 526, 528, 535, 542, 552, 573, 574, 575. For a very different interpretation of the reader see Garrett Stewart, *Dear Reader: the Conscripted Audience in Nineteenth-Century British Fiction* (Baltimore: Johns Hopkins University Press, 1996). Rather than seducing the reader, Jane, in Stewart's analysis, uses the reader as "a model of psychic need itself" (p. 237). "Figured as eavesdropping alter ego in *Jane Eyre*, as narratorial censor in *Villette*, the reader is subjected in both cases to the otherness that keeps the enunciating subject – as narrating drive – from coinciding with itself" (p. 250).

4 See especially Rosemarie Bodenheimer's elegant article, "Jane Eyre in Search of Her Story," *Charlotte Brontë's Jane Eyre*, ed. Harold Bloom (New York: Chelsea House, 1987), pp. 97–112. The small number of other studies of Jane as a narrator include: Carol Bock, *Charlotte Brontë and the Storyteller's Audience* (Iowa City: University of Iowa Press, 1992); Nancy V. Workman,

"Scheherazade at Thornfield: Mythic Elements in *Jane Eyre*," *Essays in Literature* 15:2 (Fall 1988) 177-92; Janet H. Freeman, "Speech and Silence in *Jane Eyre*," *SEL: Studies in English Literature – 1500–1900*, 24:4 (Autumn 1984) 683–700; and Mark M. Hennelly, Jr.,"Jane Eyre's Reading Lesson," *English Literary History (ELH)* 51:4 (Winter 1984) 693–717. In a recent book-length study of *Jane Eyre* Jerome Beaty pays careful attention to the differences between "the virtual present, the moment of the fictional action" and "the narrator's present, the moment in which she is writing this part of her autobiography,"(p. 102) but he does not find Brontë deliberately seducing and misleading her reader. Instead, he sees the author's and narrator's goals *unintentionally* diverging from the reader's actual experience of the novel. See *Misreading Jane Eyre* (Columbus: Ohio State University Press, 1996), especially pp. 213–22.

5   Despite Jane's triumph as a writer, Janet H. Freeman uses this scene to argue for Rochester's ability to silence Jane: "Jane, still loyal to her idea of the plain and simple truth, is no match for the slippery ironist who insists on telling her that she is a good listener, that she was "made to be the recipient of secrets." See Freeman 693.

6   Bodenheimer, p. 101.

7   I am grateful to David Czuchlewski for sparking my interest in Jane's relation to Revelation.

8   Most biblical scholars agree that the John who wrote the Gospel is not the same John who wrote the Book of Revelation. While St. John Rivers may be named after the writer of the Gospel, Jane clearly associates her cousin with the author of Revelation. If Helen Burns teaches Jane to love the Christ of the Gospels, St. John labors to make her fear the Christ of Revelation.

9   See, for example, Carolyn Williams, "Closing the Book: the Intertextual End of *Jane Eyre*," *Victorian Connections*, ed. Jerome J. McGann (Charlottesville: University of Virginia Press, 1989). Williams notes that Brontë uses Bunyan's *The Pilgrim's Progress* as both a model for Jane's progress and "a negative model, finally positioned within [*Jane Eyre*] in order to be contradicted" (p. 81).

10   Bruce M. Metzger and Michael D. Coogan, *The Oxford Companion to the Bible* (New York: Oxford University Press, 1993), p. 654.

11   Elaine Showalter, *A Literature of their Own* (Princeton: Princeton University Press, 1977), p. 121.

12   D.H. Lawrence, *Apocalypse*, ed. Mara Kalnins (New York: Viking Press, 1982), p. 14. "The power-homage in a man like Judas felt itself betrayed! So it betrayed back again: with a kiss. And in the same way, Revelation had to be included in the New Testament, to give the death-kiss to the Gospels."

13   Carolyn Williams, p. 63.

14   See Elizabeth Rigby's unsigned review, *Quarterly Review*, lxxxiv (December 1848) 153–85.

15   See the unsigned review, *Christian Remembrancer*, xv (April 1848) 396–409.

16   Lyndall Gordon, *Charlotte Brontë: a Passionate Life* (New York: W.W. Norton & Co., 1994), p. 285.

17   Unpublished letter to W.S. Williams (8 April 1853). BPM. Gr:F2. Quoted in Gordon, p. 285.

18   Gordon, p. 285.

19 Janet Gezari, *Charlotte Brontë and Defensive Conduct* (Philadelphia: University of Pennsylvania Press, 1992), pp. 61–2. Gezari notes that "the only clue in the text to the pronunciation of the name is ambiguous, for Adèle asks Jane's name and being given it, declares it unpronounceable: 'Aïre? Bah! I cannot say it'" (p. 102). The umlaut [sic] appears in the Clarendon edition and has its authority from Brontë's manuscript, but the first three editions of the novel (and all later versions before the Clarendon edition) omitted it, thereby helping to establish the literary tradition that has determined the usual pronunciation." Gezari does a fascinating job of noting the recurring eye imagery in the novel.

20 Letter to M. Heger, July 24, 1844. *The Letters of Charlotte Brontë with a selection of letters by family and friends*, ed. Margaret Smith, Vol. I 1829–47. (Oxford: Clarendon Press, 1995), p. 358. Letter translated from the French.

21 Richard Chase, "The Brontës: a Centennial Observance," *Kenyon Review*, 9 (1947): 495.

22 Overlooking Jane's retrospective reconstruction of events, Mark M. Hennelly, Jr. writes of this scene: "Jane's earlier account had been incomplete and misleading....The distanced and critical Rochester plays the model reader here, while the implied reader hears an analysis that is more successful than his or her own prior interpretation, which has been based on Jane's misreading (and then misreporting) of events." See Hennelly, p. 711.

23 Gilbert suggests that Brontë "consciously or unconsciously exploits psychological Doubles." Sandra M. Gilbert and Susan Gubar, *The Madwoman in the Attic: the Woman Writer and the Nineteenth-Century Literary Imagination* (New Haven: Yale University Press, 1979), p. 360.

24 Mary Poovey, *Uneven Developments: The Ideological Work of Gender in Mid-Victorian England* (Chicago: University of Chicago Press, 1988), p. 139.

25 Gayatri Chakravorty Spivak, "Three Women's Texts and a Critique of Imperialism," *Critical Inquiry*, 12.1 (1985): 243–61.

26 Jenny Sharpe, *Allegories of Empire: The Figure of Woman in the Colonial Text* (Minneapolis: University of Minnesota Press, 1993), p. 46.

27 Susan Meyer, *Imperialism at Home: Race and Victorian Women's Fiction* (Ithaca: Cornell University Press, 1996), p. 92.

28 Meyer, p. 94.

29 Sandra M. Gilbert finds "an element of truth" in Richard Chase's oft-cited reading of the sexual punishment of Rochester. See Gilbert and Gubar, p. 368. See also, for example, Dianne F. Sadoff, *Monsters of Affection: Dickens, Eliot & Brontë on Fatherhood* (Baltimore: Johns Hopkins University Press, 1982) and Martin S. Day, "Central Concepts of *Jane Eyre*," *Personalist*, XLI no.4 (Autumn 1960): 495–505.

30 As a child, Brontë and her sisters and brother had created an imaginary African kingdom. While teaching at Roe Head, at Miss Wooler's school where she had once been a student, Brontë would occasionally write down on spare pieces of paper her visions of this kingdom, Angria, and its capital Verdopolis. Six of these fragmentary manuscripts, written between 1836 and 1837, survive and are now known as the Roe Head Journal. As Christine Alexander, the editor of Brontë's juvenilia writes, "they are the most important evidence we have of Brontë's efforts to cling to her Angrian dreamworld in the face of 'this wretched bondage' her life as a teacher." See

Christine Alexander, "Charlotte Brontë at Roe Head," in Charlotte Brontë, *Jane Eyre* (New York: W.W. Norton & Co., 1987), p. 408.

31 Charlotte Brontë, "All this day I have been in a dream," Brontë Parsonage Museum: B98(8). Reprinted in Charlotte Brontë, *Jane Eyre* (New York: W.W. Norton & Co., 1987), p. 413.

32 Christine Alexander, quoted in *Jane Eyre*, p. 409. The letter to Ellen Nussey is in *The Brontës: Their Lives, Friendships, and Correspondence*, I, p. 139.

33 Samuel Richardson, undated letter to Lady Bradshaigh, *The Correspondence of Samuel Richardson*, Vol. VI (New York: AMS Press, 1966), p. 120.

34 Showalter, p. 24. Both Showalter and Gilbert have been immensely influential in making *Jane Eyre* probably the most discussed novel for feminist critics over the last twenty-five years. Other defenses of Jane include Helene Moglen's *Charlotte Brontë: the Self Conceived* (New York: W.W. Norton & Co., 1976) and Ellen Moers's *Literary Women: the Great Writers* (New York: Oxford University Press, 1985).

35 Steven Cohan and Linda M. Shires, *Telling Stories* (New York: Routledge, 1988), p. 147. See also David Rosenwasser's "A Kristevan Reading of the Marriage Plot in *Jane Eyre*," *Approaches to Teaching Brontë's Jane Eyre*, ed. Diane Long Hoeveler and Beth Lau (New York: The Modern Language Association, 1993), pp. 154-61: "It would appear that at the end of the novel the thrill is gone. Brontë gives us the 'perfect concord' of traditional closed form.... Jane has sacrificed her aggressive spirit to domestic quietude, while the pressing social problems that the [novel has] raised remain unresolved" (p. 160). Jina Politi approaches the novel from a similar perspective: "Charlotte Brontë ... set out to liberate woman from the representations in which patriarchal Victorian ideology held her. She also set out to vindicate the socially underprivileged woman. Yet *Jane Eyre* comes to celebrate the very *ethos* upon which bourgeois capitalism and its patriarchal ideology rest. What the novel originally sets out to de-mask, it then artfully conceals" (p. 90). See "*Jane Eyre* Class-ified," *New Casebooks: Jane Eyre*, ed. Heather Glen (New York: St. Martin's Press [now Palgrave Macmillan], 1997), pp. 78–91.

36 Charlotte Brontë, *Villette*, ed. Herbert Rosengarten and Margaret Smith (Oxford: Oxford University Press, 1990), p. 42. All further references are to the same source.

2 Nelly Dean: Changing tactics

1 Charlotte Brontë, "Editor's Preface to the New Edition of *Wuthering Heights*"(1850) in Emily Brontë, *Wuthering Heights* (New York: W.W. Norton & Co., 1990), p. 321.

2 Brontë, p. 321.

3 James Hafley, "The Villain in *Wuthering Heights*," *Nineteenth-Century Fiction*, XIII (December 1958) 199.

4 See, for example, Dorothy Van Ghent, *The English Novel: Form and Function* (New York: 1967), pp. 187–208.

5 Sandra M. Gilbert and Susan Gubar, *The Madwoman in the Attic* (New Haven: Yale University Press, 1976), p. 291.

6 Peter Miles, *Wuthering Heights* (London: Macmillan Education Ltd., 1990), pp. 32–3 (emphasis added).

7 J. Hillis Miller, *Fiction and Repetition: Seven English Novels* (Oxford: Basil Blackwell, 1982), pp. 48–9.

8 Stevie Davies, *Emily Brontë* (Plymouth: Northcote House, 1998), p. 88.

9 Davies, pp. 27–8, 88.

10 Winifred Gérin, *Emily Brontë: A Biography* (Oxford: Oxford University Press, 1971), p. 225.

11 Gérin, p. 7.

12 Emily Brontë, *Wuthering Heights* (New York: W.W. Norton & Co., 1990), p. 59. All further references are to the same source.

13 Davies, p. 87.

14 See, for example, Terry Eagleton, *Myths of Power: a Marxist Study of the Brontës*, (London: Macmillan, 1988) and Susan Meyer, *Imperialism at Home: Race and Victorian Women's Fiction* (Ithaca: Cornell University Press, 1996).

15 Miles, p. 22.

16 A. Stuart Daley, "The Moons and Almanacs of *Wuthering Heights*" *Huntington Library Quarterly: a Journal for the History and Interpretation of English and American Civilization*, 37 (1974): 337–53.

17 Charles Percy Sanger, "The Structure of *Wuthering Heights*" in *Brontë, Wuthering Heights*, p. 331.

18 Ibid, p. 336.

19 For a different and fascinating approach to the threshold see Carol Jacobs, "*Wuthering Heights*: at the Threshold of Interpretation," Boundary II (Spring 1979): 49–71.

3 Marian Halcombe: Appropriating an identity

1 Sue Lonoff, "Multiple Narratives and Relative Truths: a Study of *The Ring and the Book, The Woman in White*, and *The Moonstone*," *Browning Institute Studies*, 10 (1982): 158.

2 Jan-Melissa Schramm, *Testimony and Advocacy in Victorian Law, Literature, and Theology* (Cambridge: Cambridge University Press, 2000), p. 12.

3 Schramm, p. 15.

4 Wilkie Collins, *The Woman in White* (London: Penguin Books, 1985), p. 33. All further references are to the same source.

5 For more examples of Walter's lies see John Kucich, *The Power of Lies* (Ithaca: Cornell University Press, 1994), p. 91.

6 Peter Brooks, *Reading for the Plot* (Cambridge: Harvard University Press, 1992), p. 169.

7 D.A. Miller, *The Novel and the Police* (Berkeley: University of California Press, 1988), p. 164.

8 See, for example, Ann Gaylin's unpublished dissertation *Double Entendres: Eavesdropping in the Nineteenth-Century Novel*, Princeton 1995, p. 164.

9 Gaylin, p. 163.

10 Nina Auerbach, *Woman and the Demon* (Cambridge: Harvard University Press, 1982), p. 137.

11 Catherine Peters, *The King of Inventors* (Princeton: Princeton University Press, 1991), p. 217. Peters notes that Marian's conversation owes much to Frances Dickinson, her personality to Nina Lehmann, and her decision to remain a spinster aunt to Georgina Hogarth. Collins insisted that Marian was based on "many women who personally, morally, and mentally resemble her ... ." But Marian's name and looks suggest that a connection to Eliot should be explored.

12 Herbert Spencer, "Personal Beauty," *Essays Scientific, Political and Speculative*, II (New York: D. Appleton & Co., 1899), pp. 388–9.

13 Spencer, "Personal Beauty," pp. 391–2.

14 Spencer, "Physical Training," *British Quarterly Review* (April 1859) 395.

15 Nancy Paxton, *George Eliot and Herbert Spencer* (Princeton: Princeton University Press, 1991), p. 33.

16 George Eliot, *Selections from George Eliot's Letters*, ed. Gordon S. Haight (New Haven: Yale University Press, 1985), p. 97. Haight's comment is attached to this letter of 27 May 1852.

17 George Eliot, *The George Eliot Letters*, 9 vols., ed. Gordon S. Haight (New Haven: Yale University Press, 1954–78) 8: 42.

18 Paxton, p. 47.

19 George Eliot, *Adam Bede* (New York: Random House), pp. 112–13. For a fascinating discussion of this passage see Caroline Levine's article "Women or Boys? Gender, Realism, and the Gaze in *Adam Bede*," *Women's Writing*, 3: 2 (1996): 113–27.

20 George Eliot, *Letters*, 8: 56–7.

21 *Adam Bede*, p. 131.

22 Phyllis Rose, *Parallel Lives* (New York: Vintage Books, 1984), p. 226. My argument is heavily indebted to Rose's description of the relationship between Spencer and Eliot.

23 George Eliot, *Letters*, 4: 367.

24 Rose, p. 221.

25 Haight, *Selected Letters*, p. 270.

26 Rose, p. 211.

27 Frederick Karl, *George Eliot: Voice of a Century* (New York: W.W. Norton & Co., 1995), p. 642.

28 Eliot, *Letters*, 8: 50.

29 Rosemary Ashton, *George Eliot: a Life* (London: Hamish Hamilton, 1996), p. 99.

30 Spencer, quoted in Paxton, p. 18.

31 Gaylin, p. 166.

32 Collins, quoted in Peters, p. 277.

33 Kucich writes, "Fosco's great attraction to Marian ... stems from [his] recognition of their similar skills in deception ... . He fantasizes about her, not as a paragon of domestic virtue, but as a possible accomplice in crime ..." Kucich notes that "Marian's biggest 'lie' is her suppression of her feelings about Walter's marriage, a suppression in which he seems to acquiesce, as he ignores her 'sad, hesitating interest' in him. However much romantic renunciation is honored in Victorian fiction, Marian's self-suppression calls attention to her dexterity with certain kinds of silent lying." See pp. 90–93. Many critics, including probably most famously D.A. Miller, instead

conflate Walter's and Collins's identities. My concern here, however, is to consider how each of these male narrators responds to Marian's narrative. Walter takes Marian's narrative at face value. He treats it as if it were testimony at a trial. He is interested in neither its style nor its mode of delivery. Fosco, however, responds to Marian (as I believe Collins wants his reader to as well) as an artist and a woman. Walter cannot be Collins's surrogate because he is such a poor reader of what Collins has written.

34 Peters, p. 1.
35 Collins, *The Moonstone* (New York: Bantam Books, 1986), p. 8.
36 Peters, p. 1.
37 Collins, "A Petition to the Novel Writers," *My Miscellanies* (New York: Peter Fenelon Collier), p. 77.
38 Collins, "Bold Words by a Bachelor," *My Miscellanies*, p. 530.
39 W. H. Wills quoted in Peters, p. 128.
40 See *Wilkie Collins: the Critical Heritage*, ed. Norman Page (London: Routledge and Kegan Paul, 1974). None of the novel's earliest reviewers liked Laura. *Dublin University Magazine*'s review was particularly harsh, pp. 104–8.
41 Peters, p. 224.

4 Esther Summerson: Looking twice

1 Gordon Hirsch, "The Mysteries in *Bleak House*: a Psychoanalytic Study" *Dickens Studies Annual*, 4 (1975): 140.
2 Audrey Jaffe, *Vanishing Points: Dickens, Narrative and the Subject of Omniscience* (Berkeley: University of California Press, 1991), p. 146.
3 Charles Dickens, *Bleak House* (London: Penguin Books, 1971), p. 868. All further references are to the same source.
4 Jaffe, pp. 133–45.
5 See, for example, Alex Zwerdling, "Esther Summerson Rehabilitated," *Charles Dickens's Bleak House*, ed. Harold Bloom (New York: Chelsea House, 1987), p. 37, where he discusses some of the negative critical heritage.
6 Charles Dickens, *David Copperfield* (New York: Random House, 1950), p. 3.
7 David Masson, from "Pendennis and Copperfield: Thackeray and Dickens," *North British Review*, XV (May 1851) 57–89, in *Dickens: the Critical Heritage*, ed. Philip Collins (New York: Barnes & Noble, Inc., 1971), p. 251.
8 I am grateful to F. S. Schwarzbach for pointing me toward these particular reviews. His interpretation of the double narrative is the subject of his paper, "'My Portion of These Pages': Dickens as a Female Narrator," *Modern Language Association* (MLA), 1998.
9 Robert Newsom, *Dickens on the Romantic Side of Familiar Things: Bleak House and the Novel Tradition* (New York: Columbia University Press, 1977), pp. 54–6.
10 Newsom, p. 57.
11 Richard T. Gaughan, "Their Places are a Blank: the Two Narrators in *Bleak House*," *Dickens Studies Annual*, 21 (1992) 79.
12 See, for example, Deborah Nord's chapter on *Bleak House* in *Walking the Victorian Streets* (Ithaca: Cornell University Press, 1995).
13 Joan Winslow, "Esther Summerson: the Betrayal of Imagination," *Journal of Narrative Technique*, 6 (Winter 1976) 2.

14 See Nord, pp. 104–5.
15 Jack Rawlins, "Great Expectations: Dickens and the Betrayal of the Child," *Studies in English Literature, 1500–1900*, 23 (1983) 667–83.
16 Peter Ackroyd, *Dickens* (London: Sinclair–Stevenson, 1990), pp. 12–13.
17 Ackroyd, pp. 878–80.
18 Ackroyd, pp. 874–6.
19 Charles Dickens, *Dombey and Son* (London: Penguin Books, 1970), pp. 975–6.

5 Molly Bloom: Acting natural

1 Rebecca West, *The Strange Necessity* (Garden City, NY: Doubleday, 1928), p. 22.
2 Mary Ellmann, *Thinking About Women* (New York: Harcourt Brace Jovanovich, 1968), p. 75.
3 Sandra M. Gilbert and Susan Gubar, *No Man's Land* Vol. 1 (New Haven: Yale University Press, 1988), p. 261.
4 Gilbert and Gubar, p. 232.
5 Christine van Boheemen, "'The Language of Flow': Joyce's Dispossession of the Feminine in *Ulysses*," *Joyce, Modernity and its Mediation*, ed. Christine van Boheemen (Amsterdam: Rodopi), p. 76. See also Annette Shandler Levitt, "The Pattern out of the Wallpaper: Luce Irigaray and Molly Bloom," *Modern Fiction Studies*, 3 (Autumn 1989) 509. "Perhaps the most subtle example of Molly's identification with womankind comes ... when ... she remembers her period: 'I was forgetting this bloody pest of a thing pfooh you wouldnt know which to laugh or cry were such a mixture of plum and apple' ...' This bloody pest of a thing afflicts all women; the phrase '*were* such a *mixture*' validates the female universality of what she is about to describe. But 'plum and apple'? Both are red on the outside, and so we think of Molly's hesitation between white and red rose, think now of Irigaray's conjunction of white and red: 'You are quite red, and still so white. Both at once. You don't lose your candor as you become ardent' ('Our Lips', p. 70). Whereas the meat of the apple is crisp and offers resistance to the teeth, the plum is juicy, fleshy. Women contain, in this formulation, indeed are, diversity, contradiction personified."
6 Lillian E. Doherty, "Joyce's Penelope and Homer's: Feminist Reconsiderations," *Classical and Modern Literature*, 10 (Summer 1990): 343.
7 James Van Dyck Card, *An Anatomy of "Penelope"* (Rutherford, New Jersey: Fairleigh Dickinson Press, 1984), pp. 41–8.
8 Card, p. 48.
9 Phillip F. Herring, "The Bedsteadfastness of Molly Bloom," *Modern Fiction Studies*, XV (Spring 1969) 53–4.
10 Richard Ellmann, *James Joyce* (New York: Oxford University Press, 1959), pp. 443–4.
11 Cheryl Herr, "'Penelope' as Period Piece," *Molly Blooms*, ed. Richard Pearce (Madison: University of Wisconsin Press, 1994), p. 69.
12 Kimberly J. Devlin, "Pretending in 'Penelope' Masquerade, Mimicry, and Molly Bloom," *Molly Blooms*, ed. Richard Pearce (Madison: University of Wisconsin Press, 1994), p. 82.
13 Carole-Anne Tyler, quoted by Devlin, p. 80.
14 Devlin, p. 98.

15 Samuel Butler , *The Authoress of the Odyssey* (Chicago: University of Chicago Press, 1967).

16 James Joyce, *Ulysses* (New York: Random House, 1986), p. 636. All further references are to the same source.

17 James Joyce, *Letters of James Joyce*, vol. 1, ed. Stuart Gilbert (New York: Viking, 1966), p. 129.

18 Homer, *The Odyssey* (New York: W. W. Norton & Co., 1974), p. 325.

19 Harry Blamires, *The New Bloomsday Book* (New York: Routledge, 1988), p. 100.

20 Blamires, p. 100.

21 While Hugh Kenner makes a similar argument, "[A]s Penelope weaves and unweaves her web, virtually every judgement in these dense 25,000 words is substantially contradicted by a counter-judgement somewhere else. Boylan was superb, Boylan is merely coarse" etc., he leaves his discussion at this point and does not explore the implications of Molly's weaving and unweaving. See Hugh Kenner, *Ulysses* (London: George Allen & Unwin, 1980), p. 148.

22 Anni Albers, *On Weaving* (Middletown, Connecticut: Wesleyan University Press, 1965), pp. 38–9.

23 Diane Tolomeo, "The Final Octagon of *Ulysses*," *James Joyce Quarterly*, 10 (1973) 439–54.

24 Hélène Cixous, "Laugh of the Medusa," *Feminisms*, ed. Robyn Warhol and Diane Price Herndl (New Brunswick, New Jersey: Rutgers University Press, 1991), p. 341.

25 Derek Attridge, "Molly's Flow: The Writing of 'Penelope' and the Question of Women's Language," *Modern Fiction Studies*, 3 (Autumn 1989) 543–4.

26 Attridge, p. 544.

27 Attridge, p. 558.

28 Gilbert Seldes quoted in Erwin R. Steinberg, *The Stream of Consciousness and Beyond in Ulysses* (Pittsburgh: University of Pittsburgh Press, 1973), p. 8.

29 Margaret Drabble, *The Oxford Companion to English Literature* (Oxford: Oxford University Press, 1985), p. 944.

30 Maria DiBattista, *First Love* (Chicago: University of Chicago Press, 1985), p. 194.

31 Blamires, p. 235.

32 Constantin-George Sandulescu, *The Joycean Monologue* (Colchester: A Wake Newslitter Press, 1979), p. 113.

33 The material in this chapter pages 106–126 first appeared in English Literary History, Vol. 65.3 (Fall 1998) published by Johns Hopkins University Press.

34 James Joyce, "The Centenary of Charles Dickens" *Journal of Modern Literature*, 5 (1976) 3–18.

35 Fred Kaplan, "Dickens's Flora Finching and Joyce's Molly Bloom" *Nineteenth-Century Fiction*, 23 (1968) 343–6.

36 Charles Dickens, *Little Dorrit* (Oxford: Clarendon Press, 1979), pp. 19–20. All further references are to the same source.

37 Mikhail Bakhtin, *The Dialogic Imagination* trans. Caryl Emerson and Michael Holquist (Austin: University of Texas Press, 1981), p. 306.

38 Peter Ackroyd quotes from the letter in *Dickens* (London: Minerva, 1990), p. 767.

Conclusion   Refusing to tell

1 A.S. Byatt, *Possession* (New York: Vintage Books, 1990), p. 36. All further references are to the same source.
2 I am grateful to Laura Godfrey for sparking my interest in the connection between "Goblin Market" and *Possession*.
3 Christina Rossetti, *Goblin Market* (New York: Dover Publications, 1983), p. 7. All further references are to the same source.
4 In her reversed world Jane Carlyle's famous journals are given a new spin. Through the Ash marriage Byatt reimagines the story of an unconsummated marriage.
5 Byatt's fascination with the relationship between the poet and the medium is more fully developed in *The Conjugial Angel*, one of two novellas making up *Angels and Insects* (New York: Vintage International, 1994).
6 Sally Shuttleworth, "Demonic Mothers: Ideologies of Bourgeois Motherhood in the Mid-Victorian Era," *Rewriting the Victorians*, ed. Linda M. Shires (New York: Routledge, 1992), pp. 37–49.
7 Like Browning, Ash dismisses the possibility of the spirit world as a parallel universe. But Christabel, whose home is named Bethany for the site of Lazarus's resurrection, is probably more in tune with the Browning who celebrates life after death in his poem about Lazarus, "An Epistle Containing the Strange Medical Experience of Karshish The Arab Physician."
8 See the catalog description of *The Last Chapter* by Stephen Wildman, *Visions of Love and Life: Pre-Raphaelite Art from the Birmingham Collection, England* (Alexandria, Virginia: Art Services International, 1995), p. 222.
9 See Laura Mulvey, "Visual Pleasure and Narrative Cinema," *Feminisms*, ed. Robyn R. Warhol and Diane Price Herndl (New Brunswick: Rutgers University Press, 1991), pp. 432–42.
10 Nancy Armstrong, "Captivity and Cultural Capital in the English Novel" *Novel: a Forum on Fiction* (Summer 1998): 387.
11 Rochester recalls that during their courtship, "She flattered me, and lavishly displayed for my pleasure her charms and accomplishments. All the men in her circle seemed to admire her and envy me. I was dazzled, stimulated … ." (p. 309).
12 Armstrong: 387–8.
13 Cora Kaplan, "'A Heterogeneous Thing': Female Childhood and the Rise of Racial Thinking in Victorian Britain." *Human, All Too Human*, ed. Diana Fuss. (New York: Routledge, 1996), p. 185.
14 Linda Nochlin, *Representing Women* (London: Thames and Hudson, 1999), p. 10.
15 Maria DiBattista, *Fast-Talking Dames* (New Haven & London: Yale University Press, 2001), p. xiii.
16 DiBattista, p. 35.
17 Nina Baym, "The Madwoman and her Languages: Why I Don't Do Feminist Literary Theory." *Feminisms*, ed. Robyn R. Warhol and Diane Price Herndl (New Brunswick: Rutgers University Press, 1991), p. 154.
18 Nina Baym, "Matters for Interpretation: Feminism and the Teaching of Literature." *Feminism and American Literary History: Essays* (New Brunswick: Rutgers University Press, 1992), p. 223.

19 Baym, p. 231; for more about the dangers of intellectual violence in the class-room, see Lisa Ruddick's beautiful article "The Near Enemy of the Humanities is Professionalism", *Chronicle of Higher Education*, (23 November 2001), 87–9.

20 As Laura Mulvey writes in "Changes: Thoughts on Myth, Narrative and Historical Experience" "[T]he distrust of narrative closure ... had always been a point of principle for the feminist avant-garde.... We had argued in the 1970s that narrative closure resolves contradiction and stabilises the energy for change generated by a story-line. The same factors seemed to colour my perception of the rhythms and patterns of history. An ending would offer a way out of responsibility.... Changes could seem to just happen, the product of a single narrative line under which the minutiae of political struggle were lost. Heterogeneity, discordance and lack of synchro-nistication between strands of history could be unified." (p. 159) See *Visual and Other Pleasures* (Basingstoke: Macmillan Press Ltd. [now Palgrave Macmillan], 1989)

21 When I taught this scene at Princeton, a student burst into tears – the pleasures of this text are still very much alive for our students if we allow them to be.

Index